Praise for the Groundbreaking Works of
Bestselling Author Harville Hendrix, Ph.D.,
**"one of the leading therapeutic voices
of the 1990s . . ."**
(Deborah Mason, *New Choices* magazine)

KEEPING THE LOVE YOU FIND

"The very best book we have seen on how people can establish a
long-term, monogamous relationship. This book will be a classic in
the field of human relationships."

—Bob and Mary Goulding,
Western Institute for Group and Family Therapy

GETTING THE LOVE YOU WANT

"Harville Hendrix offers the best program I've seen for using the
love/hate energy in marriage to help a couple heal one another and
to become whole together."

—T. George Harris, founding editor,
American Health and *Psychology Today*

"A solid book for married couples looking for a good balance
between insight and practicality that can help make a marriage
better."

—Bonnie Maslin, Ph.D., coauthor of
Loving Men for All the Right Reasons

THE COUPLES COMPANION

"The format . . . provides a concise but powerful mix of common
sense and guidance for spiritual growth."

—Tony DellaFlora, *Albuquerque Journal*

"This marriage enrichment manual offers a year's worth of different daily workouts for the relationship gym, to be done together
at once."

—Mike Maza, *Dallas Morning News*

Also by Harville Hendrix, Ph.D., and Helen Hunt, M.A.

The Couples Companion: Meditations and Exercises for Getting the Love You Want

Also by Harville Hendrix, Ph.D.

Getting the Love You Want
Keeping the Love You Find

The Personal Companion

Meditations and Exercises for
Keeping the Love You Find

HARVILLE HENDRIX, Ph.D.
and
HELEN HUNT, M.A.

Illustrations by Beatrice Benjamin

POCKET BOOKS
New York   London   Toronto   Sydney   Tokyo   Singapore

POCKET BOOKS, a division of Simon & Schuster Inc.
1230 Avenue of the Americas, New York, NY 10020

ISBN: 0-671-86884-5

First Pocket Books trade paperback printing December 1995

10 9 8 7 6 5 4 3 2 1

POCKET and colophon are registered trademarks of
Simon & Schuster Inc.

Text design: Stanley S. Drate/Folio Graphics Co., Inc.

Printed in the U.S.A.

To our daughter Mara—
spirited, independent,
a woman we love eternally.

Writers' Page

We appreciate Jack Maguire for his invaluable help in researching quotes for the *Personal Companion* and organizing and constructing solid drafts of the entries and units that provided a solid core to the book.

Our deep appreciation to Laura Torbet, a writer with an excellent mind and a fine heart. Her capacity to grasp the subtleties of Imago theory illuminates the depth dimension of the Imago material, thus making valuable contributions to this book.

Acknowledgments

This book is the outcome of the vision, heart, and will of many people. We first want to acknowledge Elizabeth Neustadter, a fine writer in her own right, who assisted us with the manuscript in invaluable ways. She brought raucous humor and a fresh perspective to the process when everyone else seemed exhausted. She and her husband, Thomas McLaughlin, have been unfailingly supportive to us for years and we acknowledge with much appreciation all they mean in our lives.

Barney Karpfinger, our literary agent, went beyond the call of duty and helped us once again with issues that arose—unfailingly with a sense of humor.

The illustrations by Beatrice Benjamin give visual form to the difficult concepts of Imago theory, making them far more palatable and accessible. We appreciate her ability to capture subtle nuances in the complex dynamics of relationships and depict them in such vivid and humorous ways. The depth of her humor transcends entertainment and demonstrates it as a critical tool in working through the intensity of our relationship issues. Our thanks to her for sharing her talents and her joie de vivre.

Our thanks go also to Melissa Engestrom, our "wild west" assistant, for her valuable help near the final stages of this manuscript.

Last and most important, however, we acknowledge that this book owes its conception to Claire Zion, our editor at Simon & Schuster. We admire her clear vision of the Imago process having wide practical application in society. While we wanted to write a companion book to *Getting the Love You Want*, it was Claire who suggested that we create one for *Keeping the Love You Find* as well. Her insight, wisdom, and support has been unfailingly reliable for us both.

Our fondest wish is that the collaboration of us all has created a book that will illuminate the path to love for the many who seek it.

Authors' Note

We assume, if you are reading this book, that you are single. Four of our six children are single, and we are grateful to them for the perspective they bring us as we embark on the journey of relationship. In bringing their various issues and jubilation to us, we have been invited to review our own previous singleness and become updated with the current singles scene. We feel empathy for you, and we honor you as well—as we do our own children. You are about to undertake a commendable, but difficult task: *preparing yourself for a committed and intimate partnership.* This places you in a special group of people who have chosen to transcend the cultural myth that intimate relationships just magically "happen" once you find the "right" person. The people in this countercultural group are committed to *becoming,* rather than looking for, the right person. They are committed to changing those parts of themselves that have prevented them from succeeding in creating an intimate partnership. Congratulations on joining these people who are at the forefront of social evolution.

Imago Relationship Theory is clearly articulated for singles in *Keeping the Love You Find* and geared toward couples in *Getting the Love You Want.* As Harville brought the Imago Theory to couples in workshops, however, he found that many came up to him afterward, daunted by the prospect of committing to the process at home. In the same way, many singles have indicated that, while they understood and appreciated the theory, putting the theory into practice seemed an intimidating prospect. In response, we created companion books for each of the books indicated above.

This book is the companion to *Keeping the Love You Find: A Personal Guide* (also published as *Guide for Singles*). That book presented the theory and detailed the processes of change necessary for persons who want to be in a long-term, primary love relationship and have yet to fulfill their yearning. *The Personal Companion* is a daily guide that we believe will help you realize the dream of lasting love. What we offer in the pages that follow is a detailed map, a step by step guide, that will show you how to use your relationships as a means of completing your psychological development. We see this as essential preparation for creating a lasting and satisfying relationship. We also intend to guide you through the processes of self-transformation that are necessary to create the relationship of your dreams with the person of your dreams. But we do not want to pull any punches. It is a difficult journey. We are encouraged, though, by two facts: (1) the destination is achievable; and (2) the road map is clear and really involves no mystery.

While our target audience is single persons, the processes of growth and the guidelines for finding and keeping love in your life are applicable to persons in committed partnerships and in marriages, as well as single persons in casual relationships. We are confident that if you complete all the processes suggested, you will greatly increase your chances of finding an intimate partner with whom you can create a lasting and satisfying love relationship. If you are currently in a committed partnership, we are confident that you will find this book helpful in deepening your relationship.

Our thesis is that *preparation* for relationship is essential, not just desirable, if one is to keep the love they find and create a passionate and permanent relationship. An unfinished childhood, from our perspective, is the chief killer of that goal. The preparation that we have in mind, therefore, is the *type of growth that helps one finish childhood*—one that reignites our frozen psychological development. While we believe that *growth,* as we define it, can be *completed* only in an intimate, committed, long-term partnership, we know it can be *stimulated* in all relationships—especially those relationships where there is significant emotional attachment, as with friends, lovers, colleagues at work, and family. In fact, while we were writing this note, our daughter told us about a friendship in which she had experienced emotional healing and growth using these procedures. She will have to complete the process in an intimate partnership later, but she will take the healing and growth she has achieved to that relationship.

We also believe that preparation for intimate partnership is essential if we are to create a conscious society in which relationships are healing and growth producing, and children are reared without injury. We see this as our ultimate mission: *to contribute to the transformation of society by helping people create intimate partnerships that are struc-*

tures of healing. Within such contexts, the adults will thrive and children can be reared in greater support and safety. Such children, when they become adults, will create a new, conscious society, thus gradually replacing a social context in which most people spend most of their adult lives acting out or trying to overcome their unfinished issues from childhood. Your reading this book and using its processes in your current and future relationships makes you a partner in that vision.

The idea that one can and should prepare for intimate partnership runs counter to the cultural wisdom, but we know from our personal and professional experience that we do not naturally know how to be in relationship. We have to learn. What we naturally know is what we have unconsciously absorbed from our relationship with our parents and from our cultural contexts. It is obvious that what we have learned is inadequate when you consider the U.S.'s nearly fifty percent divorce rate, conflict between indigenous groups in all cultures, random and intentional violence, and war within and between nations. As a species, we have yet to learn to be in relationship with another.

We believe that committed partnerships provide the most effective context for achieving that next evolutionary step, that people must learn to live in intimate partnerships or there is little hope for the transformation of society.

It is interesting and confusing that the assumptions of our culture run counter to this position. Society offers the confusing message that, although autonomy and self-sufficiency are primary for human beings, they have to be learned. At the same time it teaches that we naturally know how to be in intimate partnerships. This adds up to the assumption, which has guided us for centuries, that once we become a self we can then be in relationship naturally, without further learning. What seems closer to experience, however, is that we have both a natural drive to be a self and a natural inclination to be in relationship, and both have to be learned. We do not naturally know "how" to create and sustain genuine contact with another person, nor do we naturally know how to become the self we are inclined to be. But we can learn both.

This point of view requires a perceptual shift, from the paradigm of the solitary and self-sufficient "individual" to a new paradigm, which is now emerging in our culture, that views "relationship" as the primary structure of reality. We think the appearance of this new paradigm is an intuitive expression of our awareness as a species that we must evolve beyond the focus on the individual, thus recovering our natural inclination to be in relationship. In the relationship paradigm, the goal of life is contact and empathy, and within this emotional atmosphere autonomy and independence flourish. Our yearning for relationship is natural, and mutual dependence is healthy. We believe that when this is learned on the personal level in intimate partnerships, its impact will be felt throughout society. We view this book as a reflection of this emerging paradigm.

We want to emphasize also that the journey to love is a spiritual process that can be facilitated by spiritual practice. Each page of this book is imbued with this practice, in the form of the meditations. This emphasis arises out of our personal experience. During a particularly challenging time within our own marriage, we discovered the power of a contemplative practice as a support for our work on our relationship. While both of us were committed to the theory of Imago Therapy, at times we each stubbornly held on to our defenses, thus sustaining our friction. We found that by inviting a spiritual awareness through contemplative practice, for as little as twenty minutes each day, we were able to effect shifts that eluded us when doing the exercises alone.

Our rational selves can carry us only so far. In order to impact ourselves and others from our deepest core, we need to tap into our essence and explore it by means other than rational thinking. Taking the time to cultivate and deepen our spiritual awareness can provide the fuel, the focus, and the energy to bring about a deeper, more profound shift in our character defenses. This deeper shift ultimately provides a wellspring of courage, strength, and love to effect more lasting change within ourselves and our relationships.

We wish you well on your journey to conscious love.

—Helen Hunt and Harville Hendrix
Abiquiu, New Mexico
1995

Introduction

Finding one's true love is a yearning people have harbored throughout the ages. This undying hope is the stuff of myth, fairy tales, poetry, and love songs. Hidden within this universal yearning are the beliefs that there is a special person who is "right for me" and in finding that person, "I will live happily ever after." From our perspective, there is a glimmer of truth in these beliefs. The larger truth is that we yearn, not for a particular person, but for a person with a certain type of personality, of whom there are many candidates. When we find a person whose personality matches the type, we fall in love and live for a while in the illusion of happiness.

Contrary to what most single persons think, the problem for most of us is not in finding our "dream lover," for he or she comes with many different names. Think about how many times you have fallen in love during and since adolescence. The problem is keeping them in our lives or staying in theirs. Romance soon turns into conflict and dreams into disillusionment. The person of our dreams fast becomes the demon of our nightmares. In horror, we discard them, dubbing them the "wrong person for us," and begin our search for another, vowing never to make that mistake again. Yet soon we find ourselves falling in love again, swearing that this new person is different, and that this time it will be better. What we don't realize is that, even though this person may not resemble our past loves in any overt way, hidden within (their) personality are subtle similarities. The new person has a different curriculum vitae but the same personality type.

Shedding light on the mystery of loves found and lost is the aim of Imago Relationship Therapy, the theory upon which this *Personal Companion* and its parent book, *Keeping the Love You Find,* are based. This companion volume not only offers a theory that will enable you to understand what happens in your unconscious mind when you fall in love, but provides a process with practical steps to help you establish and maintain a stable, loving relationship.

The thesis is relatively simple. In childhood, each of us experienced our caretakers as failing to fully meet certain, essential needs. This resulted in the creation of emotional wounds. The wounds we refer to are needs that either were, or were felt by us to be, necessary for survival. When these needs raged unchecked and unmet by our caretakers, we, as young children, were left with a fear of death. Our instinctive response to this fear and frustration was to develop an intricate pattern of protective behaviors, similar to a finely wired alarm system, designed to prevent further wounding and avert a fatal outcome. The repetition of these survival behaviors crystallized into our character defenses, and the alarm system was psychologically absorbed into our self-image. What many don't realize is that, left unchecked, this alarm system can work to sabotage rather than nurture a relationship.

During this early interaction with our caretakers, we created an image, called the *Imago,* that was composed of those traits in the caretakers that responded to our needs, as well as those that deprived us of having our needs satisfied. This inner image is an imprint of our caretakers, and it helped us to recognize our parents. It also serves as a blueprint for future partnership.

Following our blueprint, we are guided again and again to people who possess the positive and negative traits of our caretakers. When we meet our Imago, no matter if they physically resemble our parents or not, we fall in love. The sudden rush of energy that comes when we fall in love happens because we identify this person as holding the traits of nurturing that our caretakers did. The yearning we experience is the anticipation that this person will meet the needs our caretakers failed to satisfy in our childhood. With this dynamic in place, a problem immediately arises. Our selected partner, bearing her or his own childhood hurts, enters the relationship with similar expectations of need satisfaction and opposite patterns of self-protection. The collision of these mutual expectations and opposing patterns of defense results in the failure of both persons to meet each others needs. This creates a core conflict, called the power struggle. Our alarms ring out, transforming our dream of love into a nightmare of frustration and disillusionment, bringing most relationships to an end.

From the Imago perspective, falling in love and entering the power struggle are natural stages of an intimate relationship. Both are supposed to happen. Ending a relationship at the point of conflict aborts a primal growth opportunity. And the process begins yet again the minute we find ourselves falling in love anew. In order to break this cycle, we need to cultivate the understanding that our unconscious is trying to complete a process aborted in childhood. This aborted process arrested our growth, hindering our natural evolution to mature adulthood. For us to evolve into mature and whole adults, we must heal our wounds and thus begin the journey toward wholeness. This means committing with a person to a partnership that will unconsciously recreate the emotional world of our childhood. Such a person, of necessity, will possess traits that are similar to certain traits in our caretakers, and this person will be a source of romantic excitement and painful frustrations. Instead of having serial relationships that repeat and prolong the wounding, persons in conflict must learn to cooperate with the agenda of their unconscious. In this way, we can achieve the healing that will restore us to our authentic wholeness.

The goal of *The Personal Companion* is to help you become a "conscious single," by illuminating this unconscious agenda so that you can cooperate and work with your unconscious, instead of against it. The Imago process outlines the necessary journey step by step, helping you to identify for healing the childhood hurts you will bring to intimate relationships. It also serves to illuminate those defenses you use out of fear and aids you in dismantling your alarm system. By working with the Imago process, you will learn how to use close relationships in your life to restart your psychological development. This will help to end the cycle of serial relationships that repeatedly activates your childhood wounds. Each close or intimate relationship can be used as a theme park for self-discovery and growth.

However, what you can achieve while you are single and uncommitted is limited. You can discover your childhood wound in your current relationships. *But you cannot heal your wounds until you are using the Imago process in a committed relationship.* What you can achieve while in the state of singledom is to identify and begin to dismantle your alarm system by working with your defenses. The Imago system helps to illuminate patterns of behavior that come into play when you are feeling afraid and frustrated. These patterns not only keep you from experiencing the healing, growth, and love that you yearn for, but also wound your partner when used within your relationships. Each protective behavior you surrender will remove a "relationship blockade," which will contribute to your ability to keep the love you find and eventually heal the wounds of your childhood.

The next few pages tell you how to use this book to learn the Imago process and begin your journey to healing and wholeness and the relationship of your dreams.

How to Use The Personal Companion

Each entry of *The Personal Companion* uses a quote or illustration as the stepping-off point for a brief discussion of some aspect of relationships or the single life. The discussion leads to a brief task or exercise, followed by a meditation. During this year-long course of 365 entries, you will learn all about Imago Relationship Therapy and will be taken through many powerful self-revelatory and relationship-building processes.

Because *The Personal Companion* is aimed at readers who are not currently in a committed relationship, almost all of the tasks and exercises can be done alone. You can, for example, practice the skills of *intentional dialogue* without anyone whom you wish to invite into this process. You can ask someone for a *behavior change request* or practice *holding other's projections* without anyone being the wiser. But because the ultimate goal of *The Personal Companion* is an intimate, conscious relationship, the more you can involve others in the process, the more "on-the-job" training you'll get. All your current relationships—with family members, friends, coworkers, dates, less-than-committed partners, neighbors—are good practice for the intimate relationship you seek, and all your relationships will benefit from your practicing Imago skills together. You will find that if you enlist the active help of others, you will build intimacy and community all around you. When Imago skills are used with dates and potential partners, we call it "utilitarian dating." By practicing these new skills in relatively safe situations, where you don't feel at risk of losing someone you're deeply in love with, you gain tremendous knowledge and confidence for your future partnership. Also, because many of the processes in *The Personal Companion* ask you to look back at your past—at your childhood and past relationships—you will benefit from checking out your memories with people in your past: parents, siblings, past partners, school chums.

Things to Keep in Mind While Using
The Personal Companion

• You'll want to have a notebook or journal for the tasks that require writing. Always note the "day" number at the top of the page so that you can refer back to what you've written when you are asked for information in later tasks.

• Many of the self-discovery and Imago processes are presented in "units" of from two to nine days.

• You will find that from day to day the tasks vary in intensity and in the time involved to complete them. Lighter, more "fun" days are alternated with the more complex learning units.

• We recognize that the demands of this book—and of life—are sometimes strenuous and that you may get tired, or discouraged, and may need to take a break. So we've numbered the entries sequentially, rather than dated them, so that you can interrupt the process at any point and later pick up where you left off. You can also work through the book as many times as you wish; you'll gain new insights and skill levels each time around!

• We all lead busy lives, but we urge you not to stint on the time you allot to this process. In most cases, reading the entry and doing the task will take less than ten minutes. But try to set aside twenty minutes for the meditation. This is a time, not only to ground and reflect on what you are learning, but for relaxation and self-care in our high stress world.

Though you are a single person, you are about to embark on a year of giving daily attention to the skills of relationship and to uncovering, and changing, those traits and issues that have caused problems and unhappiness in past relationships. Before you even find the partner you seek, you will reap the benefits of this process. As you work through *The Personal Companion,* you will find calm and solace in the meditative practice; you will see changes in yourself that will make you a better partner in the relationship you seek; you will learn about your future partner and the issues you will face; and you will see improvement in all the relationships in your life.

Good luck on your journey!

List of Units

A journey of a thousand miles must begin with a single step.

—LAO-TZU

The life of a single person can be emotionally turbulent. Our hopes and dreams about finding a lasting love sometimes send us soaring sky high. At other times, our confusion and despair over ever finding partnership can plunge us into an abyss. It's not surprising that many singles simply give up the search. Having experienced the turmoil inherent in setting their sights on a fulfilling love relationship, they decide, grudgingly, to lower their standards and make the best of their single state.

You don't have to settle for where you are, however. You can—and will—find and keep a lasting love if you work actively toward that goal. It doesn't require extraordinary skill or luck. It simply involves walking forward with both feet on the ground. Instead of allowing ourselves to fly up into the clouds or dive down into the caverns, we need to focus on making one small step after another toward our destination. As we gradually learn new attitudes and skills, the sheer momentum of positive change will help move us along.

The Personal Companion illustrates how to realize your goal of a committed partnership—one that heals all the hurts you've accumulated since childhood and that brings you the highest joys life has to offer. Follow this guide day by day, and trust in yourself, and your journey will be both wondrous and successful.

⁂ *Today, commit yourself to doing the work in this book for one year. If possible, choose a particular time of day when you can consistently set aside at least one half hour: around ten minutes to read the entry and do the accompanying task, and around twenty minutes to perform the meditation.*

In stillness today, I vow to bring the totality of my being into this work I am about to begin.

As we strive to become more fully evolved human beings, capable of entering into fully committed partnerships, we owe it to ourselves to keep notes. Maintaining a personal journal can be a valuable experience, and it doesn't require great writing skills, large amounts of time, or even neatness. Instead, it calls for a better self-regard: a desire to take more account of our life, a willingness to express ourselves on paper, and a keen interest in retaining our most valuable thoughts, insights, and discoveries. When we keep a journal faithfully and thoughtfully, it becomes not only a log for our life's voyages, but also a unique journey in and of itself into our innermost depths.

Occasional entries in this book will ask you to perform specific writing tasks in a notebook. These tasks are a vital and irreplaceable part of your participation in the Imago process. You may also want to use this notebook, or another notebook altogether, to record important, day-to-day incidents in your life, especially those relating to love and self-growth. Or you may want to keep track of major dreams or inspirational brainstorms.

❺ *If you haven't already done so, buy a special notebook or journal today that you can use for the writing tasks in this book (and, if desired, for other journal-keeping purposes as well).*

Today, in the quiet place at my center, I hold this thought: "My life is an unwritten book waiting to be written and read."

To learn is a natural pleasure, not confined to
philosophers, but common to all.

                         —ARISTOTLE

Popular mythmakers seduce us into thinking of singledom as a preferred lifestyle. In the media, carefree singles breeze through life with their sexy partners, great clothes, trendy apartments, and exciting careers. Very pretty images, indeed, but not the whole picture. Why do most singles complain about the shallowness and unhappiness of their life—even if it does resemble the popular fantasy? Now that it's become socially acceptable to live alone, why do so many singles still long for a life companion?

The answer is quite simple. Within each human being is an unconscious yearning for partnership. As individuals, we each have emotional wounds that need healing; and on some level, we know that it is only in the context of a committed relationship that this healing can occur. Each of us harbors a spiritual drive toward wholeness that can be realized only by uniting in real love with another person.

To reflect these vital purposes, the concept of singledom needs to be redefined. Singledom is, in fact, a *stage* of life, not a target lifestyle or an end in itself. It's a rite of passage on the way to a loving partnership in which both individuals can live to fulfill their potential.

To say that singledom is a stage of life, not an end point, doesn't minimize the possibilities for personal growth. When we're single, we have invaluable opportunities to try on the world for size and to master the skills for the art of lasting love.

‎➔ *Today, take some time to write down what your hopes are, where you see yourself six months from now and when you've finished this book. As you progress, this will be an interesting entry to review.*

I honor my independence with the understanding that by living fully at this stage of my life, I am preparing for a healthy and fulfilling partnership.

*I soon realized that no journey carries one far
unless, as it extends into the world around us, it
goes an equal distance into the world within.*

—LILLIAN SMITH

The ongoing practice of meditation and prayer is a means of going deep within and opening ourselves up. This opening releases an inner spirit we can then channel into seeing new possibilities and practicing new behaviors. Real care for others begins with real care for ourselves. Meditation provides that kind of care. It enables us to get closer to the source of our Being, the place where our spirit as an individual intersects with the universal spirit. A daily time of quiet can effect change at the very deepest level of our existence.

Contemplative meditation can take many different forms. It can be a religious experience that taps into, and contributes to, one's faith. It can also be a mental and physical exercise aimed at renewing one's spirit. It can be performed in a very specific way, or it can be done simply by opening oneself to stillness and quiet in life—and in oneself. There will, of course, be some days when we find meditation easier than others. But it's the daily commitment that deepens both self and universal awareness.

❧ *Today, become more intentional around your daily meditation practice. Light a candle or stick of incense while you're meditating; designate a special corner for meditation; add an inspirational piece of art to this area.*

As I become quiet today and focus inward, I make a decision to practice meditation until it becomes an artful experience, knowing that daily contact with my deeper self opens me to the larger universe.

No one can make you feel inferior without your consent.

—ELEANOR ROOSEVELT

Single people can be their own worst enemy. At a loss to understand why they can't find a committed partner, they sometimes blame their own general lack of appeal. "I'm just not a lovable person," they say. To support this theory, they may obsess over their past relationships for evidence: rehearing all the criticism and reliving all the rejection.

It's easy and, at some psychological level, even comforting to fall back on this theory. Those who do so spare themselves the work of addressing the more complex challenges involved in building a deep and lasting relationship. They have an excuse for accepting the "inevitable"—a life alone that they know in their hearts falls short of what is possible.

If we're determined to look for personal failures in our past relationships, we will certainly find them. But such obsessions diminish the abundance of personal achievements in those relationships. We must be lovable, or no one would ever have cared for us in the first place! In thinking about past relationships, focus on evidence of our personal "lovability."

᛭ *In your journal, write brief answers to the following questions:*
  * *In my life as a whole, what people have cared about me enough to reveal personal details of their life with me?*
  * *What did each person like about me that caused them to trust me? (Try recalling actual compliments and admiring words or looks you received.)*

Entering the place of peace and safety, I see myself walking in the rain. Each drop of water is a positive word about my lovable traits. I am flooded with warmth and joy, and say to myself: "I am lovable."

Our failure to find love, to keep love, or to recover from a lost love can be so discouraging that we give up altogether. Like a hurt animal, we retreat to our cave to lick our wounds. In the darkness of our retreat, our wounds may eventually cease to be so painful, but our courage may never return. Why should it? We don't need it if we refuse to venture outside.

Accustomed to our cave and unwilling to admit our lack of courage, we convince ourselves that finding lasting love is an impossible goal. Indeed, it does become impossible if we never leave our cave of solitude to see the wealth of possibilities that lie outside.

❧ In your notebook, spend a few minutes making a list of "love possibilities." List places and situations where you might be able to make such contacts, or people who might help you meet potential dates, or people you might like to date. Promise yourself that you will try one *of these possibilities this week.*

Today in my time of solitude, I enter the dark cave that holds my despair of finding lasting love. As I relax more deeply, I become aware of a light in the cave, its rays leading me to the exit. I follow the light.

Too easily and too often, single people rate their dates and potential romantic partners against their private standard of the "perfect mate." Typically, this image includes an elaborate checklist of glowing attributes and achievements. We then compare all potential partners against our version of the singles' ads in newspapers:

> **Wanted:** Slim, sexy, smart, sensitive, and fun-loving Unitarian, 30–40 years old, financially secure and compatible with Capricorn, who loves golden retrievers, progressive jazz, and gourmet food, and who doesn't smoke, drink, or snore.

Ironically, these become recipes for disappointment in love, as one real candidate after another falls hopelessly short of the ideal concoction.

The truth is that the "perfect mate" is a myth: not a real person, but a patched-together fantasy that deliberately excludes any human shortcomings, idiosyncracies, or surprises. We may think we need such perfection to compensate for the deprivations of our earlier lives, but what we actually need is real love, born when two real people recognize, accept, and tend each other's imperfections.

🍃 *In your notebook, write a "singles' ad" describing your "perfect mate." This will help make you more aware of the personal myth that keeps you from finding real love.*

Entering my quiet place today, I become aware of my dreams of a perfect mate. Summoning the courage to release that fantasy, I open myself to the truth of universal imperfection and accept it as my opportunity to evolve toward my wholeness.

The quest to find and keep a fulfilling love relationship is a pilgrimage. In order to be successful, we must be sure to bring along on this journey our heart, mind, and soul. Using these innermost resources, we will be able to tread the path of self-transformation. We can leave behind the narrow confines of our own ego and habits, and instead make steady progress toward becoming a more fully realized human being, one who is capable of knowing, expressing, and receiving a transcendent love.

Our quest for love springs from a yearning for wholeness. Wholeness is achieved when we begin to care for another's self-interest as we would our own. We cannot expect to find this wholeness if we blindly trudge through one romantic entanglement after another, seeking only self-gratification. A whole person is one who discovers his or her highest, most sacred self on the way toward finding another. A whole person is also one who can share his or her life totally with someone else, knowing that it means a much greater life than he or she could ever have alone.

❧ *Today, compose in your journal your commitment to the quest for love.*

In a time of prayer today, I envision myself on the journey to love. I make this vow: "I will travel to the land of love."

Before we can know another person intimately and, through this experience, find real love, we must first know ourselves. But many of us never actually stop to take stock of who we are. We assume full self-awareness and fail to ask ourselves the very questions that we're most interested in posing to other people. In this unit, you will be guided toward a closer look at who you *really* are and what is *really* going on in your mind. It's the best vantage point for seeing how you can go about making positive changes in your life—the types of changes that we'll be discussing throughout this book.

– *Begin your self-knowledge inventory on an upbeat note by thinking about your current hopes and dreams. Use the following questions as prompters and record your answers in your notebook:*

- *What are my goals in life? What would I most like to accomplish?*
- *What are my fantasies? What are the things that I most often wish for or daydream about?*
- *What is my idea of a perfect job or career? Living situation? Vacation?*
- *What are the best things that could happen to me?*

Pausing for a time of stillness, I allow my mind to expand, making room for the many possibilities available to me in life. Without the pressure of having to make decisions or offer explanations, I allow myself to visualize the myriad paths opening before me.

> *Fears are educated into us and can, if we wish, be educated out.*
>
> —KARL MENNINGER

Fears and worries arise from our insecurities. The process begins in childhood, when everything is new and, therefore, unsettling. Psychologically, we're at the mercy of our rapidly changing bodies, our clumsiness in mastering new skills, the mysteries of our expanding social environment, and the mistakes of our less-than-perfect caretakers. We go through certain unique patterns of anxiety over and over until they become learned behaviors. Puberty casts us once again into a scary new world, where we learn a host of new fears and worries. And so the process continues, each change in our lives rekindling old anxiety patterns and, possibly, teaching us new ones.

Our fears and worries are forms of aversion. The bad news is that we're programmed not to think about them, and they thrive on our neglect. The good news is that we can unlearn our fears and worries; but first we must face them squarely and name them for what they are.

🐚 *Today, take a few moments to consider your personal fears and worries. Ask yourself the following questions:*
- *What are my deepest fears in my life as a whole?*
- *In what skill areas or social situations do I feel insecure?*
- *What things do I worry about most often in my day-to-day life?*
- *What specific things have triggered fears or worries in recent weeks?*
- *What behavior patterns emerge when I'm feeling afraid or insecure?*

I recognize and acknowledge the fears that have been stopping me from reaching my full potential. In times of prayerful contemplation, I visualize my fears as being a staircase that I can easily tread, spiraling upward into a calm and new daylight.

*Our feelings are our most genuine paths to
knowledge.*

— AUDRE LORDE

"I may not know much, but I know what I like!" But knowing what
we do or don't like is *not* a substitute for knowledge. It is, however,
a good starting point.

At one time or another, we've all paid a price for not being
properly attuned to our likes and dislikes. For example, you may
have repeatedly groveled to stay on someone's good side, only to
realize one day that you never liked this person very much. Or
perhaps you used to avoid card games because they seemed stupid
to you, until you broke down one weekend and discovered that you
love to play poker. Maybe you once rushed out to the bars every
Friday night because you thought it was the cool thing to do, refusing
to admit—even to yourself—that you didn't really like the drinking,
the late hours, or the smoke-filled atmosphere.

Becoming more consciously aware of our likes and dislikes helps
make us more sensitive to pleasure. As we understand our likes and
dislikes, we can begin to learn how to satisfy our own needs and
desires. There is, in fact, much that we need to know in order to
lead a happier life.

❧ *Today, spend a few moments distinguishing between the things
that you like and the things that you dislike. The following
questions will help guide your thoughts:*
* *What do I like most about my life as a whole? What do I
dislike most?*
* *What things do I regularly enjoy in my day-to-day life? What
things are recurrent sources of displeasure?*
* *What places do I most associate with pleasure? What times
of the day, the week, the year?*
* *What places do I most associate with displeasure? What
times of the day, the week, the year?*

Today, as I center into a place of deep peace within, I allow myself to
dwell upon my likes and dislikes. I move to a profound sense of
acceptance as I realize more vividly who I am, and I embrace
my uniqueness.

Who sees the other half of Self, sees Truth.

—ANNE CAMERON

When we look into a mirror, the reflected image we see is two-dimensional. The way we commonly think of ourselves—our mental self-image—has a similar flatness. Often, we do not even take the time to really see our reflection. In the same way, when we think of who we are as a person, we don't take the time to really assess ourselves from a place of joyful awareness. When we're asked about ourselves, we say things like, "I'm a lawyer." "I'm an Italian American from Philadelphia." "I'm your average, middle-class, thirty-something, single parent." The truth about ourselves is much more complex and multidimensional. And more exciting!

In order to help others get to know you better, you first need to get to know yourself better. It's an ongoing effort, but well worth it. You'll be surprised to find you're much more interesting than you think you are!

🍂 *Today, begin looking more closely at the image you have of yourself. Try answering the following questions with the first impressions that come to mind:*

- *What do I think are my best qualities? My worst?*
- *What would I change about myself if I could?*
- *What accomplishments am I most proud of?*
- *What secrets about myself do I hide from others?*
- *How do I spend time when I am alone? How do I feel about this?*
- *What things do I consider sacred in my life?*
- *What people and events have had the biggest impact on my life?*
- *What was I like as a child? An adolescent?*

Entering the stillness within me today, I visualize myself as those who truly love me might see me. In doing so, I open myself to the wonder of rediscovery.

*A true knowledge of ourselves is knowledge of our
power.*
                                        —MARK RUTHERFORD

For many of us, the most difficult and distressing aspect of our lives
to sort out is our past relationships. We're still hurting from them,
perhaps still confused or angry. Maybe we miss the people who are
no longer in our lives, or rue the day we ever met them. Perhaps we
still suffer the ever-burning coals of desire and anger, or simply sigh
with regret and fatigue over all the energy we apparently wasted.
The one common element is that we are reminded once more of our
estrangement from people we used to care deeply about, and we feel
once more like strangers to them and to ourselves.

Our past relationships may be reminders of pain or failure. However, they can also be valuable windows into the issues, wounds, and
conflicts that we must address if we are to make better partner
choices in our future. Every past liaison began in love and hope. If
we can honestly examine each relationship, we can begin to see the
damaging patterns that get repeated, the healing that we need to
experience, and the changes that we need to make in order to do
better in the future.

&ə *Today, mentally review your past relationships, with these
questions in mind:*
  • *What have I liked about dating? What have I not liked?*
  • *On the whole, how would I describe my relationships?*
  • *What have been some of my best experiences in intimate
relationships? My worst?*
  • *How do I usually feel and act when I fall in love?*
  • *What does intimacy mean to me?*
  • *What do I most enjoy sexually?*
  • *How have I and others expressed anger in past relationships?*
  • *How have my relationships ended?*

Today, in quiet, I reach into the inner recesses of my heart, offering
kindness and love to those who have touched my life, celebrating the
positive ways in which I have built upon these relationships to make
me who I am today.

The delights of self-discovery are always available.

—GAIL SHEEHY

Over the last few days, you've courageously explored your past and your present. Part of the journey may have been rough. But no doubt you're already discovering just how rich your life actually is with dreams, dramas, and possibilities. Like a diamond in the rough, you are a unique and multifaceted person. Your voyage of self-discovery has only begun. As you continue through this book, you'll have many opportunities to see more clearly into different parts of yourself. You'll also find out how your experiences within your family and within your romantic relationships have conditioned your inner self. With this knowledge available to you, you can work to resolve some of the problems that this conditioning may have caused. Above all, you'll learn that keeping in touch with who you are on a continuous basis is not only therapeutic, but also a source of much joy.

&. *Before you go on to learn and practice the relationship skills that are offered in this book, take a few minutes to think about the type of future partnership you currently desire. Write brief responses to the following questions in your notebook:*

1. Why is a committed relationship important to me?

2. What goals would I set for a committed relationship?

3. In my opinion, what are the general strengths and weaknesses of a committed relationship?

4. What do I fear most about a committed relationship?

5. What mental, emotional, and spiritual qualities can I bring to a committed relationship?

6. What mental, emotional, and spiritual qualities do I hope to gain through a committed relationship?

Moving into the calm, still place at my core, I set my sights forward. Opening myself to the Universals, I contemplate not only where I have been, but also the possibilities of my future.

Planting a seed in a garden is an act of hope. When we pat that seed into the soil, we impress upon it our desire and belief that it will grow and, in due time, bear fruit. We intentionally keep nourishing that hope as we continue to cultivate our internal garden.

This kind of *intentional* hope is an indispensable element in working toward positive self-change. We must always have faith that what we do matters and therefore persevere in the doing. We must enrich our lives from day to day by applying new skills and practicing new behaviors. As we apply these skills, we need to cultivate the whole-hearted conviction that they will eventually yield positive benefits.

Today, identify at least three things in your life that you tend to think will never happen. For example, you may feel virtually incapable of finding—or enjoying—a date. You may think that it's hopeless trying to impress your boss, to please your mother, or to manage your money so that you can go on the dream vacation you crave. For each thing that you identify, think of at least one way to plant a seed of hope and reverse these negative trends.

Today, in my time of quiet, I see before me a fertile, prepared garden waiting to be planted with seeds. I take my wish and plant it, giving it the water and nutrients it needs. I surrender my doubt and despair.

*I do not ask for any crown/ But that which all
    may win;
Nor try to conquer any world/ Except the one within.
Be Thou my guide until I find/ Led by a tender hand,
The happy kingdom in myself/ And dare to take
command.*

—LOUISA MAY ALCOTT

Too many singles spend far too much energy and effort hunting for a mate, not realizing that they can fall into all sorts of traps. Some hunters are too quick to find fault with prospective mates. Other hunters are too quick to choose a partner, settle down, and *then* worry about being happy in the relationship—only to discover that they're actually quite miserable.

It may not be your fault that you haven't found a lasting love, but it is definitely your responsibility to do what needs to be done to find one. The first step is to forget the mating game! The answers to your problems are not "out there," with the right clothes, apartment, car, and one-liners, but inside yourself. Before you can find or attract a partner with whom you can truly be happy, you need to look deeply into your soul, acknowledging your power to grow. With this acknowledgment comes a commitment to exercise that power. It's a fourfold process that requires you to:

1. Educate yourself about YOURSELF.
2. Educate yourself about RELATIONSHIPS.
3. Train yourself in the skills of relationships.
4. Do what you can to change the behaviors and character defenses that prevent you from keeping the love you find.

&❧ *Today, declare a moratorium on the mating game until you've had time to work on your inner growth with the help of this book. Write down the four stages of the process in your notebook.*

During this time of prayer, I reinforce my commitment to working through the fourfold process that will open the once-locked doors and lead to a rich and rewarding future.

Before committing yourself to a lifelong partnership, it helps to
practice simple, short-term togetherness as much as you can. Good
friends and casual dating can help. Besides eating, strolling, bowling,
watching TV, going to a movie, or having sex, what can you do with
another person that's particularly instructive as well as entertaining?
Here are some suggestions:

- Design and execute an artistic or home decoration project.
- Plant and tend a garden: all vegetable, all flowers, or half-
  and-half.
- Research and then travel to someplace that's historically or
  culturally significant.
- Join and participate in a hobby or sports club.
- Take an adult-education course together.
- Read the same list of books—or study the same subject—and
  regularly compare notes.

By spending time engaging in these types of endeavors, we can learn
valuable information about ourselves and those whom we care about
in our lives. We can begin to have an understanding of what we and
others feel is important. We also begin to learn the important concept
of teamwork as it relates to partnership.

*Today, think of at least two "togetherness" projects you could
propose to people who are important in your life. Write these
ideas down in your notebook. If you have time, do a little research
so that when you propose this idea, you will have the necessary
information to make the plans right then.*

**In my time of solitude today, I visualize myself as a partner with
significant others. I feel the power of contact and the joy of co-
creation.**

We come into the world with the history of the human species encoded in our bodies. This is strikingly apparent in the two-part makeup of our brain: the *old brain* and the *new brain*.

The new brain, scientifically known as the cerebral cortex, is the part that thinks, remembers, decides, plans, and creates—the definitively "human" section of the brain. Underlying this part is the more primitive old brain, which has two sections: the "reptile brain" and the "mammalian brain" (indicating just how far back in evolutionary history it goes!). The old brain controls unconscious functions meant to ensure survival. Our old brain is as crude, powerful, and hard to ignore as a dinosaur. Whenever a love partner does anything that upsets us, the old brain automatically responds in one of five basic ways: hide, fight, flee, freeze, or play dead. The new brain can't hope to stifle these strong primal reactions. All it can do is learn to recognize them and deal with them in a conscious and appropriate manner. In this way, we move away from the reactive state that can push real love away, and make room for real human love and understanding.

𝕒 *Review your most significant present and past relationships and recall incidents that triggered your old brain's "danger" reaction. You may remember a particular critical remark that sent you running out the door or a moment of jealousy that instantly enraged you. Identify at least three of these moments—and how you reacted—and record these patterns in your notebook for future reference.*

In my time of quiet today, I go to my center and experience in the stillness my God-essence. I envision a safe place and bring into awareness my old brain responses. I make this commitment: "I will care for the part of me that protects me."

Cocooning: The need to protect oneself from the harsh, unpredictable realities of the outside world.
— FAITH POPCORN

The older, more primitive part of your brain—the part that you have in common with dinosaurs and all other reptiles and mammals in evolutionary history—has no sense of time. Indeed, it exists outside of time altogether. In registering a "danger" situation, it can't tell the difference between the stimulus it received way back when your mother didn't respond to your infant cry and the one it received today when your partner called from work an hour late to cancel your date. As a baby, you may have responded by sucking your thumb and cooing to yourself. Today, you may respond to the same feeling of abandonment with the same type of response—downing a pint of ice cream and distracting yourself with hours of mindless TV.

The same phenomenon applies to situations that the old brain registers as "safe." When we greet people with a big smile or a kiss or a few words of praise, their old brains instinctively sense safety. As a result, they are likely to respond with much the same instinctive warmth and delight that they exhibited when they were babies and their parents smiled, kissed, or praised them.

🥄 *Today, commit to making one person feel safe in your presence. Avoid cold, hostile, or teasing behavior. Instead, go out of your way to be open, warm, receptive, and agreeable. See if you notice any difference in their response!*

Entering the silence, and recalling my safe place, I become aware of the fears others have of me. In prayer, I make this vow: "I will make other people feel safe in my presence."

*What is more enthralling to the human mind than
this splendid, boundless, colored mutability—life in
the making?*

—DAVID GRAYSON

It's safe to say that everyone reading this book yearns for a lasting
love that will thrill their senses, stimulate their mind, elevate their
spirit, and transform their life into a glorious adventure. In fact, aside
from people who have chosen to live celibate lives for religious
reasons, who in the world could possibly *not* want that?

Well, then, if so many people want that, why do so many people
fail to achieve it?

Many of us might answer that this type of love is an almost
impossible dream. It rarely occurs, and when it does, it's a matter of
sheer luck. It's not something a person can set for themselves as a
realistic goal.

Those who would say such things couldn't be more wrong! Far
from being an unrealistic fantasy, this type of love is the very purpose
of life. It's a dream that is possible for virtually anyone who chooses
to pursue it, regardless of their age, gender, sexual orientation, or
marital status. This fulfillment is vital to our wholeness as human
beings, and the process of achieving it is the making of life itself. This
book is specifically designed to help you realize your own particular
dream of love—a dream that nature intended you to realize.

&. *Today, spend a few moments writing in your notebook three
or four reasons why you sometimes think that realizing your
dream love may be impossible. Then, write and underline the
following sentence: These negative thoughts keep me from seeing the
possible dream.*

**Today, in a quiet awakening, I see my negative thoughts as storm
clouds threatening the blue skies of my dreams for real love, and I
recognize that my consciousness is the mighty wind that will blow
them from my skies.**

The stresses and strains of a solitary life can sometimes be overpowering. When we experience hardship or disappointment—such as things getting hectic at work, or having a fight with a good friend, or failing to achieve a goal we've set for ourselves—we miss that source of comfort that is naturally offered when one is in a relationship with someone who is close enough to understand. Without partnership, we can feel extremely alone, exposed, and helpless in an emotional storm.

At these times, we need to know automatically what we can do to feel more calm and secure. For some, it may be simply taking a nap or a long bath or a walk in a nearby woods. For others, finding solace may require more effort: going fishing, composing a poem, visiting a special chapel across town, or spending some time with a beloved relative. We should be well aware of the options we have, which are based on our personality and resources. This awareness will enable us to draw upon these sources of comfort when we really need them.

❧ Thinking of your past experiences with stress, grief, or disappointment, identify at least three possible ways you might go about finding solace the next time you need it. Write these down in your notebook.

I take comfort today in the fact that I have the resources to comfort myself in times of stress.

*Luck is real, and the harder you work, the more
luck you have.*

—ANONYMOUS

Although you've shifted your focus from full-tilt mate-hunting to self-awareness and self-change, this doesn't mean you're not still interested in romantic relationships. However, shyness, fear, ambivalence, and past dating disasters can be powerful inhibitors. The impulse is to stay home in front of the TV, hoping that you'll somehow bump into the person of your dreams on the way to work. The unavoidable truth is that in order to have relationships, you have to put yourself in a much better position to meet people. This doesn't mean parading up and down Main Street wearing a sandwich board that lists your virtues. Rather, it means taking advantage of as many reasonable chances of enlarging your pool of romantic partners as possible.

Explore every likely avenue! Try singles retreats, religious groups, special-interest clubs for singles, classes and activities geared toward singles sponsored by organizations such as the Learning Annex. Using these resources, we can engage in activities we enjoy within a group dynamic that encourages people to meet one another. And don't rule out using the better dating services or placing personal ads in publications that you feel would attract the kind of person you seek. Remember, no one ever met his or her partner by sitting at home waiting for UPS to deliver a dream date!

❧ *Today, think of possible things you could do to enlarge your pool of partners. Begin by checking local newspapers and periodicals for ideas. Take out your notebook and write a personal ad for yourself—even if you don't place it right away.*

In reverential stillness, I tap into an adventuresome spirit lurking deep within myself and vow to bring this playful energy into my search for partnership.

I say you shall yet find the
friend you were looking for.

— WALT WHITMAN

It's only natural to hope that the love of our life will appear like magic and sweep us off our feet. But while we're waiting for that perfect mate to show up, we'd do well to bone up on our relationship skills. And the best way to do that is to come down out of the clouds and to live in the real world, where we get to like, and learn from, many different people before finally launching on the grandest and most remarkable adventure of all: a real love relationship!

"Utilitarian dating" is the art of using friendly but noncommitted dating situations as opportunities to practice new skills and behaviors for your future partnership. The key to this type of dating is that it takes place in a low-risk atmosphere. There are good reasons for going out with someone you like but are not crazy about. Maybe you crave one-on-one conversation after a week of solitude. Maybe you haven't had a romantic evening in months. Or maybe you don't want to hang around home alone on Saturday night, listening to your favorite CDs yet again. There's no reason you shouldn't enjoy this kind of utilitarian dating. Take advantage of it as a training ground for trying out relationship skills.

🐾 *Today, make a commitment to use your casual dating situations to experiment with the new skills and behaviors that you'll be learning in this book. Make a list of people who you think might be good to practice with. If there are no "casual dating" candidates, this list can include friends and family.*

Realizing that I often live in the romantic fantasy of finding my ideal and living happily ever after, I move into prayerful contemplation and imagine myself experimenting, learning, and growing in a real relationship. I accept this truth: "Love is learned in the act of loving."

And the trouble is, if you don't risk anything, you risk even more.

—ERICA JONG

Utilitarian dating is more than just a great way to turn otherwise "ho-hum" occasions into exciting opportunities for personal growth. It's also a way to rescue yourself from a potentially disastrous rut. Single people often become so frustrated with the shallow experience of dating just for companionship that they give up expecting, or trying for, anything better. Instead, they develop a standard, mechanical behavior that gets them through the night with a minimum amount of fuss or disappointment. Utilitarian dating means daring to try new behaviors. You can start simply by asking more intimate, nonthreatening questions that will help you learn more about another person's point of view.

- "How did you feel about that movie/party/dirty joke?"
- "What do you do when you want to get away from it all?"

You can also try out personal behavior changes. For example, if you know you're too needy, try allowing more distance; if you usually take the lead in a relationship, try playing the passive role.

Most valuable of all, you can experiment with the specific relationship skills, that you'll be learning in this book. You don't need to tell the other person what you're doing, but if you'd like to, why not? You can probably convince your utilitarian dates to do the same, thereby turning them into friendly collaborators as well!

&* *Look at the list you made at the beginning of this unit (Day 23) and identify those people whom you would feel comfortable talking to about your intention to try out new relationship skills. Put a star next to their names and make a commitment to bring this work to them.*

No longer willing to be trapped in routine or tradition, I relax into my quiet place today with a commitment to take risks. I commit to exploring new behaviors and to sharing parts of myself with others that I usually keep private.

*I am beginning to learn that it is the sweet, simple
things of life which are the real ones after all.*
                                    — LAURA INGALLS WILDER

What constitutes a "spiritual life"? It is not, as some would believe, living like a preacher, a nun, or a rabbi. Nor is it making sure to attend a worship service once a week or to pray twice a day. It isn't measured in specific acts or specific blocks of time. Instead, it's a life that is infused with a special awareness of the oneness of all things, that finds purpose and beauty in each passing moment.

To people who look at the world through mundane eyes, everything is separate and often meaningless. Nothing's ever very exciting for them because their expectations are so low, and a great deal is too boring, frustrating, or downright ugly to face at all. However, to people open to the transcendent, the world is a sacred place where all things are interconnected. The result is a life full of emotional enrichment. A spiritual life invites a profound sense of belonging, an investment to be present in, and appreciative of, each and every experience, no matter how elemental. Merely preparing a meal for a friend, hugging a child, or picking up litter from the street, from a spiritual perspective, can stir the soul. Opening ourselves to the moment, we grow to understand that each separate act has an effect on the greater universe.

🕭 *Look back over the past day and try to recognize moments that impressed you as having a spiritual quality, where you saw or experienced how things are related to each other. Or find moments that might have revealed that quality if you had been a little more open to them.*

In my time of silence today, I focus on the rhythm of my breathing, on the pulsation of my beating heart. I become aware of the sounds outside: the wind, rain, children playing, or sirens on emergency vehicles. Allowing all this to be present in my consciousness, I become aware of my connection to all these things.

I have been a selfish being all my life, in practice,
though not in principle.

— JANE AUSTEN

If only there were a sensitivity meter that we could strap on our wrist to register when we're not being sensitive enough to the people around us or when we're being overly sensitive about something they've done! As single people, we can be incredibly self-absorbed without even realizing it. Then, to our surprise, someone gets huffy because of something we said that we thought was perfectly innocuous—something like, "You probably don't like opera," "Did you ever think about having a nose job?" or "I might like to go to that movie with you, if nothing else comes up." Or maybe *we* get surprisingly miffed at someone else who clearly didn't intend to hurt us. Perhaps we berate a friend just for laughing when we bite into an orange and it squirts us with juice or we sulk after not being invited to play tennis when we've never expressed any interest in the game.

Until a sensitivity meter is invented, there is only one thing we can do: Try more often and more conscientiously to put ourselves in the other person's shoes. Instead of only considering things from our own point of view, we need to expand our awareness to include the experiences of others.

❧ *In your conversations and personal interactions today, practice making a stronger effort to see things from the other person's perspective. For example, pay closer attention to their words, tone, facial expressions, and body language to determine more accurately how they're feeling, how they're reacting to what you're saying or doing, and what meaning lies behind their statements and actions. Write down in your notebook incidents where you began to see from someone else's perspective or moments when you realized in retrospect that you were being too self-absorbed.*

In my time of contemplative peace, I recognize that my experience of life is not the *total* experience of life. I encourage myself to learn from the experience of others.

We with our lives are . . . like trees in the forest.
The maple and pine may whisper to each other with
their leaves. . . . But the trees also commingle their
roots in the darkest underground.
—WILLIAM JAMES

Have you ever had a moment when suddenly, inexplicably, a wave of happiness or bliss wells up in you? When you experience a feeling that you've transcended the boundaries of time, place, and self, and that life is rich and all is right with the cosmos? For example, you may have had moments when something "came over you" as you watched a sunset or caught a whiff of freshly mowed grass or marveled at the synchronized movements of schools of fish or flocks of birds. What you've experienced is a sense of full aliveness.

On an average day we seldom experience or recognize this totality, this joy of being one with the universe. We are conditioned to be keenly aware of our separateness from other created things. Only in moments of rapture or ecstacy, enlightenment or profound caring, do we get an inkling of our deep affinity to the rest of humanity. Sometimes, if we are lucky, we experience this affinity with the entire universe.

To appreciate the vital contribution that a love relationship can make to our spiritual evolution in life, we need to look beyond our day-to-day selves. We need to recognize our essential connectedness to all human beings and, ultimately, to all of creation. Over the next few days, in this unit, you will come to a better understanding of how love for another can help restore your core feelings of aliveness.

← *Take a few moments today to recall and reexperience those times in your past when you've suddenly felt a transcendent sense of happiness and connection with the universe.*

Breathing deeply, I relax into my center, releasing for this moment all my fears and protective thoughts. Becoming aware of my own pulse, my awareness expands to include the vastness of the universe connected to and surrounding me. I hold this thought: "I am one with the All."

Creativity is inventing, experimenting, growing,
taking risks, breaking rules, making mistakes, and
having fun.

—MARY LOU COOK

From what well do feelings of full aliveness spring, surprising us with their intensity? What memory are these feelings trying to revive? They arise from our forgotten connection to everything and to everyone, from a spiritual sense of wholeness that we knew as children. The memory of this original state of oneness is the source of the primary and universal human longing for connectedness, and the unstated hope of love.

In seeking and building a lasting, conscious love relationship, we must always keep in mind that we're not looking for something we've never had. Instead, we're trying to recapture something that we lost in childhood when we were wounded emotionally and we began to think of ourselves as separate people. Though we may not always acknowledge it, our secret goal in relationships is not some movie-screen fantasy of love. Rather, we are responding to a drive to recover, with another human being, the state of relaxed joy that is our birthright.

Write in your journal about those times in your childhood when you felt especially close or connected to another person. You may recall relatives, friends, a kind woman who came to clean house and tell stories, a man behind the counter at the local drugstore who always had a friendly greeting, a relative stranger who briefly touched your life in a way you'll never forget. Remember the happiness, reassurance, and feelings of aliveness and connectedness that these moments gave you.

Closing my eyes in silence and breathing deeply, I release all worries and desires. I bring to mind my childhood, a time when I was more consciously aware of my connection with the source of life, and I focus on these words: "I am connected to all of creation."

Energy is eternal delight.

—WILLIAM BLAKE

In order to realize your full potential, and your wholeness as an individual, you must move beyond the impulse to merely survive. What you are really searching for is a feeling of aliveness. In order to achieve this feeling, you must be aware of how you live life in every moment.

Every day in dozens of ways you refer to this aliveness. "I feel good," you might declare, or "I'm so out of it"; "I feel I can do nothing wrong" or "My body feels like a lead weight." Such remarks are a running commentary on how you experience the intensity of your aliveness. Paying more conscious attention to this commentary is the first step toward actively expanding your "aliveness quotient." The more you understand how you feel, the more ability you will have to experience your feelings to the fullest.

&❧ *Here's an exercise that will help you evaluate how alive you feel at this particular time in your life. In your notebook, write each of the statements below on a separate line, leaving a blank space at the end of the line. In each blank space, rate the statement on a scale of one to five (five being the highest degree that you feel you identify with the statement right now).*

1. I feel alert and awake most of the time.
2. Most of the time, life excites me.
3. I laugh a lot.
4. I usually feel joyful in the company of a loved one.
5. Most of my feelings are clear and intense.
6. I have many creative ideas.
7. Many things interest me.

I descend into my inner depths, to the place of stillness, and relaxing more deeply still, I become aware of my pulsation—my beating heart—my breathing. Letting go of all tensions, I experience the pleasure of feeling myself fully alive.

A feeling of aliveness is what each one of us seeks in our lives. We try to achieve this aliveness in any number of ways—with our competitive games and work promotions; our cars, condos, boats, and gourmet food; our designer clothes, recreational sex, skin flicks, and skydiving; our dancing, jogging, and walks on the beach; our music, TV, and movies. Sometimes these "aliveness" stimulants seem to work—at least for a while. Other times, they not only fail to work, they also backfire by making us realize just how far away we are from a deep, genuine joy—the sense of spiritual wholeness and power that we knew as children.

We need to recognize that the feeling of full aliveness cannot come from material items. Nor can it be manifest within a relationship if we are not striving to achieve this feeling on our own as well. Full aliveness can only come from a commitment to be truly present in our lives.

&❧ *In your notebook, list all the things that you regularly rely upon for feelings of aliveness. Possible "aliveness stimulants" include: music, sex, drugs, alcohol, socializing, work, sports, exercise, reading, food, games, TV, shopping, hobbies, and travel. For each stimulant, think about the positive outcome you seek (for example, "I want to be admired" or "I want my body to feel exhilarated"). Then, think about ways in which this same stimulant can disappoint you or give you a negative experience (for example, "I feel inadequate" or "I get physically ill").*

In the quiet of these moments, I recall joyful memories of childhood: running, playing, laughing—expressing the natural joy of being alive. As I hold these joyful memories and sensations, I experience myself shedding all the artificial means I now use to stimulate myself in an attempt to feel my natural joy.

*If love is the answer, could you please rephrase
the question?*

— LILY TOMLIN

To sum it all up, love is the answer to the question of how to realize
full aliveness. In order for us to feel fully alive, we need to transcend
our separateness as individuals and, once again, feel our spiritual
connection with the source of life. But we can't accomplish this feat
alone. We can only achieve full aliveness through the path of a
relationship: a committed journey toward recapturing the wholeness
and the deep state of inner joyfulness that characterized our original
selves. We can do this only by stretching to meet our partner's needs.

Our partner in a real love relationship heals us, and we heal our
partner. Our unconditional love makes it safe for our partners to
open up emotionally. It lets their trust build over time and allows
their fullness to come back into being, so that they can feel their
oneness, their totality. And as love begets love, our partner's
unconditional love will simultaneously do the same for us.

The path toward a conscious loving relationship is part of nature's
grand design to restore our original joy. It is nature's repair process
to bring back our lost sense of full aliveness.

❧ *Today, review the insights you've gained over the past five
days about your personal sense of aliveness. Recall again your
memories of once feeling more profoundly connected with all
living things [Days 27 and 28]. Then, reconsider the ways in
which your present life fails to provide similar feelings of joy and
oneness [Days 29 and 30]. This review will help you see how
much room you have to grow, through a relationship, in order to
feel more fully alive. It will also help give you ideas for enlivening
your own life right now. Later in this book, you'll find single
entries that will suggest specific enlivening activities.*

**As I enter a time of prayer today, I recall the place of safety. In
serenity, I make this commitment: "I open all of me to the joy of
aliveness through love."**

*There are two ways of meeting difficulties. You alter
the difficulties or you alter yourself to meet them.*

— PHYLISS BOTTOME

One of the most difficult truths about relationships for most singles
to accept is that in order to be loved we must start by becoming a
lover. We must be willing to commit ourselves first and foremost to
healing the other person, so that he or she is more capable of
healing us. A real love relationship calls upon all of our strength and
commitment in order to make it work.

This is easier said than done. There are behaviors that are rooted
in us that act to ambush a developing relationship. We must work to
alter these attitudes and behaviors even though our unconscious
minds are highly resistant to change and even though it is easier to
fall back on the belief that people don't change, they just have to be
accepted as they are. Having heard this so often, we often don't even
question it. Nevertheless, it is wrong. It may be a safe and comforting
defense against the fear and anxiety that change provokes, but the
truth of the matter is that we *can* change. And to achieve not only
the type of healing relationship we want, but also the type of personal
fulfillment we need, we *must* change.

❧ *Prove that you can change for the better today. Identify at
least two specific ways that you could be more considerate or
helpful to someone important in your life. Write these down and
be prepared to look back on them as you are making progress
with change.*

**Letting myself relax today in a few quiet moments, I contemplate the
discomfort of remaining the way I am and the discomfort of changing.
I hold this truth: "Change is the constant. Stability is an illusion."**

Timing plays a critical role in any love relationship. Wise lovers recognize the right and wrong moments for a kiss, a hug, a joke, or a wrestling match. They take pains not to pursue each other too swiftly or too slowly. And, of course, they carefully plan dates, so that when they *do* get together, they're ready to make the most of it.

In the Imago process, the number one rule regarding timing is that all expressions of criticism, anger, or hurt are done *by appointment only.* It's the same wise strategy that goes into making dates for pleasure. Scheduling an appointment to express something that is potentially upsetting (preferably at the earliest convenient time) allows both people to prepare themselves emotionally. Anticipating a serious discussion, the "receiving" person won't feel ambushed and defensive. Meanwhile, the "sender," reassured that the matter will be addressed, has a cool-down period for organizing thoughts. In this way, a damaging, potentially regrettable outburst is averted.

Best of all, making this kind of appointment ensures that the troubling issue gets the undivided attention it deserves, rather than being ignored, overlooked, or lost amid all the other busy-ness of life. By setting aside time for the heavy stuff, you'll create more time for the lighter, sweeter side of love.

&❧ *Today, make an agreement with someone you care about that all expressions of criticism or anger will be done by appointment only. If you want to, schedule time with this person to do some of the work in this book together.*

Entering my sacred place within today, I honor this truth: "Respect for another is the surest sign of respect for myself."

*Most conversations are simply monologues delivered
in the presence of witnesses.*
                                        —MARGARET MILLAR

Unlike members of other species, two human beings who come together are not totally at the mercy of primitive stimulus/response patterns whenever they sense danger or conflict. Instead, they can engage in dialogue—not only to communicate with each other more effectively, but also to grow as individuals and be more capable of love. Through dialogue, one human being can temporarily suspend his or her own consciousness and allow the reality of another person's experience to enter and enlighten his or her mind. Through dialogue, two people can rise above a naked struggle for dominance and, instead, achieve a better understanding of each other and themselves.

The core relationship skill in the Imago process—the basis for all the other skills you'll be learning in this book—is *intentional dialogue.* It is a conscious, structured way of communicating that enables both partners to become better informed about each other's perceptions. Using it, two people can work through problems as safely and productively as possible. Intentional dialogue consists of a simple but powerful three-part process: mirroring, validation, and empathizing. In the four days ahead, you will learn the foundational skill of mirroring.

⋙ *Think of past conversations in which you had trouble discussing important personal issues with someone whom you cared about. Perhaps you wanted this person to know about your future plans, a secret insecurity, a minor irritation, a major grievance, a suppressed feeling. Write down those areas that you felt were the largest source of the difficulty. This review will give you an appreciation of the types of conversations that can be made easier and more effective through intentional dialogue.*

Recalling my conversations with others who are important in my life, I relax into the place of safety and let go of the tension of misunderstanding and being misunderstood. I open myself to the image of a new way of talking.

*You cannot truly listen to anyone and do anything
else at the same time.*
                                                    —M. SCOTT PECK

When we're talking with someone, we can easily become preoccupied with what *we* have to say. Instead of listening to what they have to say, we are thinking of how we are going to phrase our next thought or what we are going to make for dinner tonight. When this happens, we are listening only passively, with one ear, to what the other person is discussing. Our chances of understanding that person and successfully communicating with that person are seriously diminished. Instead of a dialogue, we're engaged in a parallel monologue: two people talking at each other, with very little active listening taking place.

Active listening, in which your attention is primarily focused on hearing *exactly* what the other person has to say, is the heart of mirroring. It ensures that you grow attuned to the other person's state of mind. This is the best way of knowing precisely who you are talking with and, therefore, how best to say what you have to say.

🍃 *Today, practice active listening with at least two people. Quiet down your "inner chatter" and remain alert to what you are hearing. Focus on the specific words and intonations of the people who talk to you. When you're alone, note all the different sounds around you: a passing car, the hum of a furnace, the distant bark of a dog, the conversation of people sitting nearby. Notice how much information your ears can bring you!*

Entering the sacred place within, I summon the courage to lower my fears and open myself to the world of others, recognizing that "active listening" is the first requirement of love.

When you mirror someone in intentional dialogue, you must make a conscious effort to reflect exactly what the person is saying, so that he or she feels heard. When we feel misunderstood, our natural reaction is to stop sharing. Intentional dialogue helps people to open up and share what is in their hearts on a deeper level.

The actual technique of mirroring is simple. You repeat or paraphrase the words your conversational partner uses—capturing the meaning of what they said as closely as you can. Repeat this process until you get it right. Here's an example in which the listener doesn't mirror correctly at first:

> "Sometimes I need to be by myself."
> "So you're saying sometimes you don't want me around?"
> "No, I said that sometimes I feel the need to be by myself."
> "Okay, sometimes you need some time alone."

Mirroring may seem tedious and mechanical at first, but the more your practice it, the smoother and more natural it becomes. As you use this tool of intentional dialogue, you and your conversational partner will deepen your contact with each other. As your skills progress and mirroring becomes second nature, you will be far less likely to suffer from or inflict misunderstandings and misjudgments.

🥬 *Today, practice mirroring at least three times in conversation with someone else. To make your mirroring sound more natural, you might preface your replies with a phrase like, "If I got it right, you said . . ." or "I hear you saying that . . ." You can wait for confirmation or prompt it by saying, "Did I get that right?"*

Retreating into an inner sanctuary, I become aware of my tendency to deflect instead of reflect what I am hearing in conversation. In quiet, I surrender my fear of listening.

*Home is not where you live, but where they
understand you.*

—CHRISTIAN MORGENSTERN

In mirroring someone, it helps to imagine yourself as a flat mirror, neither convex nor concave. A flat mirror reflects an exact image, while the other two surfaces distort an image. Distorted communication offers an interpretation rather than an accurate representation. Since an interpretation is what *you* are thinking and what *you* mean, rather than what the other person actually said, it often provokes frustration, anger, and conflict.

Often, we respond to what others say by slanting their meaning, giving their ideas a new twist, belittling their feelings, or blowing what they are saying out of proportion. However, when you literally reflect what the other person says, the person who is speaking with you experiences an immensely reassuring sense of safety. The other person can hear him- or herself in your own voice. In short, the other person feels "at home" with you.

🍂 *Continue to practice mirroring with other people who are close to you. Perfect your style so that you mirror more and more naturally, warmly, and supportively. Be sure to conclude your mirroring by saying, "Did I get it right?" to check for accuracy.*

In my safe place today, I relax my own need to be heard and imagine myself a flat mirror, neither convex nor concave, gifting others with accurate rephrases until they feel "at home" with me. I focus on this thought: "Making contact is holy work."

Talk is cheap because supply exceeds demand.

—ANONYMOUS

Congratulations! Having spent the past three days improving your mirroring skills, you've made an excellent start toward mastering intentional dialogue. Maybe mirroring still seems a bit stiff to you. Maybe your throat is a little sore from swallowing all those words that you were about to hurl at the other person before you'd taken the time to reflect. But consider what you've accomplished! You've obviously demonstrated to your conversation partners that you *are* listening, and no doubt you've already begun to appreciate how mirroring can help bring you and others closer together.

Soon you'll learn the other two steps in the intentional dialogue process: validation and empathy. In the meantime, continue to practice mirroring. No matter how casual or emotionally charged a particular conversation may be, mirroring is certain to make it twice as warm, illuminating, and satisfying for both parties.

❧ *Today, take a well-deserved break from conversations about serious personal issues. Instead, talk about funny items in the news, swap interesting stories and observations, or share ideas and fantasies for future entertainments. Just don't forget to mirror from time to time: It's easy work, and practice makes perfect!*

Today, in quiet stillness, I celebrate this truth: "Dialogue is the path to relationship."

Sad to say, there are no magic pills for the relationship blues! If anyone came up with a formula for such a pill, they would soon be a millionaire! While we can—and should—be idealistic above love, we have to be realistic about the hard work we must do to find and keep that love. Like everything worth having, love requires effort, commitment, and persistence in the face of sometimes incredible challenges. There is, however, a saving grace. As we do that hard work, we can begin seeing results very soon. We know ourselves better. We have more appreciation for the world around us—and the people in that world. We understand what relationships are really about, and we see ourselves changing so that we're better equipped to have the kind of relationship we so desperately want. We break the destructive patterns of past relationships, and we build more creative patterns for our present and future relationships.

🐾 *Today, look back over what you've learned, and how you've changed, in just the past thirty-nine days. Write down in your notebook some of the positive changes you've made, then do something to celebrate!*

Relaxing deeply in this time of prayer, I acknowledge the hard work I must do in order to realize my dreams and goals. I recognize that I have the strength and capacity to reach my potential.

Be bold. If you're going to make an error, make a doozy, and don't be afraid to hit the ball.

—BILLIE JEAN KING

Love is hard. But then, what is life without love? As far as life is concerned, love is the only game in town. It's a high-stakes game, and how skillfully we play determines how successfully we grow and thrive. We may as well learn how to distinguish the real rules from the false rules so that we can play this game to the best of our ability and win the prize of real love.

This book offers the game plan, but we ourselves have to put that plan into action. During the course of the game, we're bound to win some points but lose others along the way. We'll have to take many big risks, which often means there will be at least a few big failures. There will be times when our ambitions exceed our skills—at least for the moment—or times when we simply fumble despite our skills. During every moment, but especially when we're frustrated, discouraged, or tired, we need to keep our mind on the goal. A good way to remember, when you need encouragement, is to repeat: "Love is the only game worth playing, and any game worth playing is worth playing well."

&. *Today, title a page in your notebook "How to Get Back in the Game." On this page, write at least three things that you can do to restore your spirits when the game of love gets you down. Perhaps there's one particularly stirring piece of music you can play as an anthem or a poem you can read that expresses just the right sentiment to get you recommitted to the game. Maybe there's an appropriately inspirational place you can visit—a grotto in the park or a favorite room in a museum.*

In this time of reverential stillness, I tap into the courage at my center to prepare me for the total game of love—setbacks and scored points combined.

Every child, before self-consciousness sets in, acts spontaneously, with total abandon and full involvement. If you spend any time around children, you know this. Everything interests them. They whirl until they're dizzy, run until they fall, paint wildly, sing unself-consciously.

We all were like that once. We felt alive, and we allowed those feelings to overflow into many forms of expression. Unfortunately, life's realities intruded. Our parents didn't always respond to our cries, or there weren't enough hugs. Perhaps a new little sister came along or we were laughed at when we shared important ideas. As a result, we became afraid. We lost our sense of being fully alive, which we can feel only when we feel safe. Our child self got buried, and we ceased to laugh out loud, sing, or dance with abandon. We carry these "uptight" feelings, and our ways of coping with them, to our relationships. To release ourselves from these restrictive feelings, we need to once again discover the joy of childhood.

&❧ *Today, take a few moments out to recapture the feeling of spontaneous, full aliveness you had as a child. By yourself—or even better, with someone else—engage in some delightfully free and silly, childlike activity. Stand in front of a mirror and make faces until you laugh. Speak out loud in gibberish. Spin around like a dervish until you're dizzy (with a partner: hold hands, place your feet close together, and spin in a circle as fast as you can). Play tag with each other until you're exhausted. Or join children wholeheartedly in their make-it-up-as-you-go-along fun.*

In my twenty minutes today, I imagine myself a joyful child twirling in abandon. Holding this image, I remember: "I am essentially joy."

*You need someone to love while you're looking for
someone to love.*

— SHELAGH DELANEY

So, you've joined a single's bowling league, gone to every single's
workshop offered by local self-help centers, and loitered in the pet
store whenever you've shopped at the mall. All of these ideas
sounded like good ways to meet people when your friends suggested
them. Yet, you're still not encountering many romantic possibilities.
It's time for some serious self-assessment. Besides frequenting more
places so you can meet more prospective partners, you might also
try expanding the criteria by which you make your choices. The
narrower and more detailed your list of specifications for an acceptable date is, the smaller the field of choice becomes. Unwittingly,
you are rejecting thousands of prospective partners before they've
even had a chance to win your heart.

   To improve your social life, give both new people and yourself a
big break! Broaden your horizons! Date people who look, act, and
think differently from what you're used to. For example, if you
customarily rule out shy, intellectual types in favor of aggressive,
athletic types, do the uncustomary thing. Pursue the next shy,
intellectual type that catches your eye. If you're drawn to someone
who seems too plain—or too glamorous—for you, don't back off.
Give it a shot! Even if you don't wind up with another romantic
prospect, you'll enlarge *yourself,* and this alone will enlarge your pool
of partners.

&▪ *Sometime during the next week, make an effort to know
someone better whom you would normally discount as a dating
prospect. Perhaps you already have a few people in mind, whom
you've always looked at wistfully on the elevator at work but
never dared approach. Make a commitment to ask one of these
prospects on a date.*

**During this time of silent prayer, I allow those limitations that would
normally narrow my path to dissolve away, illuminating a wider
course for me to travel.**

Most people remain basically unconscious in their relationships. They let their old brain run their emotional agenda. The old brain is quite simple and not very demanding. It allows them to float along when things are going okay and forces them to snarl, run for cover, or simply collapse when things are going wrong. They blind themselves to the details. What they don't see, can't bother them.

Oh, but it can! One moment of passionate words spewed in anger can destroy the trust and safety that has taken so long to build. In order for a relationship to survive and, ultimately, reach the stage of real love, our *unconscious* aim must be transformed into our *conscious* intent. We must enlist our new brain—our cognitive powers—to achieve the survival objectives of our old brain. These objectives are to find safety, heal our wounds, and restore our sense of full aliveness. When the old brain works on meeting these objectives, we are acting from an unconscious place, where we cease to be in control. However, when we enlist our new brain, we gain control over our reactive states and create a greater potential for real love. This shift requires taking a clearer look at ourselves, our past partners, and the world around us, and developing the skills to cope effectively with what we see.

🖎 *Think back over the past week. In your relationships with important people in your life, what actions and reactions of yours strike you as being "old brain" or unconscious, instead of "new brain" or intentional? Write your insights down.*

In my time of meditation today, I imagine I am in a room that is dark except for one ray of light. As I focus on the light, it expands and slowly fills more of the room, bringing the room's contents into view. I make this decision: "I will become fully conscious."

We do not live in an age of arranged marriages, but that doesn't mean that we have free choice regarding our romantic partners. The image of the partner we seek begins to be etched in our unconscious mind very early in life. Called the Imago, it's a composite likeness of our earliest caretakers—the people upon whom we depended for our physical, mental, emotional, and spiritual well-being.

Our Imago stays with us as we mature, exerting an irresistible influence on our romantic attraction to others. The result is the grand mystery of love. Thanks to our Imago, we unconsciously want to get what we didn't get in childhood and seek this fulfillment from someone who is like the people who didn't give us what we needed in the first place.

During the next few days, you'll work toward deciphering your own Imago and shedding more light on the mystery of love. You'll examine the characteristics of your early caretakers and the traits and behaviors that had the most impact on your own childhood. And you'll trace the influence of your Imago in shaping your past relationships.

Think about the major relationships in your life. Identify your primary male and female caretakers as an infant (usually, the mother and the father; in some cases, a sibling, a relative, or another person). Then, identify your two most significant romantic relationships as an adult (possible choices may include a high-school crush, a college sweetheart, a live-in lover, a steady date, or a marriage partner). Write down the names of the people in your notebook, and the roles they've served. These are the people whom you will be examining more closely in the days to come.

As I sit in sacred stillness today, I renew my commitment to look within, viewing myself from this new perspective. As my breathing slowly deepens, I simply allow my awareness to move as far inward as feels comfortable to me.

*All of us . . . have been formed by experiences that
still inhabit us. Memory is not only a trip but also
a structure. . . . Our need to make sense of our lives
has continually to take account of all this.*

— JOHN BERGER

Like a baby zebra instinctively walking round and round its mother
to imprint her stripe pattern so that it will never lose her, our child
brain imprints the distinctive characteristics of our caretakers. On a
deep level, it memorizes both their positive *and their negative* traits,
creating a pattern that becomes familiar to us and to which we are
attracted. This is the image that coalesces into our Imago.

When we grow up to become adults, our unconscious mind seeks
to heal its childhood wounds and, in the process, recover its wholeness. To this end, it seeks someone who resembles our Imago. In
this way, it can continue unfinished business left over from childhood
with the same sort of emotional "caretaker." We are, in effect,
programmed to fall in love with someone who has both the positive
and the negative traits of our imperfect parents, someone who fits
the Imago image that we carry deep inside us.

❧ *Today, think specifically about your mother (or mother figure).
On a separate page in your notebook entitled "Mother," make
two lists: "Positive Traits" and "Negative Traits." In each list,
describe specific traits using simple adjectives or short phrases.
For example, positive traits may be "kind," "a good painter,"
"patient," "very protective of me." Negative traits may be "pessi-
mistic," "expected too much of me," "fearful," "stingy."*

Today, I relax into a deep place of courage, the place that allows me
to look objectively at my childhood. I offer compassion to myself for
those ways in which I was not cared for as a child yet needed to be.
Before my time of quiet is ended, I give myself a big hug.

*It doesn't matter who my father was; it matters who
I remember he was.*

— ANNE SEXTON

Never underestimate the power of your childhood mind! From the moment it came into being, it was ferociously busy recording every aspect of your early caretakers. These recordings contain the sound of their voices when they were angry, the way they smiled when they were pleased, the smell and texture of their bodies, what they ate and wore. Then it forged all of this information into your Imago. You now have this Imago as an indelible image that you use as a template in your search for a romantic partner—someone with whom you can establish a strong, caring relationship.

As a child, your primitive old brain was intensely concerned about sheer survival. Since your caretaker was primarily responsible for your survival, it makes sense that these images penetrated so deeply into your subconscious. Unfortunately, it also makes sense that the most vivid and potent of all the impressions absorbed by your childhood brain were the negative encounters. Nothing holds greater impact than a behavior from a caretaker that seems to threaten your very existence. For better or worse, the way that you learned to survive in a relationship—your entire emotional security system—is organized around your childhood experiences.

&❧ *Today, think specifically about your father (or father figure) as you knew him in childhood. On a separate page of your notebook entitled "Father," make two lists: "Positive Traits" and "Negative Traits." In each list, describe specific traits using simple adjectives and phrases.*

Going within today, I tap into the core of my strength. I reinforce this place within my mind, recognizing that I have the capacity to protect and heal myself.

*The heart has its reasons which reason knows
nothing of.*

—PASCAL

When we are strongly attracted to someone new, we are in fact reencountering something old: our Imago. This image goes back to the beginning of our lives. Our Imago is a type of ghost partner that stays with us. When we encounter this ghost partner embodied in a flesh-and-blood person, a chemical reaction occurs. We fall in love, and that fall plunges us back into the intense experiences of childhood loves and needs, joys and pains.

At first, we feel confident that this person who has so deeply stirred us will make everything all right in our lives. Unfortunately, we've almost surely been influenced by our Imago to choose someone with negative traits similar to those of our caretakers; so the odds of a more positive outcome this time around are stacked against us. The work that you're doing now, in this unit specifically and in the book as a whole, is designed to make you more conscious of what goes into your relationships. As a result, it will improve your chances of getting more out of them.

🦰 *Today, focus specifically on one of your most significant romantic relationships as an adult. Consider all the different traits that your partner exhibited during the relationship. Recall when you first fell in love and all the things you noticed about him/her then. Next, think about the first time you experienced something wrong and became more aware of different traits in this person. Finally, remember the traits that you associate with the ending of the relationship.*

In your notebook, entitle a separate sheet with the name of this person and make two lists: "Positive Traits" and "Negative Traits." In each list, describe all of the specific traits you observed, using simple adjectives or short phrases.

In wordless prayer, I trust myself and the knowledge I am unearthing to point the way to a conscious relationship that offers real love.

*It always comes back to the same necessity: go deep
enough and there is a bedrock of truth, however hard.*

—MAY SARTON

Relationships are intrinsically mysterious. We have to reconcile
ourselves to the fact that we will never be able to predict with
complete accuracy why we fall in love with someone. Or how a
certain romance will play itself out. However, as a single person
searching for a good partner, the best way to improve your outlook
is to start by probing beneath the surface of your own life.

Mining past relationships will unearth informational gems about
what your values are, why you make the choices you make, and what
to watch for in the future. If you can sort through all your memories
of past partners honestly and intelligently, distinguishing between the
"good" and the "bad" traits that you saw in them, you will eventually
come up with a rough picture of your Imago. This is the image of the
ideal partner to which you are mysteriously and inevitably lured.

You may not be able to prevent interpersonal dilemmas in the
future. But by reflecting deeply on past relationships, you can gain
invaluable insights into the sources of your romantic pains and
pleasures, the patterns that get repeated in your relationships, and
the places where growth and change must begin.

᛫᛫ *Today, focus on another significant romantic relationship that
you have had as an adult, considering all the traits that you
encountered in this person. In your notebook, entitle a separate
sheet with the name of this person and make two lists: "Positive
Traits" and "Negative Traits." In each list, describe all of the
specific traits you observed, using simple adjectives or short
phrases.*

**In quiet contemplation today, I commit myself to exploring my past
relationships with honesty. I recognize that these honest moments
create a strength that I can draw upon in the future.**

The future bears a great resemblance to the past,
only more so.

                                     —FAITH POPCORN

We are all products of our past, and so we never really leave the past behind us. It is no accident that the people with whom we are fated to become romantically involved are those who have a great deal in common with our early caretakers. Although we may not be fully aware of it, we are reliving our childhood with each partner choice, in the hope of being truly fulfilled this time.

We end up doing this because our unconscious mind has no sense of linear time. To our unconscious mind, our Imago-based adult partners *literally* function as composites of our early caretakers. By choosing partners whose positive and negative traits are similar to those of our early caretakers and who, therefore, have the same capacity to nourish or to wound us, we are trying to pick up where we left off as children. We want to be able finally to achieve satisfaction from the people upon whom we so heavily depended in our childhood.

⁂ *Review the pages in your notebook on which you have already listed the positive and negative traits of your mother (or mother figure), father (or father figure), and two significant romantic relationships. On each page, circle positive traits that are common to all four of these individuals or to at least three of them. Then, on each page, underline negative traits that are common to all four of these individuals or to at least three of them.*

As I sit in sacred stillness, I celebrate this work that leads me on my path toward consciousness.

*Your task is not to seek for love, but merely to seek
and find all of the barriers within yourself that you
have built against it.*

                             —*A COURSE IN MIRACLES*

To get a preview of the person whom you will want as your future
partner—and whom you will *need* as your future partner if your
childhood wounds are ever going to be healed—you have to look into
your own soul. Your Imago match is not an ideal person in the
abstract, a paragon of beauty and sensitivity who can anticipate and
meet a partner's every desire. Instead, your Imago match is the ideal
character and qualities *for you*—someone with whom you can join in
striving to realize a better, more holy life.

    The myth of the perfect mate is a static image derived from books,
magazines, movies, and television. It represents what is absent from
your life—a shimmering, seemingly unattainable apparition that has
no depth and allows for no change, positive or negative. By contrast,
the Imago is an image derived not just from life itself, but from your
own, unique life. It is a mysterious presence that has deep roots and
great potential for growth.

    Your Imago portrait is by no means as bright and shiny as the
perfect mate image; indeed, it's rather dark and obscure. But
the perfect mate image can only become increasingly dull and tar-
nished the more you subject it to real-life scrutiny. The Imago
portrait, however, can only become clearer and more illuminating.

  *Today, entitle a separate page in your notebook "My Imago
Preview." On this page, draw a circle and divide it in half
horizontally. Within the top half of the circle, write in all the
positive traits that you circled yesterday (Day 49)—the ones that
were shared by three or four of your early caretakers and past
relationships. Within the bottom half of the circle, write in all the
negative traits that you underlined yesterday. The result is a
preview picture of your Imago.*

**In my time of spiritual renewal, I recognize that my vision of the
future has shifted. The dark corners, harboring the fear of
the unknown, are becoming illuminated by newfound knowledge of
myself and my Imago.**

The single state has its own unique constellation of pleasures and pains. However, taken as a whole, it simply doesn't offer the rich potential for emotional and spiritual growth that we can enjoy within a committed relationship. For anyone who seeks fulfillment according to nature's plan, being single can only be an interim stage of evolution, not an end in itself. It's a time for reassessing and refining ourselves after the end of one period of close relationship (such as dependence on our parents or a long-term romantic partner or a former spouse) and before the beginning of another. With this in mind, we must try not to think of ourselves as merely "a single person." Instead, we need to think of ourselves as "a single person who is on the way to the wedding." It may be a long journey rather than a short one, but the journey will be all the more rewarding for having a clear destination.

Today, consider your last period of living in an intimate relationship. For many of us, this will be when we were living with our parents or early caretakers. For others, it will be when we were living with a lover or a marriage partner. Identify at least three ways in which you are still resolving painful issues that linger from that relationship. For each issue that you identify, think of a positive alternative that you'd like to experience in a future, committed relationship. Write these findings down in your notebook.

In a time of quiet meditation today, I hold this truth: "Committed relationship is the path to wholeness."

*The spirit is the true self, not that physical figure
which can be pointed out by your finger.*

—CICERO

Single women starve away their fat, torture their hair, and moisturize their skin, hoping the full effect will attract a mate. Meanwhile, single men are busy toning their abs and pumping up their pec-deck for the same purpose. There's nothing bad about trying to maintain a good-looking body. But there's something tragically wrong with the notion that our attractiveness as people depends on our physical appearance. Our real self is not the way we physically appear to others. Our real essence resides in our spirit—that part of us that gives life to our character and personality.

Placing too much value on appearances, and not enough on the spirit, defeats one's truest self. For no matter how much external beauty we cultivate, our whole being can only be truly radiant when our spirit shines forth in full strength. Why go to such lengths to redesign our body, just so that it appeals to another body, especially since our physical appearance will shift with age? How much saner it is to strengthen our conscious mind to grasp our fuller reality and the reality of our interconnection to others. How much more gratifying it is to stretch our heart's capacity to love and be loved! How much grander it is to ignite our soul so that it can illuminate our own life and the life of our future partner!

❧ *Today, think about all the things you do to benefit your body. Then, think about what you do to benefit your spirit. Make two columns on a notebook page and write this list down. Is the "body" list longer and more specific than the "spirit" list?*

Knowing that all attention I place upon appearances is a search and substitute for my true self, I vow today, that whenever I feel pulled to make an impression upon others, I will enter the deep silence and commune with my deepest essence.

Never miss a good chance to shut up.
　　　　　　　　—SCOTT BEACH'S GRANDFATHER

Like any other skill, good listening takes practice. Fortunately, opportunities abound! We often find ourselves in the company of someone whose need to talk is equal to or more pressing than our own. It could be a friend who is bursting with excitement about a new car. Perhaps it's a colleague at work reporting on a tricky business negotiation. Or maybe it's a date who pokes fun at our love for country music and goes on to recall the personality quirks of an ex-spouse.

We may be sorely tempted to interrupt or derail these speakers with our own remarks and reactions. Unlike our friend with the new car, we're still struggling along with our old one. We can think of a better way that our colleague could have handled the negotiation. We're defensive about our date's teasing, and nothing could interest us less than our date's ex-spouse.

However, if we refrain from speaking and, instead, really apply ourselves to listening, we can turn these initially irksome experiences into unique learning opportunities. Our friend may reveal something helpful about car buying. We may reach a better understanding of the type of negotiation our colleague is discussing. Our date may reveal feelings or interests that we might otherwise have never known. But most important, we will learn something about the other person, about how it feels to be in their shoes. We will expand our narrow horizons and feel more connected to life.

🍃 *Today, practice listening to other people more actively. Use the intentional dialogue skill of mirroring (Days 35 through 38) to show people that you are listening and to make sure that you've heard them correctly.*

In this time of silent prayer, I focus on those times when I have truly listened to others. I recognize the gift that listening is, understanding that I am gifted by added knowledge about others in my life.

No man is an island, entire of itself; every man is a piece of the continent, a part of the main.

—JOHN DONNE

Although we tend to think of ourselves as separate individuals, we are inextricably bound to the world around us. Each one of us can be seen as a part of a seamless tapestry of being—a single thread interconnected with others, part of a larger pattern that makes up the entire cosmos. As humans, we have a unique power to observe ourselves and our place in the seamless tapestry of being. This awareness is the foundation of our innate spirituality. By opening ourselves to this deeper spirituality, we can become empowered to correct the problems that are hurting ourselves as well as others. For every time we resolve a problem that hurts us, we are resolving a problem that ultimately harms the people with whom we associate. As part of the tapestry being, we must remember that a single thread can unravel the whole and every thread must be sewn to keep it together.

Take a few minutes to become more aware of your place in the tapestry of being. Examine your life today and ask yourself these questions:
- *What people do I regularly depend upon? How so?*
- *What people regularly depend upon me? How so?*
- *How is my well-being affected by my friends? My family? My community? My planet?*
- *How do my actions affect the well-being of my friends? My family? My community? My planet?*

Entering the stillness within today, I visualize every action I make as a ripple that affects all others in the pond of our total existence.

Give him enough rope and he will hang himself.

—CHARLOTTE BRONTË

Many people yearn to have a partner. They believe that they are doing everything in their power to draw a mate into their lives. But deeply rooted, insidious behaviors and attitudes often get in the way. It isn't that we don't try hard enough or find the right people, but sometimes our own behavior turns people off.

There are countless ways to turn the odds against yourself when meeting someone new. You might not allow them to get a word in edgewise, or you might brag outrageously about your new condo. You could disparage their intelligence. Or, perhaps you're late, with plenty of excuses and no sincere apology. Even talking negatively about your own past relationships can make you look bad. This negative talk alerts your date to some sticky areas in your life and can send the message that you'll speak about him or her in the same way later.

Watch out for self-defeating behaviors! They can be very difficult to detect. If you can't think of times in your past when you've sabotaged your chances, try thinking of what turns you off in others and guard against doing those things yourself.

❧ *Today, start a list in your journal of negative behaviors that you are currently aware of. You may want to approach a trusted friend and ask him or her to give you input. While it may be hard to listen to at first, in the long run it will keep you from offending someone new in the future.*

During my sacred time of solitude, I breathe in the resolve to receive new people with gentle and accepting kindness. With each breath, I feel my heart expanding.

A major milestone in our postpuberty psychosexual history is our "first love." One special person suddenly takes on universal importance in a way that no one else ever has. We experience what love *really* is: something that shakes the body, rattles the brain, and rocks the soul.

We never forget this person, and we never really leave the memories of this time behind us. Certain aspects of our first love subtly reoccur in each succeeding love relationship, as if we were forever committed to that same pattern. Perhaps we are continually attracted to redheads, hotheads, good huggers, or people who get easily depressed. Maybe we woo each lover in a similar way: buying new clothes to dazzle them, pretending to like everything they like, or playing it cool until they're forced to grab our attention. We may glory when our lover bursts into laughter at our slyest joke and agonize when they are once again an hour late to meet us. Developing an awareness of such recurring patterns helps us to become more conscious in our relationships and, as a result, more competent in making them work.

❧ *Today, think back to your first love. How did you feel and behave around this person? What was the person and overall experience like? Then, briefly consider the major romantic relationships you've had since that first love. Identify at least three things that all of these loves had in common and write them down.*

In silent reverie today, I close my eyes and revisit my "first love," knowing that the stirring of my heart was a call and an opportunity to recover my wholeness.

INTENTIONAL DIALOGUE: VALIDATION

Conversations often turn into verbal sword fights. "That's not how I see it!" "You shouldn't let something like that stand in your way." "But what about the alternatives?" We consistently parry other's remarks with our own personal thrusts. This behavior can seriously injure a relationship.

The second part of intentional dialogue is *validation*. Validation requires putting yourself in the other person's place and recognizing that what they are saying *makes sense from their point of view*. Then you communicate this recognition so that the other person feels they have been understood. It can be as simple as saying, "I understand why you might feel that way."

Validation does not mean that you have to *agree* with the other person—either openly or privately. Nor does it mean that you are encouraging them to maintain their current perspective. It simply means that you are acknowledging the other person's right to their own experience and feelings.

Learning how to validate your partner is a way to keep both of you from reaching for your swords. Through validating each other, you learn to respect—and perhaps even to resolve—your differences.

ᔍ *Think of someone with whom you often "sword fight" in conversation. Try to envision how they may view things based on who they are: their gender, age, past experiences, and present needs and desires. Then write in your notebook three ways that you could have validated them in the past.*

As I enter my safe place today, I summon the courage to face the awareness that I am absorbed in my point of view, often assuming that others experience the world exactly as I do. Confessing this omnipotent perspective, I surrender it and accept that my world is one among many. I hold this sacred truth: "Only God can see the whole."

*We rarely find that people have good sense unless
they agree with us.*

—DUC DE LA ROCHEFOUCAULD

To master the art of validation, it is important to remember that *others are not you.* This means that others are bound to have different experiences and reactions from what you would have in a similar situation.

Let's assume that you invite a friend to come with you to a party. In your mind, it's a casual invitation that offers your friend a chance to meet new people. After the party, your friend surprises you by saying, "I wish you had stayed around to make introductions instead of instantly wandering off."

Nonvalidating, combative responses on your part might be, "You're not a shy person, so I didn't think you'd need my help" or "I saw someone across the room that I had to talk to." Even if you prefaced one of these remarks with "I'm sorry," you would still be deflecting or devaluing what the other person has said.

A more helpful, validating response might be: "So, you're upset that I didn't help you meet people [mirroring]. I can understand how you felt [validation]." Other typical validating phrases are: "I can see that . . ." or "I can appreciate that . . ." In this way, the other person feels heard.

&❧ *Practice taking the time and effort to validate people in conversations. Remember, always begin by mirroring what your conversational partner has said and checking to make sure that you've got it right; then, offer your validation, to reassure your listener that what they said makes sense to you.*

In the privacy of my safe place today, I accept that other people see the world from their own perspective, and without invalidating my own perceptions, I accept their logic to be as valid for them as mine is for me. I celebrate this opportunity: "To see the world through the eyes of another is to add another world to my own."

*The test of a first-rate intelligence is the ability to
hold two opposed ideas in the mind at the same time
and still retain the ability to function.*

— F. SCOTT FITZGERALD

In any communication between two people, there are *always* two
points of view. Sometimes these two viewpoints are in conflict. This
doesn't mean that the two people who hold them are enemies or
even incompatible. It just means that they are two individuals with
different reactions based on their unique life experiences. In fact,
these different viewpoints can enhance the relationship as a whole.

When letting another person into your life, it is important to honor
their unique identity. In this way, your life can become all the more
mentally, emotionally, and spiritually fulfilling. The most effective
dialogue keeps both points of view equally in mind. When this
happens, both people—even if they are very different—can function
well together from a place of mutual understanding and respect.

Validation is a powerful tool that can help you forge more meaningful relationships with people. It's an expression of respect that says,
"You and I can grow closer and closer together and still remain
distinct individuals." It's a way for your soul to break out of a self-
centered prison into the heavenly freedom of a "Me-You" partnership.

🍃 *Begin a page in your notebook with the phrase "I can see how
you would think that (or feel that)." Write down other phrases
that you can use to validate others. Commit yourself to practicing
validation techniques with those you care about. Notice how you
are able to maintain your own point of view without offending or
belittling others. And notice how good it feels when you allow
others to express their feelings and viewpoints.*

From the holy place at my center, I realize that I can allow others to
exist and remain myself. I ponder this thought: "The oneness of the
world is available through the eyes of the many."

Love is . . . the open sesame to every soul.
                                        — ELIZABETH CADY STANTON

In order to feel fully alive and to recapture our joyfulness, we have to reintegrate the unconscious, instinctual old brain with our clever new brain. But we cannot merely *think* our way to aliveness. The old brain can only be altered through experience. And so we need to combine thinking *and* doing. We need to bring back to life the parts of ourselves that were split off, denied, or lost during childhood. We need to heal the numbness, pain, and fears that restrict our feeling of aliveness and keep us from realizing our connection to the universe. The most effective way to achieve this healing is through a committed relationship.

People who have been disappointed in love don't want to hear that they *need* a relationship to feel fully alive. They want to believe that they can be autonomous and restore their spiritual wholeness on their own. But this is a delusion. While there is a great deal that we can accomplish on our own, we can't go the whole way toward self-realization without the critical process of experiencing the conflict, and the ultimate lessons and resolution of the conflict, in a committed love relationship.

❧ *To better appreciate the power that relationships can have to help you come alive as a human being, recall at least three important things you've learned about yourself or three latent qualities that have emerged in the course of your past relationships. Write your realizations down.*

During this twenty minutes of reflection, I recognize that the conflicts that I experience in partnership reveal aspects of myself that contribute to my wholeness. Being open to the wholeness in myself opens me to the wholeness in others and in the universe.

*Inside myself is a place where I live all alone and
that's where you renew your springs that never
dry up.*
                                            —PEARL S. BUCK

Meditation is an ancient spiritual practice and a part of a wide variety
of cultures and customs. Why have so many different people in so
many different contexts been drawn to establish some form of
contemplative practice? Meditation can be seen as a way to make
contact with our innermost feelings, to open ourselves to our spiritual
depths, and to connect with the whole of reality. One could say that
we meditate to renew the spirit within, to reconnect with the
universal energy that fuels our life and gives it meaning.

Meditation is using our mind to do its best and noblest work. We
spend too much time in a semiconscious state, unwilling or unable to
notice things too closely or think about things too deeply. There are
periods when we shift our minds into overdrive. But usually we do
this in order to handle many different matters simultaneously, which
too often leads to a chaotic or fragmented emotional state. Through
meditating, we learn *mindfulness*—the ability to focus all of our
attention on a single issue using prayer, contemplation, or meditation.
In this way, we can give our full attention to whatever happens to be
the most important issue we are facing. It's the type of mindfulness
we need in order to find, develop, and conduct a lasting love relationship.

❧ *Bring a renewed energy to your meditation today. We often
fall into routine, and each daily meditation offers us the chance to
practice with our full commitment and enthusiasm. Perhaps, if it's
warm, you could meditate outside. Or you could meditate in your
bathtub. You could light incense, focus on a special picture, or
listen to some new relaxing music.*

**Right now I am imagining a point of light in my mind's eye. Breathing
deeply and relaxing, I bring all my attention to that point, knowing
that as I hold my focus there, I will create a sacred intersection with
all else.**

Call attention to a person's good points, and you'll look all the better! Everyone not only likes compliments but *needs* them to feel more secure about themselves and the impression they make. Offering this security is a thoughtful expression.

We may have to remind ourselves to compliment people more often, and we should never forget that there's a big difference between *compliments* and *flattery*. A compliment is the end result of a spontaneous and sincere appreciation of something positive in the other person's appearance, behavior, or personality. Flattery, by contrast, is a calculated effort to curry favor with them by speaking about them positively, whether or not we've actually been impressed. Complimenting brings two people closer together in a natural way. Flattery sets up a fooler-fooled dynamic that's very risky.

Of course, when we're face to face with someone whom we want to like us, we can certainly compliment him or her *intentionally*. This is not the same as premeditated flattery. Here's a tip to help you tell the difference: If you find yourself silently admiring something about a person, go ahead and tell him or her. That's a compliment. If you find yourself trying to think of something positive to say, stop thinking, or you'll wind up simply offering empty flattery.

❧ *Write down things that you genuinely like about some of your friends or coworkers. With these points in mind, make an effort to compliment at least five people at work tomorrow.*

Today, in my twenty minutes of solitude, I recognize how appreciative I am when people share their sincere admiration with me and I promise to offer them the same in return.

> *Fear is that little darkroom where negatives are developed.*
>
> —MICHAEL PRITCHARD

From childhood on, we learn to fear different things. These fears are based on our own personality and experiences. Each person's list is unique. For example, take Liz, a thirty-five-year-old, high-energy woman who grew up with quarreling parents. She owns her own catering business and once broke her collarbone in a late-night car wreck. Her "fear" list might include losing her youth, being all alone with nothing to do, or being yelled at by other people. She may also be fearful of driving after dark and failing as a cook. Mark is an African-American who was bitten as a child by a German shepherd. He also starred on his college debating team and twice lost long-term girlfriends to other men. His fear list might include racial prejudice, dogs, saying something stupid, and being rejected as a lover.

Whatever our list of fears might contain, it's a life spoiler. Fears constrict our spiritual openness.

They trap our free spirit, keeping us attached to our past troubles. Instead of living with an enthusiasm and vitality for life, the fear conditions us to live from a stifled place of wariness. And our fear activates our old brain, which in turn inundates us with all sorts of negative attitudes and behaviors.

🕊️ *Today, list at least three fears on your "fear list." For each fear, ask yourself:*
- *Why might I have this fear?*
- *How does it spoil things for me in my present life?*
- *How might I go about overcoming this fear?*

Today, I enter my place of safety and make a commitment to free myself from the fears of my past. I meditate on this thought: Fear is in the eye of the beholder.

Unhurt people are not much good in the world.
—ENID STARKIE

It is fashionable these days to be cynical about romance, but in our hearts, we should never diminish or demean. However disappointing, foolish, or downright miserable the romantic experience can be, it's one of nature's miracles. Not only does it feel supremely wonderful, it is also the catalyst for healing and change. In blinding us to reality, romantic love performs a valuable service. We unwittingly choose someone to love whom we would never knowingly choose—someone who has many of the faults of our early caretakers. Paradoxically, this person has the potential both to reopen old wounds and to heal them completely. It appears to be a recipe for disaster and heart-break. If we were not in romantic love's thrall, we would turn tail and run, for we have actually chosen someone who will, indeed, frustrate AND HURT us as our caretakers did. But that kind of person, when responsive to our needs, is the only kind of person we will allow to help us realize our full potential.

❧ *Today, recall at least two incidents in the past when you realized that your romantic partner was capable of wounding you in the very same way that a parent or early caretaker wounded you. Write these two incidents down.*

❧ *As I relax into my quiet place today, I rest in the wonder that pain is a natural consequence of my growth toward wholeness. Knowing this, I make this vow: Fear will never divert me from love, for love is the path to wholeness.*

An important element in any close relationship is safety. Familiar routines, such as going out for brunch every Sunday, give couples a sense of tradition and permanence. Carefully planned budgets and vacations offer couples a comforting blueprint for the future. Agreed-upon rules for handling household chores, scheduling independent activities, or even fighting help couples feel more secure about being together on a day-to-day basis.

But these same sureties can also put limits on a relationship's ability to grow. Nothing revitalizes love better than novelty and a sense of adventure. Those routines that keep us feeling safe must be balanced with times of unchartered adventure. To avoid getting into a rut, any relationship needs to occasionally venture into the un-known. If you are not dating right now, go off somewhere with a good friend or sibling for an afternoon, evening, or weekend without planning precisely what you'll do or where to go. If you are dating someone, spring something spontaneous on them! By creating your adventure as you go along, you're likely to find whole new worlds of excitement in each other's company.

❧ *Sometime soon, take off with someone you like for a "magical mystery tour" date. Ramble around a neighborhood or country-side that's unfamiliar. Consult no guides and follow no maps. Instead, go wherever your imagination takes you. Browse in antique shops that catch your eye. Stop to watch children—or adults—at play in a park. Find a romantic-looking restaurant for dinner. Or, if you come across a circus, buy tickets for that day. If you pass a club where they're playing your favorite kind of jazz, drop in.*

Relaxing into my breathing, and entering my safe place, I access my courage and imagination. Shedding commitment to routine and safety, I open myself to adventure. These words guide me: The unknown holds the potential of joy.

> *. . . life is thorny; and youth is vain;*
> *And to be wroth with one we love;*
> *Doth work like madness in the brain.*
>
> —SAMUEL TAYLOR COLERIDGE

Have you snapped at someone recently, only to find them looking at you with large eyes that reflected their surprise? Or have you come home feeling absolutely furious over an offhanded comment that someone made to you on the way to the elevator? If this is going on, chances are it's your old brain at work once again!

We like to think of our brain as the part of us that thinks, plans, creates, and makes decisions. It is the center of our *consciousness* and reason, which are the states of mind that are generated by the most recently evolved part of our brain, the cerebral cortex. But *unconsciously* our old gray brain lies in ambush, waiting to spring on anyone if it feels that our protective walls are about to be—or already have been—breached. No matter how steeped in civilization we feel we are, nothing can temper or obscure our intrinsic—and sometimes primitive—human nature. At times, the intensity of our response can surprise us. But when we remember that our old brain is what closely connects us to our earliest humanoid ancestors—and back beyond them to other mammals and even reptiles—the responses begin to make sense.

This doesn't mean that it is okay or acceptable to respond in this manner, however! One of our new brain's constant jobs is to try to keep our old brain from spinning out of control! The more we can identify what it is that sets our old brain to growling, the easier it is to aid our new brain in this monumental task.

❧ *Today, think back over the past week and try to identify moments when your reaction was too much "old brain" and too little "new brain." Write these reactions down.*

In quiet contemplation, I visualize myself throwing meat to the protective energy that lives within my old brain, assuaging the fierce need to protect and defend, so that the consciousness awaiting me in my new brain may take a more active role.

*Our business is to wake up. We have to find ways
in which to detect the whole of reality in the one
illusory part which our self-centered consciousness
permits us to see. . . . We must be continuously on
our watch for ways in which we may enlarge our
consciousness.*

— ALDOUS HUXLEY

Most of us resist taking an honest look at past relationship frustrations. We strive to suppress conflictual memories, hoping that someday they will disappear altogether. Inevitably, however, these memories return unbidden to haunt us. We are fortunate that these thoughts and memories are so persistent. As long as we flee from or fight them, they will continue to upset and dominate us. But as soon as we face and start studying them, they will begin to teach us, making us stronger.

Becoming a more conscious person will enable us to enjoy conscious relationships in the future. Becoming conscious means mastering the types of situations that frustrated you in the past. To do this, one must answer some pretty tough questions: What caused conflicts between you and previous romantic partners and why? How did these conflicts play out?

As a single person, you are in an excellent position to work on these types of questions, because it is much more difficult for couples in conflict to be objective. Even if you have painful memories, you are a conflict survivor and have a certain degree of emotional detachment. During the next few days, you will be reviewing your past relationships. In this way, you can begin to discern more clearly the patterns of frustration that have consistently tormented you.

❧ *Today, choose the three romantic relationships in your past that caused the most frustrations and begin to write down an abbreviated history of each. Make a commitment to study these three relationships more thoughtfully in the days to come.*

Drawing upon courage in this time of stillness, I commit myself to viewing my past relationships with honesty and fairness.

> *It is only that my illusion is more real to me than reality. And so do we often build our world on an error, and cry out that the universe is falling to pieces, if any one but lift a finger to replace the error by truth.*
>
> —MARY ANTIN

Many singles cling to fantasies of partnership. They cherish illusions, believing that true love automatically brings complete happiness, and that love alone will surmount any crisis. But fantasies can be devastating. Singles who refuse to see beyond them loose sight of reality. They fail to acknowledge unconscious patterns and don't appreciate the amount of hard work that goes into achieving a solid relationship. They don't realize that romantic love alone cannot support even the most impassioned lovers through a major conflict.

Inevitably these confused, unhappy, and hurt singles become confused, unhappy, and hurt couples. The combination of these two singles creates an even greater degree of pain and confusion, and this pain compounds with every new relationship started that is based on fantasies and illusions. The only way to break the cycle is to look more objectively at the harsh realities of past relationships. Instead of dwelling on the shattered fantasies, try focusing on the actual events that frustrated you, one at a time.

❦ *Choose one of the three relationships mentioned yesterday, and divide a notebook page into three vertical columns. Label the first column: "1. Frustration." Underneath, list specific behaviors that caused you discomfort or pain. For example, "S/he would make appointments with me and then always be late." "S/he would often get angry and defensive." "S/he often criticized me in front of my friends."*

Relaxing into a time of reverence, I let go of my fantasies of a perfect partner. Instead, I allow myself to acknowledge that with hard work on myself, the real love that will be available to me is more fulfilling than any fantasy.

*He who knows others is learned; he who knows
himself is wise.*

—LAO-TZU

When we think about past romantic partners, we tend to fixate on
the frustrations we felt. They didn't like our friends. They never
cleaned their hair out of the sink, even though they knew it bothered
us. They nagged us about not being supportive enough.

Our former partner behaved in ways that frustrated us. But how,
specifically, did we *feel* about each frustration? Did our former
partner's jealousy make us feel mistrusted or overly dominated?
Then there's the issue of our *reaction*—how we behaved as a result
of our feeling. For example, if we felt belittled by our former spouse's
put-downs of our best friend, did we react by trying to put down their
best friend? By ignoring the remarks? By praising our best friend?

Identifying how we felt in the face of each frustration will unearth
useful information about ourselves. This information will help us to
lower the frustration potential in the future.

🍂 *Today, continue thinking about the same person you thought
about yesterday (Day 68). On the same page in your notebook,
label the second and third columns: "2. Feeling" and "3. Reaction." For each frustration that you listed yesterday in the first
column, jot down the feeling that you had in the second column—
ideally in one word, like "angry," "frightened," "humiliated."
Then, for the same frustration and feeling, note your reaction in
the third column, that is, how you behaved as a result; for
example, "I sulked," "I stormed out of the house," "I drank to get
over it."*

**Moving into my inner sanctuary, I accept responsibility for my part
in the negative dynamics that occurred in past relationships and
honor myself for my willingness to do so.**

Nothing in life is to be feared. It is only to be understood.

— MARIE CURIE

Exploring who we were during our childhood offers us profound realizations about how we function as adults. Similarly, analyzing past relationships can offer new awareness and insight essential for healthy future relationships. Your efforts to reach a better understanding of your past relationship frustrations are aimed at keeping you from falling victim to these same frustrations with future partners. It's human nature to do things the way we've done them before, unless we educate ourselves to do things differently.

You may be reluctant to look once again—and then twice or three times or more—at past episodes that caused you turmoil and anguish. You may wince at the possibility of reopening old wounds. Or, alternatively, you may simply worry about boring yourself to death or wasting your time by rehashing scenes that you can no longer do anything to change. However, a far more painful prospect would be to find yourself reexperiencing the exact same kinds of problems with a future partner, only to suffer from them even more acutely because you've done nothing to rehabilitate yourself from your previous injuries.

❧ *Today, focus on another person that you chose as a significant romantic partner from your past (Day 67). Entitle a separate page in your notebook with the name of this person, and divide that page into three columns: "1. Frustration," "2. Feeling," and "3. Reaction." Fill in all three columns, as you did for the first person you thought about (Days 68 and 69).*

Moving into the calm, still place at my core, I breathe deeply, aligning my heart with the work I am doing. I commit myself to this process that, though initially difficult, will bring rich rewards in my future.

*'Tis not love's going hurts my days, but that it went
in little ways.*

— EDNA ST. VINCENT MILLAY

How does one gain the "deep experience of love?" Does the secret lie in having many lovers, or extremely dramatic love affairs? The reality is that each romantic relationship is an important one within the totality of our development. For each relationship highlights various layers of who we are. As we examine these relationships, we begin to find the path that leads us not only to our core but to the deep experience of love.

The dynamics in any serious romantic relationship are more complex than they appear. While confusing at times, this makes for exciting, interesting, and informative discoveries. In this unit, for example, you're looking beyond the basic frustrations to become more aware of your feelings regarding those frustrations and of how those feelings shaped your reactions. Elsewhere in this book, you'll learn even more about how your most fundamental hopes and fears affect your adult relationships. With this deeper knowledge, you are more capable of achieving real and lasting love in your life.

When you're in the thick of a relationship, you're in no position to be objective. After it's over, you may not take the time and effort to look back. Now you are performing that important spiritual work and, in the process, becoming increasingly aware of who you are and what types of relationships you help to create.

❧ *Today, focus on the third person that you chose and complete the same three-columned exercise for this person that you did yesterday.*

In wordless prayer, I focus on this thought: "Only by cleaning out the frustrations of the past will I be ready for a partnership in the future."

*Coincidence, if traced back far enough, becomes
inevitable.*

—HINEU

The most noteworthy common denominator in all your romantic
relationships is, of course, you! You bring the same strengths and
weaknesses, the same register of emotions, and the same learned
behaviors to each relationship. The difference between relationships
has to do mainly with the other person, the time, the setting, and the
circumstances. But then, just how much difference does all that
really make?

If you can find patterns of frustrations, feelings, and behaviors that
persist from relationship to relationship, you're on the track to
realizing how much you yourself influence the tenor of your relationships. At first, this dawning realization may be disturbing. Few people
like to discover that they have unconsciously set themselves up for
the same sorts of frustrations, bad feelings, and negative reactions
time after time in their relationships. Ultimately, however, this
realization is surprisingly liberating. If we become more conscious of
the power we inevitably bring to our relationships, we can learn to
use that power wisely and compassionately. In this way, we can
finally achieve the wholeness of spirit, flesh, and feeling that we've
always sought in loving others.

❧ *Today, review each of the three pages you've written in
your notebook about a past romantic relationship. Compare the
"Frustration" columns on each page and identify similar frustrations. Do the same with the "feeling" and "reaction" column.*

**I breathe deeply in this time of quiet reflection, drawing upon an
inner strength and wisdom to guide me as I discover new truths
about myself.**

By taking a more objective look at past relationship frustrations—and how our feelings and reactions were affected—we begin to heal the hurts from these relationships. We can also better empathize with our past partners. They, too, experienced frustrations that somehow never got resolved as they functioned at the mercy of their own patterns and conditioning. For the benefit of both yourself and your future partner, you need to use past frustrations to create a more realistic picture of what you truly desire in a relationship. This will avoid certain negative feelings and reactions. This picture, subject to ongoing modification and shared with your partner, is the only reliable blueprint for realizing happiness in love.

🍃 *Today, entitle a page in your notebook "Desires." Thinking about the recurring frustrations in your past relationships, write on this page what you want in future relationships. For example, if you got frustrated when your partner was late for appointments, you might write: "I would like my partner to try harder to be on time and to call me if s/he is going to be more than ten minutes late." To help offset your anger, you might add, "I would like my partner to apologize when s/he shows up late."*

During this time of meditation, I allow my heart to expand with compassion for those I've been in relationship with, as well as myself. I allow my feelings of compassion to aid me as I seek to avoid recreating frustrations within my future partnership.

*Nature has been for me, for as long as I can
remember, a source of solace, inspiration, adventure,
and delight; a home, a teacher, a companion.*

—LORRAINE ANDERSON

After hard work, and especially after deep soul-searching, nothing feels better than immersing ourselves in nature. Lounging in soft grass under a woodland canopy, strolling along a sandy shoreline, or gazing at a sun-dappled valley from atop a rocky summit restores our spirit. Breathing deeply of a freshly mowed lawn or taking time out to view the sun as it drops below the horizon helps to remind us once again of our place in the seamless tapestry of being.

Our human nature makes us eager to live and to grow, and it connects us with all other living beings in a vital network. When we tap into this network, we recharge our energy and commitment to achieve our full, natural potential. We witness the handiwork of Creation, and once again, we are struck with wonder at the exciting possibilities of life. This time-out with nature allows us to restore our faith that our wounds and weariness will be healed.

🍃 *Treat yourself for all the good work you've been doing in examining your past relationships over the last few days. In the coming week, go somewhere outdoors where you can commune with plants, animals, and the elements. Take a walk in the park or in a field, or canoe across a stream. When you have found an especially good spot for ambling, drifting along, sitting, or reclining, let go of all nettlesome thoughts and simply sense your connection with the natural beauty all around you.*

Entering the deep place within where God dwells, I release my worries into the wind so that I may draw upon the peace residing in my core.

It takes two to speak the truth—one to speak, and another to hear.

—HENRY DAVID THOREAU

We all want people to be truthful with us, and the only way to hear the truth is to listen closely. If you don't, you won't hear the whole truth of that person's message. The result will be a conversation, and perhaps a relationship, filled with confusion, misconceptions, and failed chances at intimacy.

Listening for the truth does not mean listening only for facts or ideas that agree with *your* sense of things. Suppose, for example, that a date, referring to a party you both attended, complains, "Those people were boring! All they could talk about was golf!" Having listened superficially, you might snap back, "So you think golf is boring?" or "I enjoyed talking with those people!" Neither of these statements shows that you've heard your date's truth. Your date did *not* say that golf is boring, nor was your date referring to what *you* may have experienced. If you'd really been listening, your response might have been: "You're saying you were bored because all you heard people talking about was golf, right? [mirroring, followed by a pause] Well, I can understand how you would be bored with that [validation]."

Listening for the truth means suspending your own preoccupations and prejudgments so that you can become more fully attuned to the speaker. Later, you can proceed to communicate your truth, the whole truth, more confidently and effectively.

❧ *Today, practice listening more attentively in your conversations with people and write down the names of those whom you feel you've achieved this with. Use the mirroring and validation skills you've already learned (Days 35–38 and Days 57–59) to make sure that you have heard the other person accurately.*

Relaxing into my breathing, I see my heart as a flower that opens to allow the truth of others to penetrate my awareness. Just as flowers are observed and valued without comment, I commit to offering those people in my life a deep and true time of really listening.

It may be tough finding a mate these days, but at least it's not as it was in the Middle Ages, when marriages were prearranged, right? Wrong! The bottom line is that our partner in love, though apparently chosen by our conscious mind, is, in fact, predetermined for us by someone who is completely irrational. For it is our own inner self, the part of us that is fixated on our Imago, that hurtles us toward our romantic love.

Just as parents in the Middle Ages arranged marriages for wealth and/or alliances, our unconscious mind selects a partner to suit its particular needs. Since we don't realize this, we behave as though we are making a logical, analytic choice. If only life were so simple!

It is true that in our era we marry someone to whom we're romantically attracted. But the process of mate selection is not to be confused with love, nor do love and marriage necessarily go together, as most of us assume. Mate selection is about the *need* to find our Imago match, not love. Romantic feelings are not love, but a chemical reaction designed by nature to trick us into seeking a long-term relationship with this Imago match. And love, if it appears at all in marriage, comes as a result of our conscious commitment toward healing our partner, which helps our partner heal us.

&❧ *Today, take another look at the Imago portrait you made on Day 50. Remind yourself that this person is not someone that you would choose of your own free will; however, it is someone you need and are capable of loving more than any other person.*

I close my eyes in quiet today and breathing from my inner strength, I acknowledge the truth that I frequently make choices unconsciously and without full awareness.

*What a lovely surprise to finally discover how
unlonely being alone can be.*

— ELLEN BURSTYN

As single people, we can frequently wind up yearning for someone else in our lives simply to relieve the overwhelming loneliness we feel. What's wrong with that? All too often, we find out for ourselves what's wrong. Acting impulsively from a place of despair causes us to latch onto the first person who comes along. We then find ourselves entangled in an inappropriate relationship that's boring, unhappy, or downright abusive—in any event, doomed to failure.

The cure to loneliness does not lie outside of ourselves. And the impulse to grab some other person to distract us only keeps us from finding real love. Rather, we must cultivate our solitude and take a closer look at all the resources we have as individuals to make our own day-to-day lives richer and more meaningful. We must allow our body, mind, and soul more freedom to know the pleasures that the universe has to offer. In this way we can come to value our personal sense of aliveness even more. And we must learn to derive greater enjoyment from our own company by reflecting more positively on our experiences. In this way, we can bring a fresh optimism to the work we are doing to ensure a better future. Only by conquering our loneliness can we appreciate our unique strengths as individuals. From this place of strength we can form a lasting, fully conscious love relationship with someone who will also value and nourish those strengths.

🐚 *Sometime during the coming week, do something special that you seldom do alone. Dine in a fancy restaurant, go to a hit play, take a long stroll at sunset, rent a canoe and paddle down a woodland river. Whatever you do, cherish your own delightful company!*

Today, in my safe place, I decide to become a friend to myself. I savor this thought: "I can be alone without being lonely."

Singlehood is a dynamic state of being. We move away from childhood dependence or an unhealthy attachment to a past lover and develop an independent self that can enter into a lasting love relationship. During this period in our evolution, we need to make some effort to pace our progress according to our capabilities and our long-range interests. We don't want to leap into a love affair or a marriage prematurely, from a rash desire for companionship because we panic at the thought of being alone. Nor do we want to snooze away our single life, letting chances for self-growth and love pass us by. To achieve our own personal best as singles, we need to look around periodically and see how far we've come. Only then can we determine how far we have to go and at what rate we need to proceed in order to get where we want to be in a timely and satisfying manner.

❧ *Today, create two sections on a notebook page. On the first page, write your thoughts about where you were two years ago: what your life was like, what you were doing for self-development, and where you hoped you would be by today. How much have you advanced or retreated or gone around in circles since then? Next, think about and write down where you want to be two years from now. How can you manage your time and energies so that you achieve your goals, and enjoy the trip?*

Entering into prayer today, I go within to commune with my deepest self. There, at the point where I intersect with the universe, I ask for guidance on my journey to wholeness.

*A divorce is like an amputation; you survive, but
there's less of you.*
                                        —MARGARET ATWOOD

Many single people think of marriage as an experiment in living
rather than the real thing. If it works, fine; if it doesn't, there's
always divorce. This attitude alone makes the prospect of marriage
all the more difficult to take seriously. In fact, it's completely the
opposite of the right attitude. When we contemplate marriage, we
need to think about it as a *way of life* that is vital to our personal
growth, not simply as a householding venture with another person.
In the event that trouble arises during a marriage, we should be
prepared to get rid of the *problem* we are having, not the *person* with
whom we are having that problem. Otherwise, the problem will
continue to haunt us even after the person is gone.

We need to recognize the unconscious agenda of our Imago in
mate selection and marriage and cooperate with that agenda. By
cooperating we can achieve wholeness. Otherwise we will continue
to suffer, coming across the same old problems like B movies on
late-night television. Divorce is *not* the way to become fully liberated
as individuals. The real way lies in successfully solving the problems
within a marriage, as difficult as that may be. When thinking about
entering into a marriage, we must envision the bond of true partnership as a lasting testament, a commitment to real and lasting love.

☙ *Today, think about your attitudes toward divorce. Would you
be willing or able to enter into a marriage without considering the
option of divorce as a safety exit? If you have doubts, try to
strengthen your resolve by WRITING DOWN AND memoriz-
ing this statement: "Real love, and therefore personal fulfillment,
only comes through working to build a lasting relationship."*

**Taking time for reflection today, I look beyond the stereotype of
marriage as a prison and transform that image into a home where
true love can be found.**

Few men, I believe, are much worth loving, in whom there is not something well worth laughing at.

—JULIUS CHARLES HARE

Let's face it, few people can be as self-conscious and critical of others as the single person looking for love. However confident, positive, and accepting we may appear, when we're face to face with a potential romantic interest, deep inside we're cataloging faults: "My nose is too big." "Her clothes are always so loud." "I move like an ox." "I wish he wasn't so obsessed with cars." "I can't believe how silly I'm acting."

We can tell ourselves that nobody's perfect. But this doesn't turn off the nonstop carping, nor does it shame us into throwing away our ideal models of how we and our true love should be. What we need is a new attitude toward perfection. Assuming that two perfect people would even need each other, what could they possibly *feel* for each other besides a cool sort of mutual admiration?

Real love arises between two people who can accept the fact that they are mortal beings, each possessing a fascinating mixture of perfections and imperfections. Within the context of a real love, each partner values not just the other's strengths and virtues, but also the other's endearing weaknesses, funny quirks of behavior, and touching insecurities. If we can learn to take a more good-humored attitude toward our own so-called faults, as well as the so-called faults of others, we can start appreciating how much more vitally engaging real love is than the love of perfection.

&❧ *Spend a few minutes thinking about the "flaws" you see in yourself and the "flaws" you see in others. Try to see the funny, perhaps even endearing, side of each flaw. If one of your flaws is that you tend to panic under a deadline, the funny side might be the drama you create—the way you express your panic may be more endearing than annoying to others.*

Today, as I hold my focus on a point of light just above my eyes, I listen to the chatter of my mind. I breathe more deeply, and with each exhalation, I release a negative thought about myself and others.

*Life shrinks or expands in proportion to one's
courage.*

—ANAÏS NIN

A single person is always vulnerable to attacks of loneliness. For days on end, you can feel isolated, unappreciated, and fearful that you'll never find a true and lasting love. When the loneliness blues have got you in their grip, it's very easy to turn yellow. "I give up!" you mutter to yourself, waving the flag of defeat. "It's all a matter of luck. I'm not going to try anymore. I'm just going to get through each day, and what happens, happens."

Well, what most likely happens then is that your life becomes narrow and cramped. And unless you do something about it, those days will stretch into weeks, months, and even years. You may eventually become so numb to your loneliness and despair that they hardly register. You can become so used to the smallness of your life that you don't see how much larger it could be.

Growth in life requires courage. This is particularly true of growing through a relationship. The answer is *not* to succumb to the blues by doing nothing and leaving everything to chance. If you want to expand your world by opening it up to someone else, if you want to realize new dimensions of spiritual strength and happiness through a committed partnership, you must be brave enough to fight the blues. Begin by believing that you can achieve whatever you want, and then go out and dare to do just that.

📣 *Today, make a promise to yourself that you will persevere in developing your relationship skills and in seeking to create a more committed love. Specifically, tell yourself that you will not let occasional blue periods get you down. One way to keep your promise is to make sure that you follow the daily suggestions in this book.*

With faith in my power to create my own destiny, I promise myself that I will do my best to turn the blues of loneliness into the richness of a stream promising the potential for movement and growth.

> *She did not talk to people as if they were strange*
> *hard shells she had to crack open to get inside. She*
> *talked as if she were already in the shell. In their*
> *very shell.*
>
> — MARITA BONNER

"**I** can just imagine how painful that was!" "What happened to you makes me angry too!" How consoling it is for us to hear words like these, to know that others can appreciate our emotional pain!

The third and final part of intentional dialogue is empathy. Empathy requires actually imagining your partner's feelings. Sometimes, you may simply *realize* how they feel, in which case you might respond with: "I hear you saying that Mike's lack of support really surprised you. Am I right? [mirroring]. It makes sense that you would feel this way [validation]. I can understand how sad you must be about it [empathy]." Other times, you may actually *experience* within yourself how the other person feels, in which case your expression of empathy might be even stronger, such as (using the example above): "I, too, feel your sadness." In either type of empathic response, you are sharing a moment of deeper communication. It's a healing experience in which two people can transcend their differences and achieve a spiritual oneness.

🍃 *Express empathy in intentional dialogue with at least one person today. Begin by mirroring, and go on to validate their statement. Conclude your response by empathizing with the feelings that they've expressed (or, if they haven't mentioned specific feelings, with the ones that you imagine they have). Don't be discouraged if this process initially seems awkward. It will become more comfortable—and more rewarding—with practice!*

Accessing the deep place within where all is silent, I surrender my self-preoccupation and open myself to imagine and experience the feelings of others. I experience this truth: "Love is THE resonance of two depths calling to each other."

*Where Mercy, Love, and Pity dwell
There God is dwelling too.*

—WILLIAM BLAKE

Empathy brings out the best and holiest part of ourselves—our natural inclination toward compassion, healing, and connectedness. According to current psychological theory, we were instinctively empathic as young children but became increasingly self-protective as we experienced our inevitable woundings. Too involved in our own self-interest, we grew less capable of relating to others. Expressing empathy in our intentional dialogues now enlarges our capacity of relation and builds more satisfying relationships.

When you first start practicing empathy, you may have some trouble identifying and talking about feelings. After all, we are trained by our culture to ignore or suppress emotions. But as we train ourselves to recognize and reconnect with the feelings of others, an inspiring transformation occurs. Not only are we liberated from our own personal defensiveness, but we regain a whole new dimension of insight and power. More and more, our emotions draw us toward, rather than away from, the people we care about.

The moment you begin practicing empathy, your conversational partners will react positively and gratefully, no matter how clumsy your efforts may seem to you. The more you practice it, the more adept you will become. The magic of empathy is that it works to heal both the giver and the receiver.

&❧ *Remain alert to how others express their feelings in conversations with you today. Listen for specific words or tones. Watch for revealing gestures, facial expressions, and postures. Take every opportunity to imagine how your conversational partners are feeling and to incorporate empathy into your intentional dialogues with them.*

Moving into wordless prayer today, I let go of my isolation and imagine myself connecting with others through my heart. I focus on this truth: "Oneness occurs in meeting."

Love is what you've been through with somebody.

—JAMES THURBER

Empathy is easier to express when our conversational partner is talking about something negative that does *not* involve us. It is easy to empathize with the discomfort from a boss's overbearing demands or a disastrous evening at a dinner party. It's much more challenging to be empathic when the negative feelings stem from our behavior. How willingly can we empathize with their disappointment at our not phoning? Their embarrassment over our flippant joke?

Admittedly, expressing empathy in these situations isn't easy. But it is precisely in these situations that your empathy can be most valuable to you, the other person, and the relationship as a whole. By quelling your inner defensiveness and first *acting* to heal instead of *reacting* to hurt, you can help pull both of you through this difficult confrontation.

You need to remind yourself that the negative statements you're hearing are not primarily about *you,* but about the *speaker's* feelings. Thus, your first response—after mirroring and validation—should be to focus on the speaker's feelings more intently. Then, you can honestly say, for example, "I can imagine how upset you are that I didn't phone." "My remark probably made you feel foolish and unappreciated."

❧ *Think about conversations you've had with other people close to you who expressed negative feelings toward you. How might you have responded more effectively, using empathy? How might this kind of response have improved the situation? Write these down in your notebook.*

Entering the safe place in my mind today, I recall a negative feeling expressed toward me. Seeing myself bathed in a golden light, I am shielded from reacting in kind and recognize that the other's words were descriptive of their feelings and not of me. I relax my protective instinct and respond with warmth and understanding.

Once a human being has arrived on this earth,
communication is the largest single factor
determining what kinds of relationships he makes
with others and what happens to him in the world
about him.

—VIRGINIA SATIR

Congratulations! In learning how to express empathy, you have made a major step toward becoming a more skillful communicator. Your reward will be closer, more engaging relationships with others and, as a result, a more spiritually fulfilling life.

Expressing empathy is the final step in intentional dialogue. By doing so, you are temporarily putting yourself through what the other person has experienced so that your ultimate response will be more pertinent, more heartfelt, and more effective.

In a potential argument, you won't get very far fighting against the other person's feelings. The other person *knows* what he or she feels. Empathy enables the two of you to come closer together emotionally, so that each of you feels more secure around the other.

In future units of this book, you'll discover how intentional dialogue forms the foundation for other skills, such as expressing your anger and requesting behavior changes from the other person. Meanwhile, continue practicing intentional dialogue so that it comes to you more easily and naturally.

🙾 *Celebrate your new skills in intentional dialogue by practicing them under the best possible conditions. During this week, go somewhere special with someone you care about. Make it a relaxing place where the two of you can talk intimately and enjoyably: a quiet, romantic restaurant, a secluded cove along the beach, a winding trail through a pine forest.*

Today, in my time of quiet, I celebrate the miracle of dialogue. I steep myself in this truth: "Love begins when my partner becomes an 'other,' a 'not-me' in my consciousness."

To do good things in the world, first you must know who you are and what gives meaning in your life.

—PAULA P. BROWNLEE

Certain deep issues of self-development can appear—and be resolved—only in a committed, day-by-day partnership. But while we are single, some of the underbrush can be cleared away. We can at least identify and begin to address our most fundamental issues of selfhood, so that they won't be quite so burdensome either in our current relationships or future ones. We can also practice learning skills that help us get along better with other people—especially people with whom we desire more intimacy. And we can start framing realistic goals that we'd like to achieve within a relationship.

People who go into a relationship already knowing their own self fairly well, and already working hard to improve their relationship skills, are much more capable of caring, sharing, and committing than people who have not prepared themselves with that knowledge and work. And people who have a fairly clear vision of the love they want and the firm intention to make that vision a reality are much more equipped to handle real love. For it takes these skills to survive the powerful psychological confrontations that occur in a serious relationship.

🍂 *Today, review the self-knowledge inventory that you made on Days 9–14.*

As I retreat into my stillness today, I renew my commitment to the choice I've made, understanding that this choice—pitfalls and rewards combined—will usher in wholeness.

Even when romantic love fails, it provides us with a glimpse of our better self and a reminder of our potential for wholeness. Although the promise of bliss turns out to be premature, it does briefly reconnect us with that lost state of relaxed joyfulness we experienced as infants. However crushed we've been by love, most of us have fond memories of the good times and want to feel that way again.

Romantic love is nature's anesthesia. It bonds us to our Imago match by increasing our pleasures, creating a better chance that we will stick around long enough to bond. It also helps give us strength and endurance for the arduous work of self-repair that goes into building a conscious relationship. While under the influence, we have the feeling that we can, will, and must do whatever it takes to achieve a lasting and happy union. With it, we feel we're beginning the only kind of life worth living. Without it, we find it all too easy to stay in the unfulfilling safety of our singleness.

❖ *"How will I know when I'm really in love?" you might ask. The answer, of course, is that one just knows. Today, take a few moments to write about this truth. Think of a time in your past when you were "under the influence" of romantic love. How did you feel at that time? Then, think of a time when you were steadily dating someone you were not necessarily in love with. How did you feel then in comparison to the time when you were really in love?*

Letting myself relax into the sacred silence today, I hold this thought: "Falling in love is the ecstasy of reconnecting with my unremembered self."

Sometimes we can lose all sight of where we're going or why we're going there at all. Life seems bleak, and we find ourselves lost in a fog of hopelessness. While this is one of the most difficult times to pick ourselves up and move on, it is essential that we recognize our ability to penetrate the darkness. Once we understand this, the darkness becomes less scary. And we can truly appreciate that it is within the darkness that we find the rich mysteries that, once solved, lead us closer to wholeness.

A dark night of the soul calls upon the best that is within us—the radiant spirit that each of us possesses as a child of the universe. We must let this light shine forth and allow it to illuminate the gifts to be had in the darkness. We must allow ourselves to hope for the best, because this hope will carry us through. In working to see into the darkness that lies not only all around us but deep inside ourselves, we can find the richest treasures life has to offer.

❧ Today, think of at least two spiritual and emotional crises that you have come through during past relationships. For each crisis, recall how you felt at the time, how long it lasted, and how it finally ended. Was it darkest just before you found a solution? How did you manage to emerge again into the light? In the future, whenever you feel lost in the darkness, return to these memories for reassurance and, possibly, a sense of direction.

As I step into my deep place today, I discover that my core is essentially "light," and when I am there, there is no darkness at all.

In the coming world they will not ask me, "Why were you not Moses?" They will ask me, "Why were you not Zusya?"

— ZUSYA

We can't help envying people who seem to be luckier than us. Thus David, who has a big nose and tiny eyes, grouses to his friends, "If I were as handsome as Ted, I wouldn't have any trouble getting a date. But with my face, what can I expect?" Or thus Rachel, who didn't go to college, tells herself, "Ann is so much smarter than I am. It's no wonder Max likes her better than me." But we have to guard against using that envy as an excuse to give up trying to realize our full potential. Chances are good that the main reason David can't get dates is because of his self-belittling attitude and not because he doesn't look like a movie star. As for Rachel, her resigned defeatism probably had a lot more to do with alienating Max than her lack of a college education. It always seems easier to assume that our lack of success lies within those areas one could deem as surface faults. The reality, however, lies further beneath the surface. When we envy others, we're inclined to betray ourselves.

🐝 *Today, identify at least two situations in which you have envied someone. For each situation, ask yourself:*
* *How might I have hurt myself because of this envy?*
* *How might I have put myself down—directly or indirectly?*
* *How might this envy have prevented me from acting in my own best interest?*

In my twenty minutes of silence today, I descend to my inner core, where I feel my limitless worth, and from that place, I surrender all the self-depreciation hidden in my unfavorable comparison of myself to others.

Each of us has our own inner world, our idiosyncratic way of seeing things that makes us unique. Most of us, however, do not think much about this as it applies to others. We assume *they* think the way *we* do. When they don't, we assume they're wrong.

This one-sided way of thinking is a particular problem in relationships. In trying to be more objective and less subjective about our romantic partners, we not only need to consider the differences between individual perceptions, we also need to take into account the different ways men and women in general are socialized.

Too often we perceive the world from the inside out—using our narrow ways of understanding to explain all that we encounter in life. To understand our dates and romantic partners, we must start developing a way of seeing that moves from the outside in, so that we can see and comprehend the other person's point of view as well as our own. In this way, not only are we better able to empathize with others, but we can also expand our own awareness and create a more interesting foundation to draw from.

🙠 *Today recall and write down a time when your perception of a situation differed greatly from the person you were with at the time. In looking back, can you see a way in which you could have been more objective?*

Today, in my time of meditation, I access the courage at my core and entertain the truth that my perspective is relative, that others live in a world that is true for them, that we all share a common world that we experience uniquely.

It's never easy working on self-growth, and you've been working especially hard lately. You not only deserve a break, you need one! Just as an athlete's muscles require short periods of rest to heal from the wear and tear of exercise, your spirit requires a break so it can replenish itself.

Today, toss your relationship work aside and give yourself a treat. Tell yourself that, for an hour or two, you'll do absolutely nothing but lounge. Don't engage in any activity that requires you to think, exert yourself physically, or achieve a goal. Resist the temptation to grab the golf clubs, the crossword puzzle, or the shoeshine kit. Instead, turn off your internal guilt detector, sloth signal, and irresponsibility alert, and let yourself drift. Life's challenges and difficulties can wait for another moment to agitate you—this is your moment to relax!

ɕ *Today, think of three ways that you lounge around for an hour or two. Then, pick the easiest, most inviting way and do it.*

Sitting quietly today, I breathe deeply, experiencing how each breath relaxes me more deeply until I am completely at rest.

Providence has hidden a charm in difficult
undertakings which is appreciated only by those who
dare to grapple with them.

— ANNE-SOPHIE SWETCHINE

Establishing a supportive environment in which healing can take place is an important task for a single person engaged in the process of change. This support system can be composed of friends, coworkers, current romantic partners, a twelve-step support group, or a private therapist. Each of these contexts for discussing your inner self or for expressing yourself in new ways involves a degree of risk, shame, exposure, ridicule, or fear. We may not feel comfortable confiding in a coworker. We may be reluctant to try out unfamiliar behaviors on a steady date. The bond with a potential supporter may be too fragile, the relationship too compromised, the past history too painful or conflict-ridden. We may feel overly vulnerable revealing our shortcomings, our insecurities, our desires, and our goals to even our best friend. But we must keep in mind that change won't happen if we just work from inside ourselves. To reach a higher level of being, we must get outside help.

ᏋᏏ *Today, identify at least two people whom you could rely on for support. Then, choose one and make a special effort this week to involve this person in your "change." You don't have to make a formal announcement. You could simply strike up a conversation about an issue raised in this book, for example: childhood social-ization, male-female stereotypes, or the difficulties associated with being-single.*

During this time of quiet prayer, I see myself as a castle that has an impenetrable wall barring all entries and exits. I hold this truth: "In order to heal I must create a drawbridge that allows for a deeper sharing."

It takes a great man to make a good listener.

—ARTHUR HELPS

A friend starts talking to you about her miserable day. Her sink backed up, her client threatened to sue, her cat got sick on her best silk blouse. You *do* care about her, but you're not so keen on the subject matter. Your mind slides into neutral, and you pretend to pay attention, nodding while murmuring "Oh, no!" and "How awful!"

Listening carefully and considerately to what people are telling us is not always easy. When we're initially bored with the topic, we're inclined to slip into automatic pilot. Regrettably, this course of action ensures that our boredom will increase. If, instead, we decide to listen *intentionally* to the speaker by mirroring, validating, and empathizing, we automatically become more engaged in what we're hearing and more capable of being a true friend to our listener.

Hard as it may be to listen when we're bored, it's even more difficult when we sense that we're being criticized or contradicted. We stop paying close attention and start planning our counterattack while the other person is still talking. Again, this course of action is natural and understandable, but it only aggravates matters. If we can resist the urge to tune out the speaker and, instead, use intentional dialogue skills to make sure that we understand the speaker better, we can communicate much more effectively when it's our turn to talk.

➶ *In all types of conversations over the next few days, practice being a better listener by applying intentional dialogue skill: mirroring (Days 35–38), validation (Days 57–59), and empathy (Days 82–85).*

Entering my place of safety and calm, I visualize myself as a mirror. Reflecting back the reality of others offers a caring view to those who honor me with their feelings and thoughts.

Falling in love can be so wonderful! Our bodies tingle with excitement and our partners seem perfect. We seem to float above the tedium and torment of the real world as if in a dream. Unfortunately, this kind of romantic love is the height of unconsciousness, sustained as it is by the idealization of our partner and our anticipation of total and effortless fulfillment. But once Cupid's arrow is dislodged, we begin to see who our partner really is, and the power struggle begins.

During the early, romantic stage of a relationship we feel hopeful and optimistic. Each partner is voluntarily providing what the other one wants and needs. Later in the relationship, the romantic bubble bursts. Both partners start withdrawing some of their unconditional giving, while continuing to expect to have all their own needs met. Since their Imago led them to choose partners with their caretaker's failings, it is likely that their partner will fail them as well. And then what happens? The unconscious relationship inevitably moves from the lighter-than-air romance to the deadweight of a power struggle.

🕊️ *Today, mentally relive a time when you fell in love and try to identify the elements that made this romantic period seem so "dreamlike." Record in your journal how you felt, physically and emotionally. Describe how you idealized the person with whom you were falling in love.*

I open my heart today to my deepest yearnings. I give myself a quiet period today for spiritual restoration, recognizing that my deepest desires are the markers of my wounds and my need for healing.

*Power, however it has evolved, whatever its origins,
will not be given up without a struggle.*

— SHULAMITH FIRESTONE

With the end of the romantic phase we realize that our partners are not the paragons they once appeared to be. Old hurts are reactivated, and our disillusionment turns to anger.

Since our partner no longer willingly gives us all that we need, we change tactics. We try to *make* them love us! We attempt to maneuver them into caring through demanding, crying, withdrawing, shaming, criticizing, even cajoling—whatever we think might work. We negotiate like entrepreneurs for time, love, and favors, measuring our success against an economic yardstick of profit and loss. The power struggle has begun.

Many people who confuse romance with real love simply bail out at this point. They go from romance to romance, wondering why real love seems so elusive. Others who remain after the power struggle starts find themselves trapped in a vicious cycle of expectations and disappointments. The way to real love doesn't lie in avoiding the power struggle or occasionally taking time out from it. Instead, it lies in transforming the power struggle into a struggle toward growth.

🐚 *Recall the "falling-in-love" relationship that you thought about yesterday and try to remember when the romantic phase ended and the power struggle began. When and how did you first begin to realize that your partner wasn't as "perfect" as you had once imagined? When and how did you first begin to have serious fights? Write these realizations in your journal.*

With a spirit of honesty and courage, I enter my quiet place and take a fearless look at my past. I honor this wisdom: "It is only in remembering that we become free from the event remembered."

*The heart that breaks open can contain the whole
universe.*

— JOANNA ROGERS MACY

Romantic love is meant to happen between two people who uncon-sciously sense their Imago match in each other. Romance is nature's alchemical magic for bringing two seemingly incompatible people together to work toward mutual growth. It's the appetizer that hints at the full and nourishing meal that a relationship can be. But the romantic phase passes, ushering in the power struggle. In the power struggle, we unconsciously reenact our problematic relationship with our primary caretakers, in the hopes of resolving childhood issues. The power struggle becomes the impetus that propels us toward change.

The key to a happy resolution is *consciousness*. With awareness and intentionality, we can move beyond self-related matters to concern for and intimacy with another person. This serves nature's purpose as well as our own, because real love for others is essential to the survival of the species. The creation of real love is nature's way of repairing and completing itself, through a loving partnership.

🗫 *Review the insights you've gained over the past few days regarding how you tend to think and behave during the romantic phase of a relationship and how you tend to enter into the power struggle. You may want to write down two of these tendencies on a notecard and tape it to your bathroom mirror. This will help you remember them so that in the future, you will work through these stages in a relationship with greater awareness and skill.*

In a time of contemplation today, I open my spirit to a fuller consciousness. I focus on this thought: "History repeats itself unless we learn from our past."

> *Suddenly many movements are going on within me,*
> *many things are happening, there is an almost*
> *unbearable sense of sprouting, of bursting*
> *encasements, of moving kernels, expanding flesh.*
>
> —MERIDEL LE SUEUR

We all have dormant energies that are eager to be expressed. Some of those energies are attached to specific dreams or yearnings that we seldom, if ever, pursue: our love of dancing, our interest in politics, our plan to someday carve our own totem pole. Other energies are deliberately suppressed because we don't feel it's right to indulge them, such as our anger at our boss or our frivolous desire to own an expensive Italian suit.

Then there's a large reservoir of raw energy that, without a suitable outlet, could build up in uncomfortable ways. It is like enthusiasm waiting for a cause—anything from taking an adult-education course to cleaning out that annoyingly messy closet. Built up energy can bring us closer to the boiling point; it is imperative that we create "release valves" to help us ease the pressure. As long as we ignore those energies, or put off expressing them, we will remain only partially alive.

🕭 *Title a page in your notebook, "Enlivenment Intentions." Then list at least ten ways in which you could use more of your energy. Be as specific as you can, and phrase each entry as a positive statement of what you are intending to do, such as:*

- *I'm going to join the company baseball team.*
- *I'm going to arrange a special party for Mary's birthday.*
- *I'm going to scream out loud when I feel like it.*
- *I'm going to start bird watching next week.*
- *I'm going to learn to use a computer.*
- *I'm going to tell Randy how I feel about his work.*

Moving into the courage that pulsates at my center, I see my dormant energy as a screening device that does not allow the fullness of who I am to come through. I celebrate this truth: "I have the power to dismantle the screen."

We are each a walking encyclopedia of everything that happened to us in childhood. We harbor information, for example, about our mother's slight lisp or the low, calm pitch of our father's voice. We've never forgotten our uncle's distinctive scent and his characteristic sniffle or the piano music our aunt played on Christmas Eve. This kind of retention may seem improbable since we often can't recall what we ate for breakfast.

Nevertheless, these memories are all there in our unconscious mind, waiting to connect with the appropriate stimulus. Many of them combine into a shimmering apparition of "the person who will make me whole."

When we're out in the world, a part of us is scanning each new love prospect for the real-life counterpart of this apparition. Waves of incoming information are matched up: lopsided smile = yes; running shoes = no; scent of tobacco = yes. We unconsciously know that only the people who pass this screening will generate the right chemistry for romance, love, and in the end, a committed relationship that can heal our childhood wounds.

Today, recall and write down at least three times in the recent past when you caught yourself "screening" strangers and forming instant, almost instinctive opinions. For example, "This one I'd be interested in knowing better," "He'd probably be a flop in bed," or "She has no idea how foolish she looks."

Sometimes when I consider the power of my unconscious to shape my daily choices, I am in awe. As I relax into my depth, I know that surrender to the process is my only choice.

*There is in all things an inexhaustible sweetness
and purity, a silence that is a fountain of action and
joy. It rises up in wordless gentleness and flows out
to me from unseen roots of all created being.*

—THOMAS MERTON

The question of our essential connectedness to the larger universe has consumed the attention of investigators in many fields, from science and religion to psychology and philosophy. Modern physics now tells us that everything in creation is essentially one big field of pulsating energy that happens to take on different forms at different times according to different contexts and perspectives. This means that underneath the appearance of separateness, we are all joined in an energetic dance.

We feel this oneness in a real love relationship. It's an intensely spiritual and soulful experience that transcends analysis. It's a merging with the infinite force that is the source of all life, all power, and all beauty.

Today, go someplace where you can catch a glimpse of the vastness and richness of the universe: a cliff facing the ocean, the roof of a tall building where you can see out to the horizon, a lawn where you can lie down and look up at the sky without any obstruction, a bench overlooking a big meadow with countless blades of grass waving in the wind, a welcoming spot at the foot of a tree from which you can gaze upward into the vast canopy of leaves, a desert arroyo where you can marvel at the myriad rocks and grains of sand.

Sometimes when I consider the vastness of the cosmos, the complexity of a single grain of sand, the artistry of a cloud-filled sky, I am awed that I am a part of all of that—and that all of that is a part of me. Today, in my sacred moments of quiet, I allow myself to bathe in this wonder.

To be really great in little things, to be truly noble and heroic in the insipid details of everyday life, is a virtue so rare as to be worthy of canonization.

—HARRIET BEECHER STOWE

In our hunger for the illusion of love, we miss the point of real love entirely. Real love glorifies each moment of life and finds the wonder of each moment, whether it is spent drinking champagne or eating a Hershey bar. It's all a matter of being connected, through love, to the source of life, to the energy of the universe. When we have that connection, each moment of life, no matter how trivial, calls forth our nobleness and heroism. Everything counts, and our life as a whole has value.

As single people, we can prepare ourselves for this state of high, spiritual attunement by resolving to exercise the best parts of ourselves. We can stop wasting so much time worrying, arguing, criticizing, or complaining. Instead, we can focus each moment on what we can do that's positive, both for ourselves and for others: helping someone carry heavy packages, running a simple errand for a busy colleague, saying a kind word to a stressed-out neighbor, picking up an orange peel that's lying on the sidewalk. These may be small, trivial, everyday things, but they give us vital practice in living more thoughtfully, spiritually, and lovingly.

👡 *Over the next day, as opportunities present themselves, make a special, quiet effort to exercise compassion by choosing to do two small, simple things for others.*

I make boundaries for myself to allow for a time of quiet and surrender my addiction to the big, stimulating moments, to ego-aggrandizements. I hold this thought: "In reverence for the elemental, I experience the holiness of the whole."

Some people who tell themselves that they *choose* to remain single are, in fact, only rationalizing their inability to deal with the demands of a relationship. Their words are familiar: "I need my space," they say. "I just never found the right person." "My work takes up all my energy." "I could never really be happy living with another person." In many cases, these people have repeatedly run into the same problems and pains with others. Emotional wounds from childhood are reopened again and again, and these people always wind up in the same negative bind. They convince themselves that they're just not marriage material, that they're better off alone. Society tolerates their singleness, they reason, so why not be content to make the best of that state? We can, of course, remain single, but it goes directly against our natural drive to unite with another, and it leaves us living a limited life. Only through connecting and interacting with another person with whom we share our innermost heart and soul can we ever hope to heal and to realize our highest potential.

🔊 *Today, think about times when you've rationalized your single-*
ness, telling yourself it's your fate in life. Since rationalizing is a
form of psychological self-protection, ask yourself what you are
trying to protect yourself from.

In my quiet time today, I visualize myself living my life to the fullest.
I see myself ceasing all forms of self-protection, releasing each fear,
one by one.

The trouble with some women is that they get all
excited about nothing—and then marry him.

—CHER

When we meet our Imago match, we know it. Some describe the "knowing" sensation as bells ringing or fireworks going off in their head. Others use more active metaphors: "I fell head over heels for her" or "He swept me off my feet." Does this mean that *every* time we get excited by someone it's because of our Imago? Not by a long shot! We must also consider the lust factor, which causes similar spine-tingling reactions.

Our sexual desire can focus on many outsiders besides our Imago match. Socialization predisposes us to be aroused by anyone who possesses the stereotypically ideal sexual endowments. Besides that, we can easily get all shook up by someone who has more "body" confidence, who's maybe more adept at sexual techniques, or who's more skillful in manipulating us into sexual situations than others have been. Maybe this person is our Imago match, maybe not. Finally, there's the element of sexual challenge. We may get a thrill out of establishing a sexual relationship with someone who is basically prudish or who was once the lover of someone we've always admired or who is enticingly "forbidden"—our teacher, our student, our boss, someone else's spouse, or someone of another race. Any of these people could be mistaken for real love candidates, when, in fact, they are not. How do we tell the difference between an object of lust and an Imago match? By becoming more familiar with our Imago portrait and looking for the telltale signs!

🍂 *Today, refamiliarize yourself with the Imago portrait you made on Day 50.*

During this time of contemplative prayer, I acknowledge my innate ability to choose a life partner who will contribute to creating wholeness for us both.

*Life is either a daring adventure or nothing. To keep
our faces toward change and behave like free spirits
in the presence of fate is strength undefeatable.*

—HELEN KELLER

All humans fear change, even when we know in our minds and hearts
that change is good for us. How much safer the old familiar ways
seem! It is much easier to go out to the same places with the same
people. We all find it difficult to take the risk of finding a new place to
go or to introduce ourselves to a seemingly interesting person whom
we'd like to meet but are afraid to approach. Even if we suffer by
following the familiar, it's a suffering we know. More than anything
else, it's the unknown that scares us. And so we become prisoners
of the old ways, never tasting the excitement that is, after all, the
flip side of fear.

   If we're ever going to break out of that prison, we must take risks.
We must dare to try new ways of thinking and new ways of acting.
Even when we can't be certain where they will lead us, it is the
ability to take risks that matters. Only after we take a dare will the
true adventure of life begin: the thrill of growing stronger—mentally,
emotionally, and spiritually—the thrill we were born to realize.

*❧ Promise yourself that this week, come what may, you will try
out a new, positive behavior that you've so far been afraid to
practice. Identify a specific occasion (or occasions) when taking
this dare seems the most appropriate.*

**Each time I enter the silence, I am aware I am inviting change at the
deepest level. Today, I connect with the God within to allow any fear
of change to surface. Breathing more deeply, I release the fear.**

Our past relationships can continue to cast a spell over our present-day lives. Though we are well aware that yesterday's lovers are no longer around, they haunt our subconscious minds, living on in the ways that we imagine, seek, and conduct new relationships. Like Scrooge, we meet the ghosts of the past in our new relationships. We rehash the old fights, recall the good times, and carry torches for the dreams gone by. It's hard to start a fresh relationship when we're so entangled in unfinished business and unresolved feelings. Even if we do manage to find a new love, our past, hovering over us, can bring doom and gloom into a new relationship before it even has a chance to get off the ground.

Your past relationships have had their day! It's time that day was over, once and for all. In this unit, you will discover how to say good-bye to past loves in a fair, honest, and self-liberating way. By acknowledging the good times as well as the bad times, you can finally send those ghosts of the past back to their eternal rest.

🍃 *Today, identify a major love relationship in your past that continues to haunt you. Write a few sentences in your journal about what still attracts you or why it ended. This is the love to whom you will be saying good-bye over the next few days.*

In my twenty minutes of quiet today, I allow memories of a past love to fill my consciousness. In touch with my sadness, I acknowledge that I must release the old in order to make space for the new.

A very big part of the saying-good-bye process is grieving. Many people's natural impulse is to swallow their hurt and anger. Shedding tears and moving into our suffering acts as an important release valve, allowing us to let go of the anger, pain, and sadness. It eases our emotional distress, opening us up to the possibility of new relationships.

Few relationships end calmly and cleanly. They either explode in a blast of thundering accusations or just dwindle away in silence. The fundamental truths about the relationship—good and bad, dream and reality—never get expressed. The saying-good-bye exercise provides the perfect closure that life didn't give you! You begin by imagining that your former lover is sitting in front of you, ready to listen. Then, out loud, you describe, and say good-bye to, three different aspects of your relationship with that person: first, the *positive* feelings and experiences, second, the *negative* ones, and third, the *dreams* that didn't come true. Normally, you would cover all three aspects in one saying-good-bye session. In this unit, you'll be concentrating on one particular aspect each day for three days.

❧ If you have a photograph of a former lover, take it out and look at it. If not, imagine that your former love is sitting in front of you. Say out loud the positive feelings and experiences that you associate with this person. After each feeling or experience, state, "I say good-bye to that." For example, you might say something like, "I always felt so proud of how you looked, and I say good-bye to that," or "We used to walk the dog together after having supper, and I say good-bye to that."

In the stillness today, I move into my place of safety. With confidence and courage, I speak the truth, knowing that it will set me free.

*If my hands are fully occupied in holding on to
something, I can neither give nor receive.*

— DOROTHEE SÖLLE

Saying good-bye to former loves does not mean that we forget them.
Even if we *want* to forget them, how could we? They irrevocably
changed our lives. Together we created memories that we still
cherish and we learned lessons that help us even today.

Saying good-bye to former loves means declaring our true independence and freedom. Instead of continuing to cling to them in spirit as
we go through life, we must liberate ourselves so that we can walk
confidently in the present and into the future. No longer will we ca-
ress them, even as we snuggle with someone new. Nor will we point
the scolding finger at them, even as we fight with someone new.
Instead, they are now out of our lives entirely, lightening up our
current relationship.

We still have our memories of our former loves, fond and not-so-
fond, but we are not haunted by them. We may still want to revisit
these memories from time to time in the future, maybe for the
purpose of self-examination or maybe just nostalgically, for old time's
sake. But no longer can these memories drop in uninvited. Whenever
the inclination strikes, we know where they are: safely in the past.
Meanwhile, we are advancing into the future, boldly and confidently
on our own.

❧ *Today, imagining that your former love is sitting in front of
you, state out loud the negative feelings and experiences that you
associate with this person. After each feeling or experience, state,
"I say good-bye to that." For example, you might say something
like, "I always felt so inferior around you, and I say good-bye to
that," or "You would complain about me in front of friends, and
I say good-bye to that."*

**In deep prayer today, I open myself to all that I feel, knowing that
whatever is unspoken chains me to my past. I recognize that I hold
the key to these chains.**

There is a way to look at the past. Don't hide from it. It will not catch you—if you don't repeat it.

—PEARL BAILEY

Deep down in our psyche, we may resist letting go of a former love relationship, even one that was over a long time ago. To do so feels as if we are betraying the whole idea of love or acknowledging that our judgment was flawed or that there are some things we cannot fix. We once believed our feelings for that person would last forever. And so, we unconsciously make sure they do. Somehow, this means that we still care; we haven't broken faith.

Saying good-bye to old loves is not giving up on love itself. And it is neither healthy nor noble to keep alive relationships that are over. The truth is that each one of us is irresistibly drawn to fall in love again and again with our Imago match. This image stays with us until we finally meet someone with whom we form a real and lasting love: one that heals our childhood wounds and restores us to our original wholeness as a human being. Our past partners and relationships are only precursors of this real and lasting love, providing us with valuable clues to the traits of our Imago and to the ways in which we need to grow.

&. *Today, imagining that your former love is sitting in front of you, state out loud the dreams you had for the relationship that did not come true. After each dream, state, "I say good-bye to that." For example, you might say, "Our dream was to start a bed and breakfast on a farm, and I say good-bye to that," or "I always thought that we'd be friends forever, and I say good-bye to that."*

Knowing I will forever be a prisoner to my past if I do not surrender it, I enter my quiet place and allow myself to experience my emptiness. In faith I claim this truth: "Experiencing the Void opens me to the Fullness."

Each new day presents us with a new chance at life. So does each new relationship, provided we are really free to pursue it. Through saying good-bye to past partners and to the specific feelings, behaviors, and goals that we developed when we were with them, we become psychologically free to say hello to new and exciting love possibilities.

We all bring an unconscious program of hopes, fears, and behaviors to our adult love relationships that has its roots in our unmet childhood needs. This unconscious program reruns itself mercilessly, playing a major role in sabotaging our adult relationships, leaving us bewildered and alone again. The path to freedom lies not only in saying good-bye to the wrecked relationships of the past, but also in doing what we can to shed light on the internal programming that drove us to them: our Imago. With this greater consciousness, we can find a real and lasting love—one that is not going to leave us and that we don't want to leave.

≈ *Congratulate yourself on being free from the past! Do something new to honor the occasion: Start that mystery you've been wanting to read, explore that sporting goods store that just opened around the corner, or watch tomorrow's sunrise over a fresh cup of coffee!*

Today in my time of quiet, I become aware of new light filling me, banishing the shadows of the past. I take refuge in this thought: "One passes through Darkness in order to experience Light."

Heaven is neither a place nor a time.

— FLORENCE NIGHTINGALE

Many religions and cultures speak of a longed-for state of primordial perfection, a paradise of relaxed joyfulness. Under various names—the Elysian Fields, Avalon, Nirvana, El Dorado, or the Garden of Eden—this golden state of peace and joy is characterized by a perfect communion in nature among people, mountain peaks, beast, bird, and forest—an idyllic picture of timeless bliss. But according to the ancient stories, a disturbance, some fall from grace, an unwanted cataclysm destroyed our chances of enjoying this paradise. We were driven from "the garden," and thereafter we search in vain for paradise and our spiritual unity.

Today, we see this search reflected in the enormous popularity of books and self-help tapes on finding happiness, overcoming alienation, and eliciting "peak experiences." Behind this popularity runs a powerful drive. Our longing for connectedness, for moments when we pierce the veil of our everyday existence, stems from a hazy memory that at one time we were not separate but joined to all other humans and to the universe. In this unity we felt safe and supported. And now our fundamental yearning is to rise above the barriers that keep us from realizing this oneness. Heaven is not a place or a time. Nor is it a myth at all. It's our original, and best, state of being.

❧ *Today, seek a state of relaxed joyfulness by devoting even more time and attention than usual to the meditation below.*

Today in celebratory prayer, I summon joy to be a companion for my soul on my journey toward wholeness. I claim this truth: "Heaven is within."

What if years and years go by and we don't meet *anyone* who "clicks" with our Imago picture? It's an understandable concern, but one that invites the wrong kind of worries about love being a matter of luck. True, it is almost certain that we will never find an *exact* match for our inner Imago. After all, our early caretakers and our childhood home situation were unique in their myriad details. And we, in turn, have combined those details into a complex collage of infinite subtlety based on our own perceptions. But equally true, we are bound to encounter many people who have the material for becoming *close-enough* Imago matches for us. It is these people to whom we're unconsciously drawn, even if the apparent resemblance to our Imago is slight. Even if we find ourselves lacking in likely candidates, we must persevere. There may be many internalized reasons as to why we haven't found someone to "click" with. As you continue this process, internal blocks will be removed to make you a more available partner.

Fortunately, the Imago is a somewhat fuzzy, impressionistic por-trait, rather than a crisp photograph. In order to get a close enough match to trigger the romantic reflex, our unconscious mind reworks and fine tunes the image of the other person who is already emerging as a likely candidate, exaggerating the likenesses and diminishing the differences in order to achieve the verisimilitude that we seek.

&. *Today, review your past romances and try to identify at least two times when you came to realize that the other person did, in fact, remind you of your father, your mother, or some incident or quality in your childhood—a fact that you did not realize when the romance began. Write these down.*

As I enter the stillness today, I relax and trust the wisdom of an inner "compass" to lead me to the person who will call me to my wholeness.

*The great thing and the hard thing is to stick to
things when you have outlived the first interest, and
not yet got the second which comes with a sort
of mastery.*

— JANET ERSKINE STUART

The road to realizing a fully satisfying, committed relationship is a lengthy one, and we can be assailed with doubts many times along the way: Is it worth it? Am I strong enough to make it?

The truth is, every step we take toward learning more about our inner self and our deepest motivations is progress. So is every step we take toward changing our behavior for the better. In this way, we develop a new, more dynamic vision of what we want out of our life and out of a partnership. When we first decide to repaint our home, the task seems huge. But if we tackle that job, wall by wall, we soon find ourselves with a beautiful new home. In the same way, each insight we gain and each new skill we practice helps create and define our future.

In your own journey toward finding real love, rely on this book as your comfort and guide. If you persevere with the Imago process, you will eventually know the blissful experience of sharing the road with someone you care about with all your soul and who will care just as much about you.

&. *Today, think of an event in the past when you almost gave up on a goal, but persevered to achieve it. Try to recall exactly how you felt, and how you kept yourself going. Tap these memories for inspiration as you continue your journey with the Imago process and write them down.*

Knowing that the road to love is long, feeling the weariness of learning all I need to know, I turn inward to the strength of my core and drink from the waters of my aliveness. Feeling refreshed I make this vow: "I will persevere to the journey's end."

We can never overestimate the influence our caretakers had on us. When we were children, we were frantically intent on learning how to behave in this world, and so we took an abundance of mental snapshots, detailing our parents' behaviors and permanently preserving them, like photographs, for later reference. Now, in every situation we encounter as adults, we unconsciously leaf through this album of behaviors to see if any of them fit; and we will pick one, even if it's negative behavior.

If yelling and screaming kept us in line as a child, we are likely to "copycat" that behavior as adults. However much we hated and feared it back then, we find ourselves on automatic pilot. If our mother cowed us with stony, hurt silence, we "copycat" that behavior in our adult life to get what we want. We may cringe at the idea that we perpetuate behaviors we abhorred in our parents, but the reality is that when we are irritated, frustrated, or angry with close friends or loved ones, we "copycat" the behaviors that "worked" for our parents.

❧ *Spend a few minutes today thinking of times when you've caught yourself "copycatting" your father's or your mother's negative behavior, especially in your relationships with others.*

In solitude today I access the inner reserves of courage that will enable me to see the ways I emulate my caretakers' behavior. I hold this truth: "Consciousness is the key that crumbles the great barrier to freedom: fear."

My father was often angry when I was most like him.

                      —LILLIAN HELLMAN

In love relationships, we often wind up treating our partner in the same negative manner that our mother or father treated us, especially when our partner fails to meet our needs. We do this because our Imago match calls out those negative traits in ourselves that we unconsciously borrowed from our parents. Even worse, we tend to act with our partner like the specific parent with whom we had the most difficulty in childhood, because we saw this parent as the most powerful. And, therefore, pictures of this parent were the ones that dominated our personal photo album of behaviors. When we're struggling for power with our partner, we unconsciously identify with this parent because, from the vantage point of our old brain, he or she had the most sheer survival power. We may have hated, for example, our mother's whining and cowering, but it did intimidate our father, and he would eventually give up. So we, too, wind up whining and cowering with our partner. Or perhaps Dad's anger may have been brutal and scary, but when he used it against Mom, he usually got his way. So we, too, resort to being crudely and fearsomely angry at our partner.

Then, when our partner points out that we are "just like" our mother or our dad, we are shocked. Consciously we know that we shouldn't dominate our partner the way our difficult parents dominated us, but unconsciously we do so, because we let our denied self dominate us.

⁂ *Today, think of a past love relationship. Identify at least two ways that you behaved in the same, negative way that one of your parents or caretakers behaved in order to get your own way.*

Today in quiet contemplation, I recall the wise adage that an unexamined past tends to repeat itself. I open myself to all that I have been and to full consciousness of all that I can become.

Our psychological and spiritual wholeness as individuals is only attainable when we integrate our innate male and female energies. Balance between these two opposite forces creates an emotional and psychological whole that we can draw upon. We're inclined to lose sight of this need and, instead, feel pressured to conform to societal ideals about how to present ourselves as a "real" man or a "real" woman. The sad result is that we forfeit the freedom to be our true selves—for we are each a unique mixture of so-called male and female energies.

If we hope to overcome this social conditioning, to repossess our true selves, and to establish a real and lasting love relationship, we must cultivate both the male and female aspects of ourselves. We must stop looking at culturally defined pictures of "male" and "female" when scanning the world for a partner. This unit will help you to become more aware of the cultural biases that separate men and women, to honor the equal value of male and female energies, and to develop your own contrasexual energies, so that you will not be dependent on your partners to provide what is lacking in yourself.

Today, think about the pressures you have experienced in the mating game to be what society considers "masculine" or "feminine." What aspects of yourself did you have to hide, suppress, or change? How did this make you feel?

Realizing that I am a larger, greater, more exciting person than I appear to the world, and that I contain both male and female energies, I relax into my wholeness.

*Every man takes the limits of his own field of vision
for the limits of the world.*
— ARTHUR SCHOPENHAUER

One of the most troublesome facts of relationship conflicts is so
glaringly obvious that it's often overlooked: *your partner is not you.*
And one of the main reasons your partner experiences the world
from a different but equal perspective is s/he is a different gender.
Part of every single person's mission is to understand these gender-
related differences and, beyond that, to *transcend* them.

Egoists that we are, however, we have difficulty accepting differences in our partners without making value judgments. "How can
you not like opera?" "You really think that's funny?" Even the
slightest differences in tastes get disparaged, let alone the more
fundamental differences in temperament.

The first step toward accepting the "other," whether it be an
entire gender or our partner in particular, is not to assume that
others think the way that we do. Men and women experience the
world differently, if only because of the different roles society thrusts
upon them, and every individual has their own idiosyncratic inner
world. To understand our partner, we must stretch to see and
validate his or her point of view and accept their logic as being equal
to ours.

&. *Spend a few minutes recalling a time when you were upset or
taken aback just because someone didn't think or behave as you
did. Think especially about a time when a simple difference in
opinion or taste sparked a conflict or when you couldn't accept
the fact that your partner responded differently to a certain event
from you. Write them down.*

**In trying to overcome my imprisonment in my own inner world, I
open myself to the experiences of others in order to expand my own.**

Do you think that love is an accomplished thing, the day it is recognized? It isn't. To love, you have to learn to understand the other more than she understands herself, and to submit to her understanding of you.

—D. H. LAWRENCE

Real love comes to us only if we persevere in bringing our good intentions to life. It is both a cause and a consequence of those intentions, an action and a state of being, an achievement that becomes a gift. Love is the fruit of hard work and discipline. It cannot be purchased or manufactured. Instead, it comes to us as we meet the conditions for its arrival. The passion that it brings to our life is a result of creating safety for our partner, which is accomplished by meeting our partner's childhood needs.

To do this work, we must always remain conscious of our desired outcome and act accordingly. This requires extinguishing our unconscious, old-brain tendency to react without first thinking things through. Sometimes we will need to function as heroes; other times, we will need to exercise humility. Just how long it will take for us to replace our old-brain protective program with a new-brain strategy that ensures our partner's safety depends upon the degree of our childhood wounding and how conscientiously we—and, eventually, our partner—work to remove it. For some couples, this may take a few months. For others, it may take many years. But the reward is priceless and timeless: living in the grace of being fully safe, loved, and reconnected to the universe.

In the next few days, make a special effort to behave in ways that create a safe, welcoming environment for one person who comes into contact with you. Perhaps this means being aware of the volume of your voice or being a more attentive listener.

As I move into this time of sacred stillness, I am awed by the rhyme and reason that lies underneath what used to seem like chaos to me. I recognize the grace of the divine.

*Believing ourselves to be possessors of absolute truth
degrades us: we regard every person whose way of
thinking is different from ours as a monster and a
threat and by so doing turn our own selves into
monsters and threats to our fellows.*
                                        —OCTAVIO PAZ

The most powerful tool—perhaps the only real tool—we have to
explore and understand the "otherness" of our partner's gender and
self is dialogue. Engaging in dialogue with another is much like
purchasing and downloading a new computer software package. All
of a sudden, we have access to new ways of thinking and new ideas.
This enriches us, for when we are confronted with and allow in
someone new, their otherness becomes a mirror of the unknown,
undeveloped, and rejected aspects of ourselves.

The goal of dialogue is not conversion of the ignorant. It should
not be undertaken to overpower the other with the truth of our
superior point of view. Rather, the goal of dialogue is understanding.
It says to the other: "I respect your otherness. I want to learn from
it. I also want to help you learn more about what you may consider
my 'otherness.'" Dialogue assumes equality.

❧ *Today, make a special effort to engage in dialogue with a
person of the opposite gender who is important to you (including
family members, friends, and colleagues) about his or her perspective on things. Think of yourself as an adventurer in a strange
new country that people of the opposite gender have lived in all
their lives. Ask questions that will expand your own outlook and
opinions. For example, "Why did that movie excite you, or make
you cry?" "How do you feel when a friend criticizes you?"
"What's your idea of a perfect evening?" Be alert for details that
challenge your preconceptions of what it is to be a "man" or
a "woman."*

**In today's time of prayerful focus, I honor this truth: "No one has
omnipotent vision to see the whole of which one is a part."**

Fluid hardens to solid, solid rushes to fluid. There is no wholly masculine man, no purely feminine woman.

— MARGARET FULLER

Within each of us is a *contrasexual* self. In a man, it's his repressed femaleness; in a woman, her repressed maleness. It's a part of us that we lost during the socialization process and that we seek to regain vicariously through a relationship with a member of the opposite gender. However, to form a relationship that can offer a real and lasting love, we must grow beyond the need to depend on the other person to supply this lost part. We need to take it upon ourselves to recognize and develop our own contrasexual self.

Getting in touch with our repressed contrasexual self demands that we think and act in a consciously *transcultural* way—refusing to buy into the stereotypes that society imposes on us as men and women. For a man, this might mean making himself vulnerable by talking about something that he's kept private, performing a reflective and sensitive creative activity like writing a poem, playing a nurturing role by doing volunteer work with children, or making sincere attempts to appreciate traditional "women's stuff," such as cooking, watching romantic movies, and flower gardening. For a woman, this might mean performing a brave athletic activity such as hiking a mountain or river rafting, being assertive by speaking up in public situations, taking the initiative in arranging a date, or making sincere attempts to appreciate "men's stuff," such as watching football games, playing poker, or reading business magazines.

&⬧ *Think of a specific activity that you can perform to get more in touch with your contrasexual self—an activity that involves acting in a transcultural way. Resolve to perform this activity today or sometime over the next few days.*

Reflecting on my lack of wholeness today, I enter the deep space within and make contact with my missing self. I celebrate this reality: "I am both male and female."

Androgyny suggests a spirit of reconciliation between the sexes.

— CAROLYN HEILBRUN

Culturally imposed gender roles are easy to spot in the area of caretaking *within* a relationship. While both men and women need the nurturing that they didn't get in childhood, it is women who are *trained* to nurture and provide most of it within the relationship. When the scales of any relationship dynamic are tilted too far in one direction, both people are bound to suffer, for it impedes each person from reaching their full potential. Real love is not possible in such an unbalanced relationship. For instead of healing each other's wounds, this imbalance only serves to cripple each person within the relationship even more. To correct this disparity, men must consciously work on developing their nurturing skills, and women must make space for these new skills to emerge. Most women automatically fill the role of caretaker, leaving no room for the man to cultivate his own nurturing skills. In other words, each person must move closer toward *androgyny:* an inner nature where the male and female natures are better balanced.

❧ *Today, think of a past relationship and identify three ways in which the caretaking within the relationship was consciously or unconsciously left to the woman: the cooking, cleaning, concern about emotional issues, or making up after an argument.*

If you're a man, think about ways that you might have taken on some of the caretaking. If you're a woman, think about ways that you might have held back and given the man room to move into a caretaking role.

In the spirit of reconciliation today, I allow images of my roles in relationships to come to mind, one by one. This truth is mine: "Transcending roles, I achieve authenticity."

We are inherently androgynous creatures, embodying both male and female energy. Reconnecting with our innate androgyny does not mean becoming asexual, bisexual, or hermaphroditic, and it certainly doesn't mean being unmasculine or unfeminine. It means realizing the *inner* balance and wholeness that allows us to connect with a full range of modes of being. A whole person is a man secure enough to permit the feminine aspects of his personality to emerge, or a woman secure enough to permit the masculine aspects of her personality to blossom. A woman who can access her masculine energy is very powerful. And there's something incredibly appealing about a gentle man.

The move toward androgyny brings the man and the woman back together on common ground. To achieve this within our culture requires being *conscious and intentional* about who we are and how we behave. As we practice becoming more attuned to the "other" and learn to behave in ways that allow our contrasexual self to develop, we will evolve into people who are prepared for real love partnerships.

🙠 *Today, identify and write down five gender distinctions that society imposes. Decide to work intentionally to overcome those distinctions through dialogue with the opposite gender and through activities that help you connect with your contrasexual self.*

Knowing I cannot be whole without claiming and developing my contrasexual energies, I enter my deep place and make this vow: "I will become all God created me to be."

In real love you want the other person's good. In romantic love you want the other person.

— MARGARET ANDERSON

When we first *fall* in love, what, exactly, do we feel? The very expression sums it up: We feel unreal, off-balance, overwhelmed, and overturned. This state of unreal love is known as romantic love. We don't function well as individuals anymore. We are constantly caught daydreaming and find ourselves stumbling over cracks in the pavement. Our conscious minds are obsessed by our need to be with the other person. Meanwhile, thanks to our internal Imago, our unconscious minds are actually yearning to *be* the other person. No wonder we're disoriented!

Romantic feelings inevitably run their course after they've done their biological work of bringing two people together who have the unique possibility of healing each other's emotional wounds. A period of struggle follows. That's when real love begins to develop, if we let it.

At first, real love doesn't feel as exciting as romantic love. After all, a major component of falling in love is surprise, and surprise wears off pretty quickly. But if we keep on cultivating conscious efforts to care for the other person's welfare as much as we care for our own welfare, real love evolves. And even though it may not be as initially flashy and captivating as romantic love, real love can blossom into the sweetest, most satisfying feeling of all: the feeling of being involved in something that is much larger and more meaningful than ourselves—something that gives us absolute faith and unending joy.

&❧ *Today look back over a major love relationship in your past and ask:*
- *In what ways did I simply want to* have *this person?*
- *In what ways did I want to* be *this person?*
- *In what ways did this person mirror back denied parts of myself?*

Write down your findings.

This truth becomes a balm for my soul: "Beneath the glitter of jewels lies a gift that is far more precious."

"I'm happy enough being single. Why not stay that way?"

"Can't I lead a perfectly fulfilling life all by myself?"

"Being single, I have more time and energy to improve myself. What's the point of giving up that freedom to get married?"

These questions pop up from time to time in any single person's life, especially under two very different types of circumstances: when things in general are going unusually well or when a specific relationship is being unusually problematic. The answer to all these questions is the same. The single life, like it or not, is by its very nature a limited one. Like all species, we wander the world in search of fulfillment. As human beings, we are all connected to each other through the great tapestry of being, the living universe. The state of being single represents a partial disconnection. In order to realize our potential, we need to reconnect through one special person to whom we make a full commitment. Only that person can provide us with the growth experiences we most profoundly need. That person functions as a mirror in which we can see ourselves and a wall against which we can push.

꒰ *Today, select a relationship skill you've learned so far and practice it.*

In reverential stillness, I allow myself to become aware of my dependency upon another for my wholeness. I deepen this awareness by pondering the wonder of my dependence upon the Transcendent for my being.

The search for love is hard enough all by itself. And yet, during this search, we find ourselves assaulted on a daily basis by pressures from work, demands from our family members and friends, rude treatment from strangers, and gloomy headlines prophesying more violence, worse pollution, and greater economic hardship. No wonder we sometimes fail to realize the day-to-day miracles of our lives: the smiles we trigger from those who care about us, the dew-spangled freshness of the morning air, the sweet, tangy taste of an orange, or simply the wondrous feeling we get from a good, deep, breath.

Even in the most punishing environment here on earth, we're surrounded, day after day, by intimations of heaven. Unfortunately, all of us find ourselves snagged by our everyday disturbances. It is important to remember to widen our lens and make time for those moments when the sacred of everyday life can call to us. The more we learn to see these intimations, and to savor them, the more spirit and energy we'll have in every aspect of our lives.

❧ *Today, do something that will allow you to notice and experience the beauties of living! Stroll through the park, lounge on your back porch, prepare an especially delicious meal, frolic with your dog, hug a tree, or buy a bouquet of flowers for your living room.*

Breathing deeply, I relax into my depth. With each breath I take, I imagine the air as love. As my lungs fill with this elixir of nature, I hear these words deep within: "God is everywhere."

Many love relationships fall apart, or get stuck in the "bargaining" phase of the power struggle. In this phase, each partner tries to get what he or she wants by negotiating for it. "If you try harder to be less critical, I'll try harder to be more considerate." "If you'll go camping with me, I'll go to the ballet with you." "If you'd take me out to nicer places, we'd have sex more often." Rather than acting like a couple in relationship, we find ourselves living the life of game show contestants—constantly wheeling and dealing to win the "Grand Prize."

For most couples, this type of bargaining leads to suspicion, resentment, and cold-blooded account keeping. Bargaining is used by both partners to resolve the power struggle in the relationship, but it doesn't work. Maybe the two people stay together a bit longer, but almost always they tire of keeping score. The unconscious mind is singularly unimpressed with the conscious bargaining and sees the "Grand Prize" as being bogus without a deeper response. For what it really needs to heal its wounds and to recover a sense of aliveness is *unconditional* love, not a return of favors.

🍂 *Spend a few moments trying to recall at least three bargains you have struck with romantic partners in the past. How did they work out? Did they succeed or fail to enhance the overall quality of your relationship?*

I am challenged by the concept of unconditional love, of giving without expectation of anything back. Today in my prayer, I ask for wisdom to understand how this works and the courage to try it.

"I assumed you would back me up on this."

"If I have to tell you what to do, it won't mean anything when you do it."

"You should have known how I would feel about this."

Do any of these statements sound uncomfortably familiar to you? Do you tend to assume that a clairvoyant ability permeates a person the minute they find themselves stumbling into love? The fact is, we all occasionally find ourselves indignantly hurling these or similar expressions at someone else. Unfortunately, our accusations seldom bring change. In the long run, they only drive that person further away from us. We must get over the fantasy that the people we care about should read our minds. Many of us wrongly assume that if we request what we want, the response will not come from a heartfelt place. The reality is that, most often, people want to succeed at love.

To avoid disappointing ourselves and people who are close, we must communicate our expectations clearly. Mind reading keeps us blindfolded—in the dark.

🙠 *Today, recall and write down at least two times in the past when you became upset because a partner or friend didn't do what you wanted. Had you made your expectations clear, or were you expecting them to read your mind? Now recall at least two times when the situation was reversed, and you were accused of not fulfilling an expectation that was never directly expressed. How did you feel?*

Although I know I am essentially connected to others, I also know I am separate. Today, in my quiet time, I surrender my tendency to assume that my connection to others includes my knowledge of their thoughts or their knowledge of mine.

A *projection* occurs when you assign a negative aspect of yourself to another person and respond as if the trait actually belonged to them instead of you. It's like watching a movie. You are the projector and the person you are in conflict with is the screen. It may look as if the issues that are causing the problem are on the screen, but in reality they are coming from you, the projector.

Projections are the culprit in many conflicts. Dealing with them is challenging, especially if we are the target. Sometimes, we do not possess the trait we are accused of having or the trait is amplified because the projector has repressed that trait in him- or herself. We are bound to feel unjustly represented, and our natural reaction will be defensive. This is the very heart of the problem: our heated response only confirms for the projector that what he or she felt or said was true. From the projector's point of view, it must be true, since it apparently touched a nerve. Now we are being every bit as disagreeable as the projector accused us of being. In the throes of conflict, clarity and logic are lost!

&. *Today, recall a major conflict you had in the past when you accused someone of negative traits that actually belonged to you. Write down the root of the conflict and what angered you about the other person. Try to see in yourself the trait that angered you at the time.*

Entering my quiet place today, I access the courage to meet the parts of myself that I assign to others. I ponder this truth: "By owning all aspects of myself, I can achieve wholeness."

Mrs. Hopewell had no bad qualities of her own but she was able to use other people's in such a constructive way that she never felt the lack.

—FLANNERY O'CONNOR, "GOOD COUNTRY PEOPLE"

When we are the target of a projector, someone like Flannery O'Connor's Mrs. Hopewell, there are two ways to respond. One is the natural, but ultimately destructive, way: denying, getting angry, and fighting back. The other way is more difficult, but far more constructive in the long run: *holding* the projection instead of throwing it back at the other person.

Holding the projection does not mean agreeing with it or "owning" it. It simply means acknowledging it and responding with our intentional dialogue skills. First, we mirror the observation, then we validate the other person's right to his or her own perception, and finally we express empathy with his or her feelings.

For example, suppose someone accuses you of not being there when they need you—something that is actually a bigger fault of their own and, therefore, a projection. Rather than moving into conflict by defending your position, you might try responding with, "So, you are concerned that I'm not there when you need me. Is that right? [mirroring]. I can understand why that would upset you [validation]. I imagine it makes you feel abandoned and angry [empathy]." In this way, a potential power struggle becomes a validation of feelings.

⋙ *Today, recall and write down a time when you were the target of a projection, that is, when someone accused you of a negative trait that actually belonged to them. Remember how you reacted, and what the consequences were. Try to imagine how you would have handled the same situation by* holding *the projection instead of denying it, getting angry, or throwing the projection back at the other person.*

With an attitude of prayerful reverence, I hold in mind the challenge of keeping others safe in my presence by not creating conflict over their projections toward me.

You must do the thing you think you cannot do.

—ELEANOR ROOSEVELT

When we hold a projection instead of throwing it back at the person who made it, we avoid confirming the projection by being defensive. We also prevent the projection from succeeding in its secret mission of getting us into a conflict. Intellectually, we can appreciate these truths; but emotionally, it can be very difficult to keep in check our natural inclination to fight back against something that we recognize as a projection. The knack of holding projections, like any skill worth acquiring, takes persistence, time, and patience. To develop more constructive and conscious behaviors than we now possess, we must indeed do the things we think we cannot do!

It helps to realize that holding projections is a means of proving that we are definitely *not* the disagreeable individual whom the other person is seeing. By holding projections, we demonstrate to the other person our positive support as an empathic listener, and we gently guide the projector to look more closely at his or her own thoughts, feelings, and behaviors. Over time, the hostile energy that's sending the projection will dissipate. More and more, the other person will see us for who we *really* are; and eventually, their projections will fade.

❧ *Today, resolve to hold any projections the next time someone is upset with you. When you do this, you'll be amazed at how constructive the process proves to be, and it will be all the easier for you to follow it in the future. Set aside a page in your journal to record each time you successfully hold a projection, and each time you have recorded five, treat yourself to something special: a movie, a new CD, a book.*

Responding to the person who has hurt me with their misperceptions, I claim this truth: "The more I love, the more I become whole."

We can be our own worst enemies and not even realize it! One especially self-defeating behavior is to expect others to appreciate things the way we do and become resentful when they don't. With great emotion and grand gestures, we pour out our feelings about life and love. When our audience of one doesn't respond with similar dramatics, we're infuriated. We feel embarrassed, shamed, even rejected, as if the other person were intentionally being downright mean. When we're upset about an unfair situation at work and our lover doesn't join us in being downcast and miserable, we get indignant.

It might be nice if our partner always reflected our feelings. Indeed, this is the type of highly appreciated caring behavior that we practice through intentional dialogue. But to *insist* that our partner always be on our wavelength is nothing short of presumptuous. We need to guard against great expectations that are, in fact, wholly based on self-interest. Instead, we need to keep in mind that the other person is not us, but a person in his or her own right.

🍂 *Today, recall at least two times when you were angry at someone close to you for not feeling exactly the same way you did. How would it have helped you if they had felt the same way you did? How would it have injured you and them? Promise yourself that you will guard against this tendency in the future.*

Sometimes I feel alone when others feel different from me; at other times, I feel abandoned. This makes me angry. Today, in my time of quiet reflection, I surrender my need for others to be like me.

> *Who ever loved that loved not at first sight?*
> —CHRISTOPHER MARLOWE

All lovers believe they have been lucky to find someone so special. "No one else has ever felt what I feel," they think, "no one has ever experienced love like this." In a way, this is true, for every Imago match is an intricate dovetailing of two people's unconscious pictures. One person's Imago match is another person's disastrous blind date. "What does she see in him?" is exactly the point of the Imago.

A person encountering his or her Imago match has a powerful and eerie sense of *recognition*. This feeling of familiarity stems from the resemblance of the other person to the observer's unconscious portrait of his or her early caretakers. It accounts for that often-heard statement about falling in love: "Even though we just met, I feel as though I already know you." If, for example, a man grows up with a depressed, emotionally unavailable mother, he my be *consciously* looking for a life mate who is quite different—someone with a big smile on her face. But *unconsciously,* he may be repeatedly drawn to yet another serious woman with a sad, faraway look in her eyes—someone who does, in fact, fit his sense of his mother. It seems as if he's meant to be with this person. And he is!

❧ *Today, recall at least two incidents in your romantic past when you were first getting to know someone and had this sense of recognition: "I feel as though I already know you." To get a better sense of your Imago portrait, try to remember what, more specifically, seemed so familiar about each person you recall. Is it the same trait or behavior for each person?*

I know by my yearnings that I am un-whole. As I relax today into the holy place of quietness, I listen to my desires, knowing they are connected to what I can become. I decide: "I will answer the call to wholeness."

Do you ever find yourself wondering how the other gender thinks? What's it like to live in their world? What fantasies and fears they harbor that you know little about? What issues are important to them that a person of your gender might regard as insignificant? Do you also find yourself trying to understand how they respond to various stimuli—both emotionally and physically?

Of course you wonder! The mysteries surrounding the opposite gender call out to all of us—not just in terms of romantic or erotic attraction, but also in terms of getting more in touch with that inner part of us that is contrasexual. We expand our awareness every time we connect with someone who has had different types of experiences based on their socialization. The more actively we seek to shed light on these mysteries, the more fulfilling our relationships with people of the opposite gender will be and the more fully alive we ourselves will become.

ॐ Today, spend some time actively researching the opposite gender's world. Skim through a magazine, read a chapter in a book, or watch a television program that is clearly targeted to the opposite gender.

Sometimes I find myself a prisoner of my own point of view, diminished by depriving myself of the experience of others. In my time of reflection today, I see myself growing in grace and stature as I allow the world of others to enrich my own.

Being single can be a wonderful stage in life. While we are single, we can work on becoming ever stronger, more independent human beings. We can set ourselves loose from childhood ties to our family members and their ways of doing things. We can explore all sorts of roles, relationships, and lifestyles. We can experiment with who we are, who we want to be, and who we might become. And, to give our lives direction, we can relish the thought that we do have an eventual destination to give our life direction: a real love union in which two independent beings commit themselves to each other.

Meanwhile, we are free to take full pleasure from the single journey as it unfolds. We have no one to check in with, no one to call if we're running late. We can change our plans without having to worry about how someone else feels—or taking their agenda into account. If we travel with alert hearts, minds, and souls, each experience we have along the way will give us a stronger, keener sense of self and transform us into someone worth living with.

&. *Today, recall at least five instances in your single life when you've felt particularly independent and joyful. In the future, try to recall those moments whenever the demands or conditions of the single life seem unbearable.*

In my twenty minutes today, I hold this thought: "My journey *to* love can be preparation for the journey *of* love."

Many argue; not many converse.

—LOUISA MAY ALCOTT

While both men and women have a history of seeking support within single-gender groups—for example, women gathering in their kitchens and men gathering at the local bar after work—now the groups are more polarized, politicized, and exclusionary. Women meet to worship "goddess power" and to extol the natural "cooperativeness" of sisterhood. At the same time, men are getting in touch with their inner "wild man" and banding together in fishing and golfing groups. All too often, the result is an increase in antagonism between the genders. Each act that further polarizes the sexes adds another foot or so to the chasm that yawns dauntingly between the two. No rapprochement is possible when each faction is "opposed" to the other and when both factions reinforce gender-related fear, resentment, indignation, and anger.

What is needed is *synthesis,* not separation. Both men's and women's movements need to imagine different roles for the future. The emergence of separate men's and women's movements is analogous to partners who go into individual therapy, rather than couple's counseling. Both may evolve, but their growth occurs separately and often leads to further estrangement. The answer lies in creating a *dialogue.* Only then can rigid, self-limiting role definitions begin to break down. Only then can men and women come to know each other better and, therefore, know the denied, disowned, or lost contrasexual parts of themselves.

❧ *In the coming day, make a special effort to engage members of the opposite gender in conversation. You don't have to engineer discussions that focus on male-female issues. Any kind of conversation—which by nature involves listening—can open the door to better understanding and appreciation.*

Today, as I enter my sacred space, I become aware that the divisions I see in the world are projections of splits in myself. I make this decision: "To listen to others as practice in learning to dialogue with divisions in myself."

A fascinating paradox rests at the heart of real love. Our achieving wholeness of self is directly related to our partner. While this may seem a circuitous route, the reality is that through helping someone else to heal, we heal ourselves.

Therefore, the focus should not be on finding the "perfect mate," but rather creating in ourselves a "conscious mate." This means cultivating the awareness to pay unfaltering attention to a partner's needs and helping to heal their childhood wounds. To do this, we must stretch beyond our comfortable boundaries. Like an aerobics exercise, stretching is uncomfortable and even hurts at times—but doesn't it feel good days later!

The search for real love calls us to drop our defensive behaviors so that we can share our most private thoughts, feelings, desires, and concerns in a loving and gentle manner. By doing this, we create a safe space for our partner to share themselves. And by directing our caring energy more toward our partner and less toward ourselves, we start bringing to life parts of ourself that atrophied during childhood. For our old brain doesn't know the difference between the feelings of love that we give ourselves and the feelings of love we offer to others. Therefore, according to our old brain, through loving our partner we are loving ourselves.

❦ *In the coming day, practice unconditional loving. Be as nice to two people who are close to you as you would be to yourself. You'll find that expressing this type of love is, in fact, being nice to yourself at the same time.*

During this twenty minutes of quiet, I ponder the reality that relationships, like bank accounts, require large deposits to yield worthwhile returns.

We cannot remain consistent with the world save by growing inconsistent with our past selves.

—HAVELOCK ELLIS

We may take childlike delight in being around a lover, but we can also suffer in a relationship from feeling like a child. After all, thanks to our Imago, we see in the other person the shadow side of our caretakers—the negative traits and behaviors that, as children, we had to work so hard to live with. It's no wonder that we automatically respond to our lover's anger as we did to our mother's rage, however faintly the two people may resemble each other on the surface. If we were compelled as children to campaign for our father's attention with an endless barrage of stories about what went on at school, who we played with, and what we watched on TV, we are very likely to think that we have to be an unrelentingly lively and entertaining companion to hold our adult lover's interest.

Thus, our love relationships are filled not only with moments of liberating, child*like* activity, but also with moments of crippling, child*ish* reactivity. If watched closely, we will all find ourselves acting, at times, as if we were five years old. And no partner who involves themselves in relationship for adult love wants to have to repeatedly contend with a child in adult disguise. Unless we can break the spell of these blasts-from-the-past, we can never get beyond the power-struggle stage with our love partners.

🍂 *Today, thinking about a past love relationship, identify at least two ways in which you derived childlike enjoyment from it. Then, identify at least two ways in which you inflicted childish behavior on the other person.*

In prayer today, I contemplate the presence of the past in the present. I celebrate the opportunity to live in the moment and commit myself to becoming fully awake.

Anger is a powerful force in our lives—what the ancient Greeks called "eros" converted into negative energy. Anger inevitably surfaces from time to time, and we can't just ignore it. One way or another, it will have its stormy impact on our thoughts, feelings, or behavior. We need to remember that anger can be a useful emotion, if used and expressed carefully and consciously. However, if we do not learn how to do this, it can wreak havoc on ourselves or the people around us.

Some people stifle the experience of anger by tightly clenching it into their muscles, a physically self-punishing strategy that can cause headaches, insomnia, hypertension, high blood pressure, and worse. Others contain their anger, denying any physical or emotional expression of it, at the cost of their peace of mind. Many try to toss off their anger on others before they've processed it themselves. These reactions are not healthy. Both the mind and the body need to *discharge* anger in a safe, healthy, and even satisfying manner. In this unit, you will learn techniques that will help you to ground yourself physically and emotionally when bolts of anger strike.

🥬 *Think specifically about a time in the past when you were angry. How did you express—or stifle—your anger? Did you become physically tense trying to repress it? Do you cast it into an argument before you've had time to process it yourself? Write down your answers in your journal and reflect on them.*

As I enter the place of deep peacefulness today, I become aware of the pulsating energy at my core. I hold this thought: "Anger is one expression of my life force."

As civilized beings, we're not supposed to resort to violence. In fact, we're morally, ethically, and perhaps legally liable for any damage we inflict. How, then, are we going to *physically* express a savage and primal life force so that it doesn't stay locked up in our bodies or result in a jail sentence?

The answer lies in the "Anger Kit," to be used whenever you find yourself burning with anger. Your kit may include boxing gloves and a dummy or padded mat for pummeling while you yell, scream, and curse to your heart's content. It may contain soft-soled shoes for stomping around the floor furiously until you're exhausted. It may have a tennis racket, baseball bat, or Bataka (a foam bat) that you can use to strike your bed, over and over, until you burst into tears. Or maybe the bed itself can be part of your kit: something you can lie down upon and pound with your fists and feet as you shout out, "No! No! No!" until you—and the bed—have had quite enough. Anything that will help you express your angry feelings can be part of your Anger Kit.

❧ *Be prepared! Plan your own Anger Kit right now, so that it's ready the next time you feel angry. Lovingly gather or purchase each item and stow them all in a special box, maybe painted red to stand for anger. Just make sure that when you use them, you don't wind up hurting yourself or any belongings that you care about!*

In this time of quiet, I allow myself to feel that place inside of me that contains my rage. Using this moment of prayer, I make a pact with myself: "I will seek healthy ways to express my anger."

*I have a right to my anger, and I don't want
anybody telling me I shouldn't be, that it's not nice
to be, and that something's wrong with me because
I get angry.*

— MAXINE WATERS

When our anger is focused on another person, it seems impossible to stop ourselves from taking it out on them. An indignant fire burns within us, and it seems painfully unjust that we must suffer from that anger instead of making the other person suffer. We're too hot and bothered to see that it's never in our own best interest to dump our anger on the other person before we've come to terms with it ourselves.

If you really feel that you won't be physically or emotionally satisfied until you've vented your anger on the appropriate target (or what *appears* to be the appropriate target at the time), why not do it with a proxy? All you need is a soft, well-upholstered chair or a chair well-covered with pillows. You can even pin a picture of the person on the chair. Then, you can start talking to that person about how s/he hurt you and how angry you are about that. Let yourself go, raise your voice. If you feel the impulse, start pounding the chair (the imaginary person) until you feel the anger is out of your system. If you break into tears, let yourself cry. Not only will this proxy attack help you process your anger physically and emotionally, it will also improve your chances of eventually having a more humane and productive dialogue with the flesh-and-blood target person.

❧ *Identify a chair in your home that you will use as a target proxy whenever you feel the need for dumping your anger on someone. If you're angry at someone today, use it right away. If not, promise yourself that you will use it the very next time that you are.*

In my time of quiet meditation, I reflect on those times when I allowed my anger to overrule my rational voice. I understand that it is important to express my anger, but that it must be done constructively.

*Anyone can become angry—that is easy, but to be
angry with the right person, to the right degree, at
the right time, for the right purpose, and in the right
way—this is not easy.*

—ARISTOTLE

We should not discount anger, assuming that it is an emotion
best ignored, avoided, or outgrown. Anger may not be the most
appropriate or civilized response in many situations, and sometimes
our otherwise legitimate anger may be out of proportion to the
situation at hand. But anger itself is a sign of life—a manifestation of
energy that needs to be respected and handled in the best possible
way. As human beings, we will always have to *contend* with anger,
but in working to *tend* our anger well, we learn a great deal about
self-management and personal growth.

Many of us vocalize our anger to others before we listen, physically
and emotionally, to what it really has to say to us. By confining
ourselves to the verbal expression of anger, we "feel" that anger
only in our mind, throat, and mouth. Next time, try feeling that anger
with your whole body. Let yourself see in your mind the person or
situation that is the target of your anger. Then take several deep
breaths, to prevent yourself from blurting that anger aloud. Continue
this visualizing, deep breathing, and silence until you can feel the
anger in every part of your body. Then let the angry scene in your
mind dissolve and enjoy the resulting sensations of bodily aliveness.

ご *Today, resolve that the very next time you feel angry, you will
express it more constructively. To prepare yourself, practice deep
breathing during the meditation. As your breath flows, feel the
expansion in your body. It is this expansion that will help you
release your anger in the future.*

**In a reverential stillness, I take a moment to acknowledge the power
that lies in anger. I recognize that anger can be an important tool and
an emotional source that adds to my aliveness. I celebrate my ability
to feel my anger.**

> *To persevere, trusting in what hopes he has, is*
> *courage in a man. The coward despairs.*
> —EURIPIDES

Reading about self-development and relationship skills is a far cry from actually doing something about them. While the descriptions of how to achieve change and become fulfilled appear quite simple and straightforward on paper, the process itself is a difficult journey full of loops, curves, and double-backs. It's not like losing that pesky ten pounds or improving your patter at cocktail parties. It demands clear intention, steady focus, lots of creativity, and the conscientious, day-by-day practice of new attitudes and unfamiliar, uncomfortable behaviors.

There is no fast detour to avoid the rocky terrain of the self. The needs of the unconscious for wholeness and aliveness are nonnegotiable and unignorable. The psyche is committed to its own completion. Every living thing wants to reach its full potential, whether it's a tree struggling and twisting its way to the sky through rocks and desert sand or a human being trying to overcome painful past conditioning. Anyone trying to bypass the hard work of integrating the self and building a healing relationship is driving down a dead-end tunnel. Drugs, skydiving, one-week stands, or weekend spiritual makeovers may provide fleeting pleasures, but they are no shortcuts to bliss. Ultimate happiness can only be found in staying on the course toward wholeness and togetherness.

❧ *Today, take a closer look at the ways in which you try to achieve happiness—the behaviors and activities that you find yourself relying on for pleasure. Are any of these behaviors or activities frequently disappointing or self-destructive? If so, how could you go about weaning yourself away from them? What healthier behaviors or activities could you replace them with?*

As I sit in sacred contemplation, I visualize a tree whose branches seem to brush the sky. I recognize that I, too, can reach my full potential, which is as endless as the sky itself.

Our childhood caretakers' interactions are forever imbedded in our memories. These patterns of interaction have a profound effect on how we treat those who are close to us as adults. We may think we are acting of our own free will, but we're really at the mercy of our childhood conditioning. Because our response patterns were inputted when we were children, we're predisposed to have certain types of reactions based on those that were modeled for us by the first people to teach us about relationships: our mother and our father, or whoever our childhood caretakers were.

Suppose, for instance, that during your childhood years, your mother was frustrated at your father's TV habits. You may have intuitively felt that your mother was hurt and angry because your father ignored her. She reacted by being silent and brooding and may even have complained to you about his behavior. Though you may have hated her passive behavior, you understood that your father scared everyone. Now, as an adult, you may tend to respond to similar situations in the same ways. You may be especially sensitive about people ignoring you, and so you retaliate with silence and complain to others. You may then hate yourself for being so passive but be unable to break out of your fear of the other person's reaction.

🍃 *Think about how your parents typically quarreled. What were their frustrations? What feelings did they express and what were their reactions? What were your thoughts about all this? Think about and write down how this may have influenced your own quarreling habits.*

As I move into a sacred stillness, I hold this truth: "The depth of my inner resources can set me free."

Two souls with but a single thought,
Two hearts that beat as one.

— MARIA LOVELL

"**I** can't remember when I didn't know you," lovers say, though they may have been together only for several days or a few weeks. Their old, instinctive brains have matched the image of their lover with the Imago portrait of their early caretakers, binding the present to the past. Bells immediately go off, and we believe wholeheartedly that this relationship will last forever. The result is a feeling that they are participating in something infinite, that their temporal life is invested with eternal meaning, that they are dwelling in a kind of *timelessness*.

Lovers who believe in reincarnation or some form of previous existence may feel that they literally have been with each other in a past lifetime. Lovers who simply have faith in the power of magic may be convinced that their meeting was destined to occur. They view their meeting as a sudden and unprecedented springing-to-life for each of them, like the awakening of Sleeping Beauty in the classic fairy tale. Whatever the explanation, it has a ring of truth to it. When we meet our Imago match, it taps a spiritual core in us that has always been there, but that we haven't before realized quite so intensely.

🐚 *Today, recall at least two incidents in your romantic past when you were first getting to know someone and had this sensation of timelessness: "I can't remember when I didn't know you." Those particular times, when the past seems irrelevant, are occasions when you were realizing that person's connection to your inner Imago.*

Although I consciously experience myself as living from minute to minute, hour to hour, I sometimes have the experience of eternity, a sensation of timelessness. In my time of quiet today, I allow myself to feel this connection to the timeless flow.

Discouraged by the bad dates we have or the good dates we fail to have, many of us long to possess Aladdin's lamp. If only we could rub that lamp and summon the genie inside to bring us the mate of our dreams! How much frustration, despair, embarrassment, and work it would save!

Innocent as this fantasy may seem, if we entertain it too often or too deeply, it can have a sinister effect. Subconsciously, we can condition ourselves to equate real love with unreal luck and a true lover with an imaginary dream. We can become ever more passive and ever more wistful, assuming that our lives would be complete were we to find such a lamp. But we must always bear in mind where genuine magic really lies. The real treasure lies in a fully committed relationship that we have earned ourselves, by working to turn our frustration, despair, and embarrassment into patience, joy, and confidence. And no amount of rubbing a lamp can bring the satisfaction of real love!

🙠 *Today, say farewell to the "Aladdin's lamp" fantasy. First, play it out in your mind one last time: rub the lamp, summon the genie, and envision the "perfect" lover. Next, imagine yourself throwing a big bucket of water on the lover and seeing him/her completely melt. Say to yourself, "This is just a washout fantasy and a waste of time."*

Putting aside fantasy, I acknowledge the ultimate power of the God within. I enter the deep silence and make this resolution: "I will create my own magic."

> *There is more difference within the sexes than*
> *between them.*
>
> —DAME IVY COMPTON-BURNETT

Magazines and self-help books abound with lists that offer bold and basic gender distinctions between men and women. Here's yet another list to serve as an example:

women	men
emotional	rational
ambivalent	decisive
domestic	worldly
tender	strong
nurturer	disciplinarian
follower	leader
sexually passive	sexually aggressive

It's impossible to prove whether this list—or any similar list—reflects actual differences between the majority of men and women. Most people upon reading this become downright annoyed. And they should! The qualities that are cited in each list are too vague, and the sheer number of men and women are too great. The simple truth of the matter is that we are all unique individuals, each containing a myriad of personalities that make up a fascinating whole. What *is* undeniably true about this list—and similar lists—is that it only tends to perpetuate a stereotype, and *any* stereotype is unjust when it's applied to an individual.

🦐 *Prove this list fallible from your own experience. Choose any two pairs of contrasting qualities (e.g., "women—emotional; men—rational") from the above list. Then, for each pair, try to think of a man and a woman you know who don't fit that pattern, and write their names down.*

In this time of reverential stillness, I recognize the disservice provided by stereotypes of any kind. Moving past these stereotypes, I claim for myself this profound truth: "The qualities of my character make me an original."

> *If you have got a living force and you're not using*
> *it, nature kicks you back. The blood boils just like*
> *you put it in a pot.*
>
> —LOUISE NEVELSON

Within all of us is a mighty and relentless living force—the drive to express our full aliveness. We spend so much of our time trying to find or create some intellectual meaning for our lives, when what we truly want is to *feel* the fullness of our own experiences as human individuals and as participants in the vast universe of being. We don't just want to *be* alive, we want to *pulsate* with aliveness. This drive doesn't go away. If we refuse to acknowledge it or try to block it or remain in life situations where it has no outlet, it roils within us, destroying our peace of mind by constricting our thoughts, feelings, and behaviors.

When we feel safe and free to express our aliveness, we live life at its fullest. When we don't have this feeling of aliveness, we risk experiencing the very worst that life has to offer. This dynamic is true for human beings in every situation: be it in a kindergarten class, a corporation, a nation, a dating relationship, or a marriage. Millions of love poems and paintings are about feeling that aliveness or mourning its loss.

Today, spend a few minutes recalling times in different contexts when you felt that you were able to express your aliveness. Do you remember such a time in school? At a job? In your neighborhood? While working on a project or hobby?

In a time of wordless prayer, I visualize the pulsating energy at my core as a fragile bloom that must be nurtured into its full capacity for strength, love, and vitality.

Criticism is the most common reaction to frustration and the most destructive. Its misguided premise is that the pain of criticism motivates others to behave the way we want them to.

Change is scary enough, and we certainly don't need to add the pain of humiliation and judgment! There is a simple, easily learned alternative to criticism: the behavior-change request. Instead of inflicting pain by calling attention to what we *don't* like about the other person, it works gently and responsibly toward helping us to identify what we *would* like to happen. In this way, we can positively assist the other person so that he or she understands our heartfelt needs and can better provide for them. In this unit, you'll learn the skill of making a behavior-change request. Within a relationship, this request helps to heal each other's childhood wounds.

&❧ *Today, thinking of a major romantic relationship in your past, list on a page in your notebook at least five chronic frustrations that you had with this person, leaving two lines blank between each frustration. Write in the present tense as if you were completing the sentence: "I don't like it when . . ." For example, "you don't clean up after yourself." "You spend too much money." "You drive too fast."*

In the serenity of this time alone, I pause to acknowledge: "When I experience frustration, I can ask for what I need without inflicting hurt on someone I care about."

*Sink in thyself! There ask what ails thee, at that
shrine!*

— MATTHEW ARNOLD

When we meet our Imago partners, we are unconsciously drawn to those similarities they share with our parental caretakers. Our hope is to finally heal our childhood wounds by entering into a relationship with those Imago partners. To effect this healing, we unconsciously want our Imago partner to give us what we didn't receive from our parents. For it is within our Imago that we sense answers to our questions and healing for our wounds. When this doesn't happen, we're especially frustrated.

But these very real frustrations contain valuable information: they can teach us about those wounds we received in childhood that now lie buried in our unconscious. Behind each adult frustration lies a childhood wound waiting to be discovered and healed. Therefore, identifying the unmet need or desire behind the frustration is the next step. Once we understand the real, underlying cause of our frustrations, we can begin to identify the behavior we need from our partner in order to fulfill our desires.

🍃 *Review the list of frustrations you wrote yesterday. In the space you left below each frustration, write the desire that lies behind this frustration. Phrase each of your desires positively, writing what you* don't *want. For example, "I want to live with you in a clean, attractive place," rather than "I don't want to have to live with your mess," or "I want to feel safe and relaxed when you're driving," rather than "I don't want to feel scared when you drive."*

In this safe place of stillness, I allow myself to acknowledge the wounded child behind my current frustrations. With this realization, I begin to understand. . . .

Half the misery in the world comes of want of courage to speak and to hear the truth plainly, and in a spirit of love.

—HARRIET BEECHER STOWE

The worst, most counterproductive feature of criticism is that it comes across as a direct, broadscale attack: "You always withdraw when I'm upset." "You never really listen to what I say." When faced with this type of blanket assault, the other person naturally responds in a defensive manner. And it's not surprising that they are unwilling to meet our needs. Healing cannot take place when two people are caught in an offensive-defensive position.

A behavior-change request, by contrast, is a positively phrased "I" statement, rather than a "you" statement, that expresses a very specific and doable behavior that we would like from our partner. It focuses on the *desire* behind the frustration, so that instead of bombarding the other person with criticism, we can give them useful information on precisely how to give us what we want. For example, using the above criticisms: "When I'm upset, I'd appreciate it if you would comfort me by putting your arms around me and stroking my hair." "When I'm talking about something serious, I'd like you to occasionally summarize what you've heard me say, so that I know you're paying attention," (a step toward teaching them intentional dialogue skills!).

꙳ *On a new page in your notebook, write a behavior-change request for each of the desires you expressed yesterday. Make sure that each request is an "I" statement rather than a "you" statement, that it expresses what you do want rather than what you don't want, and that it asks for a behavior that is specific and doable.*

In the stillness at my core, I recognize how defensive I become when I feel that someone is criticizing me. I visualize myself becoming a person who uses "I" statements instead of "You" statements.

*Respect for the vulnerability of human beings is a
necessary part of telling the truth, because no truth
will be wrested from a callous vision or callous
handling.*

—ANAÏS NIN

Giving the other person information about what we want or need in
no way obliges them to do what we ask, but it certainly encourages
them to be more responsive than criticism would! When we communicate our specific desires, eliminating the guesswork, we help to
ensure that neither person will have to suffer quite as much again
from our frustration.

Of course, there's no guarantee that the other person will comply
with our exact behavior-change request immediately, if at all. Even if
the other person does comply, there is always a chance that we will
experience the same frustration again, to some degree. After all,
asking the other person to take one specific step toward helping us
achieve our desire may not eliminate all our frustrations. But we have
to begin somewhere—and so does the other person!

Changing one's customary behavior is difficult under any circumstances. When we ask others to change, we must go slowly—and
remember to be patient. We can't expect them to fulfill all of our
desires at once, nor can we assume that one grand act of change on
their part can completely eliminate all grounds for one of our big
frustrations. When we ask someone else to change, we must create
and cultivate a space where that change can take place.

❧ *Review the list of desires that you wrote on Day 147. Indicate
the relative importance of each desire by giving it a number from
1 (very important) to 5 (not so important). You need to learn
how to prioritize your desires so that your most immediate ones
can be met without overwhelming the other person.*

**Retreating to this holy space, I visualize change in a relationship as
similar to the progress of the seasons. I recognize that change
happens gradually, sometimes without my realizing it, and that it is
important to be patient.**

Creative minds always have been known to survive any kind of bad training.

—ANNA FREUD

Given a chance, we are capable and generally amenable to changing negative behaviors that torment our loved ones. Most of us genuinely want to be good people.

We need to remember this when we make a behavior-change request. In presenting our request, it is best to give others some latitude in making decisions. This way, we show someone that we recognize and appreciate their willingness to change and trust their commitment to the relationship. Therefore, it helps to provide them with three specific options for each request.

For example, if you wanted to feel safer as a passenger in a friend's car, the requests might be:

"I'd like you to stay within five miles of the speed limit."

"I'd like you to be sober when you're going to be driving."

"I'd like you to stay a safe distance behind every car and pass when it is safe."

While the other person is free to choose all three options, you should be satisfied—for the time being—if s/he chooses just one.

❧ *Choose one desire that you identified yesterday as "very important" by labeling it with a "1." In addition to the behavior-change request that you already wrote for this desire (Day 148), develop at least two other behavior requests that you could offer as options.*

Today, I open my mind to a deep truth: "Loving someone is being open to change. Realizing this, I recognize that any willingness to hear my request is an act of love."

> *You don't have to be afraid of change. You don't
> have to worry about what's been taken away. Just
> look to see what's been added.*
>   —JACKIE GREER

Now that you have learned how to develop and present a behavior-change request to others, you have a tool that can bring about real healing for both people engaged in this dialogue. In addition, you are prepared to assist others in making *their* requests for changes in *your* negative behaviors. When this service is performed between two people in a committed relationship, it can be a wondrously healing and spiritually uplifting experience.

If you enjoy shopping for a close friend's birthday gift, you can see the truth in the Biblical saying that it is more blessed to give than to receive. We can also learn this when we grant behavior-change requests that others make of us. At first, it may seem a fearsome challenge. We have to let go of our old, entrenched behavior, and this makes us feel vulnerable and unrecognizable to ourselves. We have to overcome both our false pride and our very real anxieties so that we can stretch into unfamiliar territory. But in making this stretch, we grow into better, stronger, more caring individuals. We learn new skills, and we lose a dysfunctional trait that may have been hurting us, as well as others, more than we realized.

🍂 *Take out your notebook and write down a behavior of a family member or past lover that really bothers you. Try drafting a behavior-change request that will alleviate your frustration. If you feel safe doing so, call the person and see how he or she responds. If you call and the response is positive, you can talk about the individual approaching you with a behavior-change request as well.*

During my time of prayer, I open to the many possibilities that await me when I gently request what I need. I recognize the joy in taking care of others by taking care of myself.

The hardest part of learning new behaviors and attitudes is unlearning old ones. As any piano teacher will tell you, when students first practice a tune on the piano, they're likely to hit many wrong notes. Despite their best efforts, they'll continue to hit a high percentage of the *same* wrong notes for many more times to come. Once our brain has latched onto a particular pattern, it's very stubborn about letting go. We must remind ourselves of this fact when we fall back on old, negative habits in our relationships or when we start thinking that it's just too much work to try doing better.

If we catch ourselves repeatedly criticizing a close friend for dawdling over the menu or borrowing our tools, we need to put more pressure on ourselves to stop dumping criticism and, instead, start making appropriately modest and specific behavior-change requests. If we realize that we're continuing to listen only half-attentively to our dates, while the other half of our mind is busy planning what to respond, we shouldn't merely bemoan our inability to change. We should forgive ourselves and try, try again to practice our intentional dialogue skills. Little by little we *can* break the chain of habit.

🍂 *Today, identify at least three bad habits that you still have. For each habit, think of at least one way you can start to break it.*

In quiet today, I accept the challenge of change, knowing that the more I surrender my old patterns, the more space I have for developing my full potential.

It is only possible to live happily ever after on a day-to-day basis.

— MARGARET BONNANO

For most of us, most of the time, each passing day is a struggle to accomplish plans-in-progress, to resolve issues that still linger from yesterday, and to start things rolling for the future. On the commute to work, we are already thinking about everything we have to accomplish that day. During lunch, we ponder what we'll serve for dinner. And while we're hanging out with a good friend, we are worried about meeting the deadline for our latest project. What happens to the here and now? It usually gets ambushed by all our other concerns. Having decided in advance what we like, dislike, fear, and desire, we're constantly anxious about life's unpredictability. We're continually being frustrated as well because life seldom—if ever—fits our agenda perfectly.

When we stop fighting our way through the day and instead open our hearts and minds to whatever the present moment has to offer to us, we start realizing how much unnecessary conflict we're inclined to generate in the world around us. We see that our situation is not nearly as complicated, overwhelming, or urgent as we thought it was a moment ago. We feel our own, fundamental aliveness coursing beneath all the surface stresses and strains, and that sensation refreshes and enspirits us.

✥ *Today, take a half-hour break from everything else and just enjoy whatever's at hand. If it's a beautiful day outside, take a walk in a nearby park. If your back is aching, lie down on the couch and listen to all the different sounds you can hear around you. If both you and your dog are in the mood to play, get out the dog toys. If a construction crew is hard at work on a building site across the road, go watch what's happening.*

Today in joyful silence, I release my hold on *making* things happen and participate with all my being in what *is* happening. Here I find a sacred place.

As lovers spend more and more time together, they are wont to say to each other something like, "With you, I no longer feel empty, incomplete, and alone. Instead, I feel fulfilled, complete, and connected." They have found in each other what they couldn't find as single people. Two imperfect halves have been made into one perfect whole—if only temporarily.

This wonderful feeling occurs when we involve our lives with someone who resembles our Imago portrait and therefore experience a transcendent sense of *reunification*. Our life as a lover seems to have taken on another dimension of reality that it was always intended to have but never did. It's as if we were finally three-dimensional after having lived so long, perhaps without realizing it, in the flat, two-dimensional world of being by ourselves. Now, many years since we enjoyed an infant child's sense of oneness with the universe, we are working toward finding love and being granted another chance.

❧ *Today, recall at least two incidents in your romantic past when you had this feeling of "reunification." In each case, try to remember and write down the qualities the other person brought into your life that gave your life more balance or completeness— qualities that were missing from your life as a single person. Identifying these qualities will give you more insight into your Imago portrait.*

In quiet today, I contemplate the mystery of love, how my emptiness is matched by the fullness of another, how my thirst for oneness is met by the generosity of the universe.

We can't help but occasionally compare one person's performance to the best performance of its type we've ever encountered. We remember those people in our lives that have been gifted with an outstanding achievement, and it's likely that we'll pass judgment if we encounter someone who does something similar, though less fantastic. Thus, our best friend's clam chowder simply cannot compete with the delicious brew our now-departed aunt Phyllis used to make.

When we silently compare in this way, we are being extremely unfair to the current relationships in our lives. What good do these comparisons do us or the other person who is with us *now*? Actually, these comparisons keep us stuck in the past and blind us to the new and wonderful things that abound in the present. Perhaps our friend's chowder is not as good as Aunt Phyliss's, but maybe they make a pasta dish that comes close to our idea of Nirvana! How much better it is to accept, value, and praise the good that's right in front of us, rather than to live in the long-gone past.

📖 *Today, consider whether you are still using old standards to judge the performance of new people. Ask yourself these two questions:*
- *Do I ever compare current friends' or dates' behavior unfavorably with that of past friends or dates? How so?*
- *Do I ever catch myself thinking that past pleasures were the best and that nothing now comes close to them? How so?*

For every "old standard" that you identify and write down, promise yourself that you will do your best to stop using it to measure the present.

I am often so attracted to living in the past that I fail to experience the richness of the present. Today I vow to surrender all comparisons and become present to each moment.

Come forth into the light of things.
— WILLIAM WORDSWORTH

The looming shadow of loneliness is always waiting to haunt the single life. We may be perfectly happy going about our normal routines for days, weeks, or months at a time, and then, all of a sudden, it hits! We find ourselves in a period of oppressiveness, obliviousness, or simple depression. We get into a rut of staying at home, not seeing people, and not doing much except keeping counsel with our own stale thoughts. We live in our sweats and cease to brush our hair on the weekends. It's here, in the darkness of the rut, that loneliness can most easily make its attack.

Solitude may be good for the soul in small doses, but on a prolonged basis it can start to wear away our zest for life. Our social skills and our chances for meeting prospective partners slowly start to dwindle. When we find ourselves lingering inside our own, solitary world, we need to prod ourselves to get out into the light of other people's company. We need to style our hair and throw on one of our favorite fancy outfits! Making the effort to look good and be around other people gives us a break and gives the specter of loneliness the boot!

&. *Plan something today that will get you more "out and about" in the near future — just as a safeguard. If it's been a while since you've been to a party, throw one yourself this month. If you miss going to jazz clubs, ball games, or bingo nights, mark some days on your calendar when you will go, come what may. If you've been putting off taking a drawing class, joining a bowling team, or going on a trip to the Thousand Islands, now's the time to get out the phone book and make that first call.*

I move into the spiritual strength at my core and flanked with this power, I can birth new life and creativity.

Our caretakers had the task of introducing us into human society as best they could, even though they themselves might not have felt comfortable around other people. Nevertheless, they gave us all sorts of guidelines during our childhood about how we should act in various, interpersonal situations. Through instruction and example, they taught us right and wrong ways to behave in order to get along with other people. Not surprisingly, these guidelines were heavily influenced by gender considerations that were reinforced by society. We were told that men are supposed to be cool, calm, and collected; while women are expected to be warm, bubbly, and giving. When men take charge of a situation, we learned, they should demand cooperation and never display any lack of a sense of personal worth or confidence. When women take charge of a situation, we learned, they should be extremely diplomatic, inspiring cooperation rather than asking for it directly and acknowledging their "weaker," feminine qualities rather than trying to hide them. In order for men and women to relate to each other as real-life adult human beings, these stage directions from children's theater need to be unlearned.

&a *Today, spend a few moments reviewing how you were raised to believe a* man *should act. Then, think about how you were raised to believe a* woman *should act.*

Turning to an inner wisdom, I acknowledge the ways in which I have been shaped by assumptions based on my gender. I shed all inappropriate assumptions, as a snake sheds its skin.

If you happen to have a wart on your nose or forehead, you cannot help imagining that no one in the world has anything else to do but stare at your wart, laugh at it, and condemn you for it, even though you have discovered America.

— FYODOR DOSTOYEVSKY

Lonely inside their single dwellings, many people have a difficult time finding someone to love in the outside world because they're too busy looking at a mirror instead of through a window. They brood over their own physical appearance, personality, intelligence, and behavior as if they were evaluating whether to date themselves! It's a comic "backward" activity that can have tragic side effects.

Whenever we start to evaluate ourselves, our mind quickly passes over the obvious good features. After all, why be concerned about things that aren't likely to cause us any problems? Instead, our mind zeroes in on the possible blemishes. We agonize over the two-inch-wide bulge of fat above our belt. We despair because we don't have anything clever to say when we meet a new date. We worry about whether our clothes look tacky, whether our laugh sounds phony, or whether it would be a turnoff to reveal our love for bird-watching. We fail to consider that the other person is not us but has an entirely different point of view—one that we should learn to appreciate by looking outward, not inward.

❧ During the coming day, practice focusing *positively* on the people with whom you interact instead of *negatively* on yourself. If you catch yourself wondering about whether the person is responding badly to your appearance, behavior, or conversation, stop and refocus your attention. Try, instead, to notice something good about the other person's appearance, behavior, or conversation.

I am intrigued by the thought that I am the creator of my perceptions and the prisoner of my preconceptions. Today in my time of quiet, I choose creativity and freedom.

As long as our mind remains preoccupied, our heart stays clenched as tight as a fist. When we allow ourselves to be fully present in the moment, our heart opens up and expands. Any time we resist a feeling state, we create a tension in our body that inhibits us. Once we release into a feeling, we are able to open up to the possibilities that abound. This type of release is at the core of every spiritual experience—prayer, meditation, a spontaneous act of compassion, or a thorough and loving attentiveness to what's going on in the here and now.

Only as we tune into the present can we sense a quality that is timeless: the essential richness of the life force and the abiding beauty of the living universe. Even if the present moment seems painful, we need to give ourselves fully to that moment in order to live *through* it. Otherwise, we will continue to live *with* it, in a state of perpetual dissatisfaction.

To hold on to the past and the future without ever letting go is to miss the presence of life altogether. To let go of the past and future in the face of that presence—if only every now and then—is to grasp eternity.

❧ *Today, do one simple thing that will allow you to live fully in the present moment. Choose a familiar, relatively trivial task, and perform it with your full, loving concentration. Or focus all of your attention on a beautiful flower, sunset, or landscape for several minutes. Experience how wonderful the simplest moment of life can be if it's lived with a devout spirit.*

In a time of reverential calm, I simply take twenty minutes to focus on my breathing. As my breathing deepens, I allow myself to be fully in this healing present.

Throughout our lives, each one of us is neurologically predisposed to express our energy in one of two ways: we either minimize or maximize. This response pattern holds true whether we are responding to major life events or to minor, day-to-day developments. The maximizers are the active ones, often dramatic and even explosive, exaggerating their feelings, and fighting their way through life. They respond to life with dramatic flair, often perceiving events as being larger than life. The minimizer is the opposite: passive, emotionally contained, often fearful and self-effacing, and habitually fleeing inward to avoid being hurt. Minimizers unconsciously try to fade into the woodwork and not draw attention to themselves.

Today, you'll review the characteristics of the minimizer to see which ones fit you. Tomorrow, you'll consider the characteristics of the maximizer. Soon, you'll find out which you are—and which your Imago match is likely to be!

&❧ *Here is a list of traits that describe the minimizer. Circle the phrases that describe you.*
- *Keeps feelings inside*
- *Restrains emotional display*
- *Denies dependency*
- *Generally denies needs*
- *Shares little of inner world*
- *Tends to exclude others from their psychic space*
- *Withholds feelings, thoughts, behaviors*
- *Has rigid self-boundaries*
- *Takes direction mainly from themselves*
- *Mainly thinks about themselves*
- *Acts and thinks compulsively*
- *Tries to dominate others*
- *Tends to be passive-aggressive.*

During this time of deep reflection, I explore how I express my energy. I acknowledge that, though it is difficult to realize at times, my areas of wounding can also be seen as areas of potential growth.

Next to the joy of the egotist is the joy of the
detractor.
                                      —AGNES REPPLIER

The old adage that opposites attract is true! Couples tend to be made up of a maximizer and a minimizer. One partner is quiet and unemotional (a minimizer), the other is exuberant and inclined to go over the top (the maximizer). This uniting of opposites is another one of nature's clever symmetries. Like romantic love, this pairing relates to each person seeking their Imago match. The minimizer unconsciously searches for a maximizer to add more dynamic energy to his or her life, while the maximizer searches for a minimizer to be a more temperate influence.

The degree to which we evolve into a minimizer or a maximizer depends on the timing and extent of our childhood wounding. The earlier our wounds were inflicted or the more severe those wounds were, the more pronounced our tendency to be either a minimizer or a maximizer will be. Our Imago, however, will direct us to the correspondingly intense counterpart.

❧ *Here is a list of traits that describe the maximizer. Circle the phrases that describe you.*
  * *Explodes feelings outward*
  * *Depends on others*
  * *Generally exaggerates needs*
  * *Is open and subjective*
  * *Is overly inclusive of others in psychic space*
  * *Tends toward clinging and excessive generosity*
  * *Has difficulty declaring self-boundaries*
  * *Distrusts own directions and asks others*
  * *Focuses on others*
  * *Acts impulsively*
  * *Usually submissive, manipulative*
  * *Alternates between aggressiveness and passivity.*
  Compare the number of circled traits on this list with the number of circled traits on yesterday's minimizer list. Whichever number is greater tells you whether you are essentially a maximizer or a minimizer.

Opening to an inner truth, I experience my form of self-expression. Once again, I recognize that the hole created by a wound is a place for the light of healing to shine through.

*Habit is habit, and not to be flung out of the window
by any man, but coaxed downstairs a step at a time.*

—MARK TWAIN

What do you do with this knowledge? For the present, just be aware
of your minimizer or maximizer tendencies and accept them as part
of who you are. Over the next few days, weeks, and months,
note specific incidents that make these tendencies clearer to you.
Eventually, when you enter into a conscious relationship, your knowledge and awareness will serve you—and your partner—well. Then,
you will have an excellent opportunity to temper the extremes of
your minimizing or maximizing as you endeavor to meet your partner's needs. If, as a maximizer, you are used to clinging to the one
you love, you can work to overcome the fears that make you cling,
so that you can allow your partner more independence. If, as a
minimizer, you're typically aloof in a relationship, you can strive to
grow beyond your worries about being smothered to become more
available and affectionate to your partner.

The better we understand ourselves, the closer we move toward
healing our wounds. Breaking habitual patterns of thinking, feeling,
and behaving—especially ones that go back to childhood wounding—
frees us to live more fully and productively. A conscious relationship
provides the ideal environment for two people to help liberate each
other in this manner, so that together they can realize their own
best selves.

❧ *Today, think of times in past relationships when your minimizer or maximizer tendencies may have caused problems. Then,
take out your notebook and write down some of those situations.
Make a vow to become more aware of these tendencies and to
work toward overcoming them in future relationships.*

**I quietly close my eyes today and meditate on all the exciting
possibilities ahead of me. I recognize that in order to be conscious in
my relationships, I must be willing to work on myself.**

The love we give away is the only love we keep.

—ELBERT HUBBARD

Real love occasionally reflects the ambiance of romantic love—its glittering qualities, lush tones, and seductive sensations—but there is a profound difference. Substance replaces fluff, surface yields to depth, and impermanence gives way to stability. Romantic love comes easily, but it is fleeting. It is nature's gift from the unconscious to lure us on the journey to our full potential. It is a transitory *state of being* created by the deep forces of the psyche. But real love is an achievement of consciousness and intentionality, a dynamic *way of being,* a hard-won prize granted only to those who persevere.

The process of transforming romantic love into real love can be compared to the journey of a child who inherits wealth and squanders it all. To return home, this child must enter the world of work, learn a trade, cultivate discipline, shed the fat gained through opulence, and surrender the illusion of entitlement. In short, this child must transcend egoistic interests and develop a transcendent self that can give as well as receive. Only then, with newfound spirit, can this child enjoy a wealth that lasts, a richness that nourishes the soul.

&. *Today, renew your commitment to "return home," to practice the skills that will help you to become a whole person, capable of transforming romantic love into real love.*

I visualize a spiral path toward my center as I relax into this time of reflection, holding this truth: "Consciously walking this path will return me to my self's true home."

In contemporary society, the word "ritual" tends to be applied very sparingly to practices that we associate with holidays or special occasions: watching for the groundhog's shadow every February 2, toasting the bride and groom after their wedding ceremony, eating black-eyed peas on New Year's Day. In fact, we each perform our own idiosyncratic rituals every day. There may be a certain personally prescribed pattern to the way we get up and get dressed each morning or to the way we travel from home to work or to the way in which we go about exercising our bodies. Some of our ritualistic habits are especially positive, such as always enjoying our first cup of coffee in the morning on the front porch. Others are more negative, like leaving unwelcome mail unopened for days until we finally force ourselves to read it. We need to pay more attention to our personal rituals so that we derive even more benefit from the positive ones and drop the negative ones—or change them for the better. In this way, we can transform our ordinary, day-to-day existence into something all the more enjoyable and inspirational.

&. *Today, identify at least three different rituals that you perform on a daily basis. Then, choose one and figure out a way to make it more positive.*

I note the degree to which I am unconscious of patterns that structure my world. Drawing from my creative spirit, I feel the freedom to create meaning in any event of my life.

The next time you look at a tree, consider all the many separate leaves that are linked to each other. Think about how much these leaves are dependent upon the life of the tree and how much they contribute to its life.

In the larger scheme of things, we are not "single" people at all. We are individual expressions of a much greater force—the life pulse of the universe. We come to feel that force most intimately when we bond with another person in a committed relationship and experience how much that single connection restores our sense of belonging to the cosmos. Until we gain—or regain—that feeling of full aliveness, we can rely on the richness and wonder of nature to remind us of the interdependence of all forms of life.

&. *Today, take a restorative walk in nature, noting how all living things interrelate.*

Today I hold this thought: "I am a node in the tapestry of being. I note that I no longer feel alone."

> *The love of our neighbor in all its fullness simply*
> *means being able to say to him, "What are you*
> *going through?"*
>
> —SIMONE WEIL

At first, most people find it very frustrating to practice intentional dialogue. It *is* hard, it *can* seem artificial, and it *does* slow conversation. It makes sense that we often don't want to do it, preferring, instead, to fall back on our old, half-conscious, automatic-pilot way of talking. At such times, we need to remind ourselves that the initially tedious process of intentional dialogue saves us time in the end, cutting through the total time and effort it would take to resolve the negative fallout from more careless types of conversation. The intentional dialogue process also eliminates the pain occasioned by hurt feelings, misjudgments, wrong interpretations, or simple inattention.

We can take heart in the fact that intentional dialogue flows much more easily and naturally with practice. Eventually, it becomes habitual and quite personal—imbued with our own particular style of mirroring, validating, and empathizing. If we stay with it, we can get the hang of it quickly, which means that we can experience all the sooner both its efficiency and the positive intimacy it creates.

➚ *During the day, make a special effort to practice your intentional dialogue skills with at least two people.*

In sacred stillness, I come to understand that what initially appears to be a clumsy device meant to slow me down is, in actuality, a key that will ultimately ensure my freedom.

Our society doesn't hold up very good models of the single state. The liberal end of the spectrum pictures it as a crazy orgy of self-indulgence, while the conservative depicts it as an apprenticeship, during which one works diligently to attract the most promising mate. People who find themselves single at thirty are still seen as being somewhat abnormal and certainly deficient.

We need to take the matter into our own hands, creating our own image of what our life as a single person can be. We do want ultimately to establish a committed love relationship, because this type of union provides opportunities for growth, joy, and connection to the universe that are otherwise unachievable. But that doesn't mean that we have to live in the shadows of life until the right person comes along.

Our single life is a time for enjoying and enriching our individual identity, so that we have more to give to ourselves, to others, and to the universe. Therefore, we must design it carefully so that it has its own special beauty.

❧ *Today, in your notebook, sketch a picture that represents your current life as a single person. Don't worry about producing a work of art. Just draw the first image that comes to mind, whether it's symbolic or literal, realistic or abstract. Then, sketch another picture representing how you could improve the quality of your life as a single person. Perhaps you'll come up with an inspirational image that you can keep in mind over the next few months.*

Today, I access the artist within. In the deepest center of my being, I draw upon the energies of creation to design myself to be consistent with my essence and wholeness.

Anger is a signal, and one worth listening to.

—HARRIET LERNER

Anger is one of the most powerful emotions we can experience. In a society leery of strong emotions, it has one of the worst raps. When we're furious at someone's cruel words or thoughtless behavior, we talk about "burning," "bursting," or "exploding" with anger. If we stifle our anger, we get "consumed" by it. Why not cool down and see this type of anger in its proper perspective, as a valuable warning mechanism that's directly tied to our sense of aliveness?

We must first realize that when anger is present, it usually pertains to a childhood wound. When we're angry with someone, it's a signal of imminent danger, a signal that we have unresolved, out-of-control feelings that could get both people into trouble. Often, this signal is out of proportion with the stimuli that provoked it. When we get that signal, we first need to discharge the emotion itself as fully and constructively as possible *before* we confront the other person. We can do this by using the guidelines we've learned in this book for expressing anger (Days 136–139). Then, after we've discharged our anger, we need to look more deeply into its causes. Aside from what the other person did, or failed to do, we must consider our own contribution: Did we have unrealistic expectations or somehow over-react? Is there a way we might have prevented the anger-provoking situation by communicating our wants and needs more effectively? Conducting this closer examination is what the anger signal is bidding us to do.

❧ *Today, review the process for expressing anger that you learned on Days 136–139. Promise yourself that you'll follow this process the very next time you sense anger toward someone about whom you have strong feelings.*

In my time of quietness today, I allow myself to experience any turbulence within my core. Realizing this is my life force experiencing threat, I breathe deeply and allow the disturbance to build and pass, releasing the fear.

Love is all fire; and so heaven and hell are the same place.
— NORMAN O. BROWN

One of the most common metaphorical images associated with love is fire. Our first encounter with the beloved features anything from "sparks" to "fireworks." He or she goes on to "light our fire." We "burn" with passion, we're "hot" for the other person's body. An obsessional quality creeps into the relationship, like the irresistible attraction of a moth to a flame. It's a sensation of *necessity* that tells us we have encountered our Imago match. We respond by saying to our lover things like, "I can't imagine what it would be like to be without you," or "I don't think I could live, or would want to live, if I didn't have you."

This sensation of need—the stuff of countless love songs and passionate poetry—reflects the connection that our unconscious mind is making between our lover and our childhood caretakers, who once wielded the power of life and death over us. Having sensed that connection, we now feel that we are at last going to get all of our survival needs met. Like fire, the power of this lover can be creative or destructive. We need to come to a more fully realized life by building a good relationship with our Imago match, or our life can be reduced to ashes. Whatever the ultimate outcome, it definitely seems to us, in the beginning, that we desperately need this fire in our lives. Otherwise, life is dark and cold.

❧ *Today, recall at least two incidents in your past romantic life when you experienced this sense of necessity. For each person, ask yourself these questions: How, more specifically, did I feel—or express—that the other person was a necessity to me? In what ways did the other person hold the power of life or death over me?*

Today, I ponder the larger truth that I am dependent and realize that my existence is an act of grace from a beneficent universe. In prayer I give thanks.

Our inborn temperament only partly determines whether we are minimizers (quiet, passive, and self-contained) or maximizers (loud, active, and expansive). The major influence is how we are socialized by our early caretakers and society as a whole.

There is not a preferable way to be, but unfortunately, our culture tends to value people who are very rational and restrained. Therefore, the minimizer, who buries his or her feelings and needs, tends to *look* like the mature, capable adult, and is more generally acceptable. By contrast, the maximizer, who copes by exaggerating his or her feelings and crying out for attention, tends to *look* out of control.

Appearances aside, maximizers may, in fact, be better off psychologically than minimizers. While their behavior may not be as socially commendable, at least they are still consciously aware of their feelings and desires. Minimizers may be more superficially well off in the world, but they are so disconnected from their emotions that they have a double burden in realizing happiness and wholeness. Before they can go about trying to get their needs met, they have to identify what those needs really are.

❦ *If you're a minimizer, write down at least two ways in which you've been praised by others for the same "repressing" qualities that inhibit your emotions. If you're a maximizer, write down how you may have been chastised for the same "expressive" qualities that make you feel in touch with your real emotions.*

My longing for wholeness is so deep that I unconsciously choose persons who complement me, with whom I do not feel my emptiness. Today, in this quiet time, I accept this mystery as a part of the process and vow to follow the path to my wholeness.

No matter how stable or loving a home we were raised in or how well-intentioned our parents or early caretakers may have been, we were all imperfectly nurtured and socialized. In every family there is always room for improvement. Consequently, we all have unmet needs and wounds from childhood because of inadequacies or misconceptions on the part of our parents when we were young or because our parents did not meet our expectations as we grew older. We became frustrated. Whatever the cause or degree of the wounding, we feel a lifelong yearning for healing.

In our adult relationships, we seek to heal our childhood wounds by trying to get what we didn't get in childhood from a partner who is our Imago match—that is, someone who has the same characteristics as our parents. Only this person can pick up where our parents left off to give us what we crave. To be better prepared to be a partner in a fulfilling, loving, and healing relationship, we need to understand the nature of our wounds and the character defenses we have adopted in response to them.

&❧ *Today, try to get closer in touch with who you were—and, if possible, what fears, needs, or problems you had—at various stages in your childhood. Thinking of your earliest memories, what were you like then? Next, go on to think about later ages. What were you like at four years old? Six? Eight? Ten? Twelve?*

In the serenity of a healing moment, I open to an inner safety, allowing myself to acknowledge those places where I feel wounded, rather than deny them out of fear.

Character builds slowly, but it can be torn down with incredible swiftness.

—FAITH BALDWIN

Each stage of childhood has its own tasks or skills to be mastered and, therefore, its own nurturing needs. Depending on the degree to which those needs are *not* perfectly met—and no parent or caretaker is perfect—we each suffer a certain degree of wounding. Consequently, we develop character defenses. We carry with us the wounds and defenses from every stage of childhood all through life until we are finally healed. It can be difficult to trace our wounds and character defenses back to childhood itself, because we keep those defenses carefully buried. We must be gentle when unearthing our defenses because we are also reactivating these wounds.

As infants, we were intensely concerned with our attachment to our parents. Our main worry tended to take one of two forms: fear of *rejection* (that is, making contact that was hurtful) or fear of *abandonment* (that is, losing contact and being hurt). If we suffered primarily from rejection, we tended to become *avoiders:* passive, withdrawn, and predisposed to shun overly close contact with our loved ones, whom we perceive as too demanding and potentially hurtful. This is a type of minimizing response. If we suffered primarily from abandonment, we tended to become *clingers:* insecure when we're alone and, as a result, constantly demanding affection and closeness with our mates. This is a type of maximizing response.

&❧ *Title a page in your notebook, "Childhood Wounds." Thinking about your childhood, and past relationships, decide whether you tend to suffer from the wound of rejection or abandonment. Are you an* avoider *or a* clinger? *When you've decided, write your wound and your character defense on the notebook page.*

Accessing courage in my space of quiet today, I move into a place where I can recognize my defenses. Instead of being angry about them, I thank my defenses for protecting me. Then I let them go, one by one. . . .

*Avoiding danger is no safer in the long run than
outright exposure. The fearful are caught as often
as the bold.*

—HELEN KELLER

When we were toddlers (approximately age 1 1/2 to 3 years) we
undertook our first bold ventures into the world beyond our parents.
We were little explorers—testing our capacity to function independently, but counting on our ability to return at any time to a secure
and loving home base. It was an immense challenge to us and to our
parents. No wonder parents in general complain about the "terrible
twos!" We wanted to enjoy complete freedom and, at the same time,
complete safety, and so we were ever vulnerable to frustration—and
caused much frustration to others.

During this period of childhood, we either experienced the wound
of *being smothered,* because our parents or caretakers wouldn't let us
have enough freedom to venture away from their safe supervision;
or, alternatively, the wound of *being neglected,* because our parents
or caretakers were too often not there when we needed their
reassurance. If we were wounded by being smothered, we evolved
into *isolators:* distant from others, insistent upon our autonomy, and
fearful of the neediness of our partners. This is a minimizing response. If we were wounded by being neglected, we became *pursuers:* chasing after our partners, seeking constant support and
reliability from them, and growing angry or panicked when we don't
get it. This is a maximizing response.

❧ *Based on your experiences in childhood and in past relationships, did you suffer most from the wound of being smothered,
making you an isolator, or from the wound of being neglected,
making you a pursuer? Write your response on the "Childhood
Wounds" page in your notebook.*

**Celebrating the sacred today, I take a moment to thank myself for the
work I am involved in. I recognize the importance of healing myself.**

When they tell you to grow up, they mean stop growing.

—TOM ROBBINS

When we were three or four years old, we wanted to know who we were as separate people in relation to the world. As young explorers, we embarked on the process of becoming a self. To do this, we had to develop a strong inner image of ourself, and strong images of the significant others in our life. Like children playing with costumes and masks, we tried on different identities for size and observed how others reacted. Any identity was up for grabs—at least for a few hours! Regardless of our actual gender, race, or even species, we practiced being our mother, uncle, a blue jay, bank robber, various comic-book and fairy-tale heros and heroines, and even tried creating a few personalities of our own. In one form or another, we were obsessively self-assertive, and we wanted this self to be validated by those around us.

During this identity search, our wounding came from one of two basic experiences: *being shamed,* i.e., having our identity tryouts rejected or disparaged; or *being ignored,* i.e., feeling invisible because our identity tryouts weren't acknowledged or appreciated. A person who has been shamed tends tc become a *controller,* a minimizing defense of dominating and criticizing one's partners to ensure one's personal safety and "rightness." A person who's been ignored tends to become a *diffuser,* a maximizing behavior characterized by submissiveness in order to be loved and passive-aggressiveness in order to get one's way.

ᏋᏗ *Today, determine whether your wounding came from being shamed, in which case you tend to be a controller, or from being ignored, in which case you tend to be a diffuser. Write your particular wound and your coping behavior on the "Childhood Wounds" page in your notebook.*

Moving into a place of inner calm, I visualize myself chained by my old ways of behaving. I recognize that only I hold the key to my freedom.

I'm not afraid of storms, for I'm learning how to sail my ship.

— LOUISA MAY ALCOTT

In our preschool years, we began competing with others to discover our personal power and its limits. Often, we have the strongest experience of ourselves when we are in reaction to, or in competition with, another. We also began to determine what belonged to us and what didn't. At this stage, we were trying to become competent managers of our newly established selves. We were attempting to gain mastery over our environment and proficiency in our social world in order to build our self-esteem. These tasks can be difficult to learn at times.

Parents and caretakers can have strong and varied responses to our efforts. However, there are two main reactions that are useful to understand as we work to understand our childhood wounds. Sometimes the child gets hearty approval; other times the child is severely criticized. Unsure of what to expect, the child suffers from a *fear of being a failure*. A child's response to this is to become a *competitor*. This is a minimizing strategy, based on aggressive competition. Another parental response might be consistently failing to support the child's achievements, possibly even criticizing them. As a result, the child suffers from a *fear of being successful* and an even deeper fear of attracting disapproval. To cope, this child becomes a *compromiser*, someone who, in a maximizing fashion, is always equivocating, manipulating, or sabotaging.

≫ *Today, identify your own wounding and subsequent character defense. Do you tend to fear being a failure and, therefore, to be a competitor? Or are you more inclined to fear being successful and, therefore, to be a compromiser? Write your answers in your notebook.*

I contemplate in prayer today the varied color and texture available to me as I sort through the individual threads of being that make up the tapestry of who I am.

The ideal is in thyself, the impediment too is in thyself.

—THOMAS CARLYLE

When we started going to school and mixing with large numbers of other children, an important change took place. The egocentricity that characterized our drive to establish a secure and competent self started to abate as a new impulse made itself felt: the caring impulse, which was expressed as a concern for our peers. We formed a wide variety of friendships in the classroom, and if we were lucky, we found our very first best friend. We looked to our parents to admire, encourage, and coach this blossoming social life.

Some school-age children find making friends at this stage difficult because their parents are overprotective or quick to voice disapproval or remiss in teaching their child the social skills that he or she needs. A child who had this kind of parent may fear *ostracism and rejection.* This child may respond in the minimizer pattern by being a *loner:* excluding others and withdrawing inside. Other school-age children are very gregarious and have lots of friends. They may be inclined this way because parents either overtly or subconsciously give them the message that self-care is bad, while caring for others is good. The wound this kind of child bears is the *fear of being needy,* and he or she compensates by becoming a *caretaker.* This is a maximizing role, featuring self-sacrifice and continual intrusion into other's lives.

☙ *Today, assess whether your wound involves a fear of ostracism and rejection, in which case you are likely to be a loner, or a fear of being needy, in which case you are likely to be a caretaker. Record your assessment in your notebook.*

As I sit in sacred stillness today, I picture myself and all my places of wounding. Tapping into the power of the Divine, I visualize myself caring for the totality of who I am.

Intimacy is a difficult art.

— VIRGINIA WOOLF

Today we look at the next task on our journey into adulthood: becoming an adolescent. One of the teenager's primary tasks is to separate more definitively from the family. A teen must solidify his or her place among peers, while establishing a satisfying sexual and emotional intimacy with someone special. At this point, the parents are charged with accepting the budding sexuality of the emerging adult in their child, while providing a model of appropriate behavior regarding the boundaries of this newly longed-for intimacy. Not an easy task, to say the least!

Sometimes, parents are fearful or envious of the adolescent's power, freedom, and sexuality. Their response to these feelings might be to pull in the reins too tightly, saying, in effect, "You're not ready, and we're not going to let you go." The child is wounded by *being controlled* and becomes a *rebel*. A minimizer by nature, the rebel is always breaking the rules and responding to life with anger and disappointment.

Other parents, also troubled by the strange new world of adolescence, take a different approach. They never stop harping on what's weird, wacky, or wrong about their child's friends, clothes, tastes, or behavior. Afraid of *being different from others,* the child develops into a *conformist*. A conformist is essentially a maximizer who is critical and controlling, forever trying to impose rules and ensure stability.

🍂 Today, determine whether you suffer from a fear of *being controlled,* which inclines you toward being a *rebel,* or a fear of *being different from others,* which inclines you toward being a *conformist.* Write your determination and how you came to it in your notebook.

In my time of stillness today, I recognize that my fear of accepting who I am has shaped my behaviors. Breathing into this acceptance, I allow myself to then experience my real self.

Identifying our childhood wounds may have been rather depressing. It seems as if there are countless wounds looming in the corners of our unconscious for each one we identify. Be assured, however, for there is a happy side. Fortunately, we can repair the damage. In doing so, we are working to grant our unconscious wish to be whole, to experience full aliveness, and to realize our spiritual oneness with creation.

The good news is that our childhood wounds can be healed when we enter into a conscious, loving relationship. Thanks to the irresistible influence of our Imago, we tend to choose partners who are like our parents and caretakers so that we have a second chance to resolve the issues that caused the initial wounding. And armed with concrete information about the wounding and the necessary tools to bring about the healing, it's simply up to us to rise to the challenge!

Furthermore, our potential partners were also wounded as children and will tend to have adopted character defenses for their wounds that are the *opposite* of our own. If we are avoiders, they are clingers; if we are pursuers, they are isolators; and so on. This means that the key to wholeness lies in helping our partners to meet our needs, as they help us to meet theirs.

& *Take our your notebook and review the insights you have gained over the past few days of this unit. Circle or underline the ones that evoke the strongest response in you. Resolve to become more conscious in the future of your particular wounds and coping mechanisms that you've identified.*

In reverential celebration, I recognize that the work I am doing now will blossom into unimaginable freedom and grace in my life.

Opportunities are usually disguised as hard work,
so most people don't recognize them.
—ANN LANDERS

Human beings have to *learn* how to love in a committed relationship. It is not a genetic legacy of the species. Our life-force energy—part and parcel of the universe—is neutral in character, not intrinsically oriented toward love. We become either caring or selfish, altruistic or miserly, in response to the quality of our experience during our journey of socialization and self-development. To the extent that we are deprived of our essence, we turn against others and ourselves. To the extent that our essence is nourished or supported, we indulge ourselves and others.

But even though we are not born knowing how to love in a committed relationship, learning to love serves our own survival directive. When we move from being ego-oriented to being interested in others, we grow as individuals. We recover parts of ourselves that we lost, we learn new, more effective ways of expressing ourselves, and we enhance our capacity to cope with life more effectively. The learning process isn't simple; but we *can* succeed provided we keep at it, doing what we can comfortably do without taxing ourselves so much that we give up.

❧ *All day today, practice making three people around you feel safer and more at ease. Be sure to try out your intentional dialogue skills whenever you're faced with a difficult, emotionally charged conversation.*

In this time of solitude, I hold this important truth: "When locked in a room with a wounded animal, the key to keeping myself unharmed is to make sure the wounded animal feels safe and not in pain."

As we struggle to learn new relationship skills, we'll be occasionally tempted to wonder, "What's the good of just *me* using these skills if the other person doesn't? How do I get the other person—my best friend, my date, or, for that matter, my future partner—to do the same?"

The magical beauty of the Imago process is that it inevitably starts sparking change in the other person, who is the beneficiary of our own improved attitudes and behavior. As our awareness expands and we cultivate healthier behavior patterns, we create a space for change within the often locked dynamics of our relationships. Like one live battery charging another dead one, our intentional campaign to make the other person feel safe, understood, and valuable will inspire that person to have the same kind of energy, if only to become closer to us, the source of so much healing power. By revitalizing the other person without a self-interested motive, we set in motion an action-reaction dynamic that will ultimately heal us.

❧ *In the coming week, make a special effort to practice one of the relationship skills you've learned on one person in particular and see if you don't notice some positive response*

While I sometimes tend to wait for others to take the initiative, today in my time of quiet, I decide to risk first and own my power to determine my outcome.

He could never see a belt without hitting below it.
— MARGOT ASQUITH, ON DAVID LLOYD GEORGE

Regrettably, many of us are programmed to attack whenever a person does something that we don't like. Do we get satisfaction out of this? Usually not. Instead, we set in motion a cycle of pain with no end in sight.

Fighting is inevitable at times, but it is important to know how to fight well. The first thing we must do is resist the self-defeating impulse to fight back. When we're upset with someone's behavior, we need to say to ourselves, "What can *I* do to make things less problematic for both of us? How can I fight fair, instead of foul?"

The fair fight involves fighting *for* fairness, instead of fighting *against* the other person. Usually, we assume that another person is causing us pain on purpose. In reality, they are simply trying to get their point across and their feelings heard. We need to remember, in the moment of conflict, that the other person cares for us but can't listen because s/he is feeling attacked. Therefore, we need to calmly share *our* feelings. By doing this, we are sharing with the other person that we are upset and offering them a chance to respond. It also means communicating how *we* would like to be treated, instead of how *they* mistreated us. Finally, it means that *we* should take on the responsibility of motivating them to do better, instead of expecting that *they* should automatically assume that responsibility. This means responding to bad behavior with a behavior-change request and not with bad behavior of our own.

🐾 *Today, review the process for making behavior-change requests that you learned on Days 146–151. Is there a situation in your life right now where you could put this process into practice? Promise yourself that you will use this process conscientiously the next time you're upset with someone.*

Whenever I feel the need to fight back or to fight unfairly, I am aware that I have allowed myself to feel diminished. In the deep silence today, I hold this image: "I am in charge of my experience and my behavior."

I'm not okay, you're not okay, and that's okay.

—ELISABETH KÜBLER-ROSS

We can easily fall into the trap of demanding perfection—in ourselves as well as in others. Once we're in that trap, it's hard to make any progress at all. We reject our body because it's too fat. We won't date anyone who isn't a college graduate. We give up practicing any form of spirituality because we fail to achieve instant harmony with the tapestry of being upon our first few tries. It's one thing to be idealistic, to have high standards, and to set ambitious goals; but it's another thing entirely to associate *anything* human with perfection. No physical body is perfect: aesthetically or otherwise. No human mind or soul is perfect: free of all selfishness, doubt, fear, or sadness. Certainly no human life or enterprise is perfect: free of all rough spots, failures, and sins.

In fact, the beauty of humanity *is* our imperfection. For it is through our imperfection and wounding that the light shines through to pave our way to wholeness. If we're ever to become more whole and alive, we must begin by accepting our basic humanity and the basic humanity of all other people. Then we can proceed to grow as individuals by being and doing *our* best, not *the* best, and by seeing and cultivating what's best in others.

🪶 *Identify two things that you don't like about yourself: one personality trait and one physical attribute. For each thing, ask yourself these questions:*

- *What would be the perfect alternative? (Don't hedge your answer; be as absolute as you can be.*
- *What could I realistically do to improve matters?*
- *What other thing that I like about myself tends to make up for this thing?*

Closing my eyes and breathing slowly during a quiet period, I focus on a greater Wisdom that resides at my core. I surrender my tendencies toward trying to be perfect and allow a deeper perfection to come into my awareness.

Many strokes overthrow the tallest oaks.

— JOHN LYLY

Acknowledging and changing our character defenses and habituated behavior can be hard and frightening. No wonder we so easily and so often resist this kind of change! Like it or not, we identify very deeply with our present character, however flawed it may be, and with our present behavior, even if we're well aware that it is a stumbling block on our way toward happiness. Therefore, the main lesson we have to learn is that *our familiar defenses and habituated behaviors are not us.* Rather, our true self is at the mercy of these defenses and behaviors.

Effecting change in our lives will not obliterate our core self, but will allow that fundamental self to emerge. But making the kind of change to free our true selves is hard work. Only by facing the negative parts of ourselves, owning them, integrating them, and then gradually modifying them can we become whole and fully alive. To attempt an end run around the hard work of self-disclosure and behavior change is a form of self-neglect or, worse yet, self-mutilation.

&❧ *Today, look back over the hopes you expressed on Day 3. You were just beginning Imago work! Think about all that you have learned and take time to write down the things that stand out the most for you. In looking over all you have accomplished, take this time to feel the excitement and renew your commitment to the Imago Process.*

In this time of divine stillness, I imagine myself shedding those parts of me that are no longer useful. This truth is mine: "Change can bring me closer to my true self."

In the beginning, all is wonderful between two lovers. They are madly in love, and their self-absorption and destructive habits seemingly float away. He quits smoking, and she stops working late every evening. In the safe, cozy nest of their new love, they are able to be more honest and intimate than ever before. Because each person is supportive of the other, they feel safe in sharing their private worries, guilts, fears, and hopes. They start to make plans for the future. It is in this moment, when reality bursts the bubble of romantic love, that things begin to go wrong.

Romantic love is an illusion, blinding us to the negative aspects of our Imago choice. Desperate to maintain our newfound sense of joy and salvation, we enlist every tactic of denial to keep the bad news about our partner at arm's length. When reality finally and inevitably pierces the smoke screen of denial, the illusion dissipates, and we're face to face with the hardest work of all: tackling the negative traits and behaviors in our partners *and* ourselves. It's the supreme challenge. As beautiful as the final reality can be, the immediate prospect is rather ugly!

❧ *Today, take out your notebook and think of the early days in a past love relationship. Identify at least two things that you and your partner used to do together then that were especially good for you and that you especially enjoyed, such as talking about intimate matters, sharing secrets you never shared with anyone else. Why couldn't you continue doing or enjoying these things with your partner? What relationship skill that you've learned in this book might have helped make continuation — or resumption — possible?*

Entering the stillness today, I marvel at the mystery of nature, seducing us with anticipation, enticing us with pleasure, using a ruse to get us into position to work its wonder of restoring our wholeness.

It is while trying to get everything straight in my head that I get confused.
— MARY VIRGINIA MICKA

Culturally determined gender roles and stereotypes have unquestionably had a destructive influence on individual growth and on male-female relationships. When we speak of "masculine" men or "feminine" women—or, for that matter, "masculine" women and "feminine" men—we are trying to fit human behavior into crude, cut-and-dried categories. In actuality, gender develops along a living continuum. In the real life of each individual man or woman, the spectrum of possible gender-designated characteristics is very broad; and the degree to which a person's feelings and behaviors range across that spectrum can change from time to time and from situation to situation.

These rigid gender stereotypes and roles act as straitjackets that impede our natural expression and growth. They are damaging to us as individuals because they force us to drop from our personal repertoire any aspects of our identity that are labeled "gender-incorrect." These repressed unacceptable traits become part of our lost and denied selves. These same stereotypes and roles also complicate our love relationships. They color our image of the "perfect mate" and force us to impose false limitations and expectations on everyone we date.

ᴥ *Today, identify at least three traits in yourself that you—or others—might consider more appropriate for the opposite gender, thanks to the forces of socialization. For each trait, ask yourself: Am I in any way, or at any time, ashamed of this trait? Do I ever try to hide this trait from other people? Are there ways that I could enjoy this trait or express it to others more often?*

Taking time for stillness, I examine the images of the opposite sex to which I seem to be attached. With courage I surrender these images and open myself to experience the reality beyond language and thought.

The power struggle has six predictable phases. These phases are similar to the stages of grief identified by Elizabeth Kübler-Ross in her well-known book *On Death and Dying:* shock, denial, anger, bargaining, despair, and acceptance. What we are grieving is the death of "romantic love," the illusion that we will live happily ever after without any hard work on our part.

Our *shock* comes from the initial discovery of our partner's imperfections. Understandably, our first response is a *denial* of what we've discovered. Then follows our *anger* that these imperfections won't go away, despite all our efforts to vaporize them. So, we try *bargaining*—"If you do this, I'll do that"—which inevitably leads to more acrimony as each partner keeps calling the other to account. Next, there's a period of *despair* when we give up trying. Then comes *acceptance* of the reality that our relationship is simply not going to be the magical carpet ride we first thought it would. At this point, the relationship breaks up or remains deadlocked in the power struggle. For those who choose to stay the course, the relationship evolves beyond an armed truce to the joyful togetherness of *real* love.

❧ *Today, thinking of a past romantic relationship, try to identify these particular phases of the power struggle. What specific feelings, behaviors, and incidents can you associate with the "shock" phase? How about denial? Anger? Bargaining? Despair? Acceptance? Write down as many as you can.*

Sometimes I have difficulty acknowledging the illusion that my needs will be met without effort on my part. Today, in my time of reflection, I consider this truth: "The power struggle is supposed to happen. Conflict is growth trying to happen."

> *The family—that dear octopus from whose tentacles*
> *we never quite escape, nor, in our inmost hearts, ever*
> *quite wish to.*
>
> —DODIE SMITH

As children, we were powerfully shaped and—inevitably—wounded by the pressure to fit into society. We received socialization messages from many sources, but the most potent socializing force was our caretakers. Whatever our society deems unacceptable—our anger, our budding sexuality, our personal interpretation of things, and our experimentation outside of strict gender roles—is carefully pruned away. This pruning continually reinforced the message that society was dangerous for us. And, within the pruning, we understood on some level that we were dangerous for society unless we thought and functioned "correctly." When we balked, trying to be ourselves and experience full growth, they responded with the battle cry of socialization: *"It's for your own good."*

Some of their messages were direct: "Stop being such a crybaby!" "You're not really upset, you're just tired." Other messages were more subtly based on what we observed: the choices they made in their lives, the ways they treated each other, and the style in which they pursued what they wanted or rejected what they didn't want. In this unit you will focus on how you were socialized, by your parents in particular, in order to understand what you lost in the pruning.

&. *Today, think about your parents' marriage as you were grow-*
ing up (if you grew up with one parent, think about one of your
parent's serious romantic relationships). Recall specific scenes
that revealed what the relationship was like, and ask yourself,
"What message was I getting from this?" For example, consider
how they showed affection or anger and ask: "What was this
telling me about how to be affectionate or angry?" Write down
your answers.

**Today in this time of reverential prayer, I focus on the safe place I've
built within. Drawing strength from this safety, I commit to looking
at past scenes in my life.**

*Every child is an artist. The problem is how to
remain an artist once she grows up.*

— PABLO PICASSO

Each of us is born with an energetic "core" self that immediately
starts interacting with the outside world. This core self connects with
the outside world through four basic functions: *thinking, feeling,
acting,* and *sensing.* As long as our thoughts remain free, our feelings
uninhibited, our body invigorated, and our senses enlivened, we have
full access to the outside world and to our inner experiencing of that
world. Our borders are open, and our core energy can flow smoothly
and naturally in and out. But all four functions are the targets of
socialization, and during this indoctrinating process—a process in
which our parents play the dominant role—our dynamic wholeness is
challenged at every turn.

On the way to becoming adults, we erected fences at strategic
places along our personal borders so that we could control the flow
of energy from our core self. Throughout our childhood, we saw
which thoughts, feelings, behaviors, and sensual indulgences were
applauded, and which were frowned upon. We heard the "dos,"
"don'ts," "shoulds" and "shouldn'ts." And we absorbed the beliefs
and stimulus-response patterns that seemed to work for others or,
at least, that others seemed to value. Our natural, inborn connections
to the outside world were thwarted, distorted, and devitalized. Now,
as adults, we are cut off from ourselves and from others we might
love more fully.

 *Today, think of at least three judgments and criticisms that
your parents imposed upon you as a child, particularly those that
wound up being translated into specific "dos," "don'ts,"
"shoulds," and "shouldn'ts."*

**Today, in my time of stillness, I recognize that growth comes from
compassion, not criticism.**

What's going on when parents flash learning cards at infants in their cribs and pray that they'll be verbal, self-motivating, and intellectually curious in time to start preschool—at age two? Socialization in *thinking* is what's going on. Thinking is what fuels society's economic and technological progress and is therefore most rewarded. We are fed new lessons daily in labeling and analyzing, explaining and rationalizing, and this feeding process was especially intense during our childhood.

Sometimes as children we were put on a strict reward-and-punishment system for our accomplishments in thinking. We got extra spending money for every "A" and were grounded for every "F." Other times, the thinking messages were more insidious. Maybe we soaked up our parents' attitudes and beliefs without realizing it, through a kind of mental osmosis. Maybe we were told, "You're too smart for your own good," or "You're too dumb to come in out of the rain." Our freedom to think our own thoughts was subverted, which primed us for this next step in the socialization process. Starved of any creative impulse that might have brought joy, we were put on a steady diet of thinking according to how we were supposed to think.

❧ *Today, title a page in your notebook "Socialization: Thinking." On this page, list several of the ways in which your parents conditioned you to think. Some may be positive, at least on the surface: "They encouraged me to read." "Mom bragged about my grades." Others may be negative: "They taught me to hate rich people." "My father said I was stupid."*

During my time of prayer, I slowly move my awareness away from the thinking in my cerebral cortex to the wisdom that is hidden in my body and my heart.

The last unit discussed how highly our society validates the intellectual process. It is therefore fair to assume that emotions are not held in high esteem. We are expected to control them through calm and rational thinking. Typically, thinking becomes the outlet for repressed feelings. We rationalize our way out of sadness, hurt, or rage. We channel our joy and affection into positive thinking and verbal compliments. Traditionally, women are cut a little slack in this area. They are allowed to cry and be fearful or sentimental. In fact, such emotional displays from women are often treated as preferable to displays of bravery or stoicism. On stressful occasions, parents are far more likely to tell their daughter, rather than their son, "Go ahead and cry, honey." This doesn't necessarily mean, however, that the daughter is getting better parenting. In many families, the daughter gets emotional support only when she cries, and so she learns to cry whenever she wants attention. Meanwhile, the son is simply left to deal with the message, "Big boys *don't* cry." As for expressing "darker" emotions like anger, jealousy, indignation, or contempt, both girls and boys are typically prohibited from expressing them.

❧ *Today, title another page in your notebook "Socialization: Feelings." On this page, list all the ways in which your parents influenced you to suppress, control, or express your emotions. For example, "They made me go to my room when I was angry," "Mom taught me to be afraid of the water," "Dad called me a sissy for crying."*

I move into the center of my being during a sacred moment, and reflect on this truth: "Feeling is an expression of aliveness."

Our society prizes action, accomplishment, and a "can-do" attitude. However, there are still substantial restrictions on our actions. We are encouraged to grow, but the pruning continues—telling us in no uncertain terms that we can grow only in the ways society deems acceptable. "Walk, don't run." "Keep your hands to yourself." "Sit still." "Don't eat like an animal." "Look before you leap." By the time childhood is behind us, we no longer question these injunctions. So great is society's need for us to behave ourselves and to subordinate our wishes and energies to those of the group that we lose touch with our own spontaneity and physicality. The sad result is a lack of confidence in our ability to act as independent beings. While girls may be allowed a bit more freedom than boys to express their *feelings*, they generally suffer far more restrictions than boys on their *actions*. Boys are permitted to play rough, girls aren't. Boys are not expected to be as concerned about their clothes, their posture, or their physical appearance as girls are. Nevertheless, both boys and girls get their unfair share of training to conform to cultural norms.

᠔ *Today, title a new page in your notebook "Socialization: Acting." On this page, list ways in which your parents influenced your behavior, activities, or physical self-image. For example, "They were constantly telling me I was skinny," "Dad made me play football even though I hated it," "Mom had rules about when we could use the living room and what we could do in there."*

In time set aside to be completely alone, I relax into myself, recognizing that I must connect with my own personhood so that, in my dealings with the world, I may act from a place of power.

If you atrophy one sense you also atrophy all the others, a sensuous and physical connection with nature, with art, with food, with other human beings.

—ANAÏS NIN

It is in the realm of the senses, with regard to our physical hedonism and our sexuality, that we are more restricted and admonished. For it is here that we most see the split that results in society valuing the intellect over the natural pleasures of the body. We are taught that there's something intrinsically evil about sensual indulgence in general and about sex in particular. "Don't touch yourself there." "Put your clothes back on!" "Do you want people to think you're a tramp?" Given the combination of silence, admonition, and ridicule that most of us receive regarding sex it's a wonder that we can enjoy it at all. We're almost led to believe that it would be better if we did *not* have bodies to give us such wild cravings or if we used them only to walk from place to place and to eat just what's essential for our survival. Some people survive this repression of their sensuality fairly well: wounded, to be sure, but still capable of enjoying random moments of sensual freedom. For others, repressed sensuality oozes out in distorted and crippling forms, from sadism to celibacy, from overly sanitized sex to pornography, or from sex addiction to frigidity. For all of us, the conditioning of our sensuality profoundly complicates every aspect of our relationships with the opposite gender.

❧ *Today, title a new page in your notebook "Socialization: Sensing." On this page, list ways that your parents conditioned you to regard—or express—your physical sensuality. For example, "My parents punished me for masturbating," "Dad accused me of thinking with my penis," "Mom wouldn't let me wear clothes that were tight."*

In this time of reverential silence, I recognize the beauty of my sexuality. I hold this thought: "My sexuality is a reflection and celebration of the divine."

> *I grew up to have my father's looks, my father's speech patterns, my father's posture, my father's opinions, and my mother's contempt for my father.*
>
> —JULES FEIFFER

Our parents aren't the only forces of socialization during our childhood. Society also conditions us through teachers, friends, ministers, priests, rabbis, books, movies, and magazines. But our parents, by far, are the mightiest force in our lives when it comes to socialization. We are molded in their image, whether or not we—or they—are fully aware of it.

Our parents gave us messages regarding all four of the functions that we use to connect ourselves to the world: thinking, feeling, acting, and sensing. When we look at the extent of those messages, we see that their cumulative effect has been to block much of our core energy. The pruning of socialization has reduced what could be a vital, thriving, and lush plant into a sickly stalk of its potential. While all of us have in some way been restrained in each of the four functions, there are likely one or two areas that are the most repressed in each individual. It is important to see where the clippers did their most damaging work. In later units, you will explore the impact that your particular socialization had on your concept of "self," compelling you to hide, lose, deny, or disown aspects of your basic nature and to develop a more socially acceptable "presentational self."

❧ *Review the lists that you made for each of the four functions of socialization: thinking (Day 189), feeling (Day 190), acting (Day 191), and sensing (Day 192). In each list, underline the most significant items. Then, determine if some functions, as a whole, were more affected than others by your parents' socialization. These are the functions in which you need the most "deprogramming" to recapture your original wholeness.*

During a time of deep reflection, I allow a vision to surface that represents those lost parts of myself, combining and swirling into a dynamic and lively whole.

*We may affirm absolutely that nothing great in the
world has been accomplished without passion.*
— GEORG WILHELM FRIEDRICH HEGEL

At this point in our work with this book we are well aware of the
roots of our relationship woes. But while insight is valuable, it is not
in itself a cure. It is, after all, *in*formation, not *trans*formation.

In order for change to occur, insight must be translated into action.
Whatever is created by experience must be corrected by experience.
In order to integrate our insights, we have to put ourselves into new
situations to learn and practice new behaviors, which will help change
our past behaviors and beliefs.

The process of changing so that we have better outcomes in terms
of relationships depends upon applying ourselves consciously each
and every day to the task of moving ahead. We may not always
succeed in that task. The process is like climbing up a mountain. We
always have the same view, but as we gain new "heights," we also
gain further insight. At times it will feel as though we are tearing
through the underbrush, only vaguely aware that we are making an
uphill journey. At other times, we may feel as though we're stuck on
a plateau or that we actually stumble backward a few paces. The
important point is not to *stand still*. Change occurs through action.
Stopping that action stops the change.

❧ *Today, renew your commitment to keep changing each and
every day by replacing your unconscious, "old-brain" relationship
behaviors with conscious, "new-brain" relationship skills. Make it
a point to practice intentional dialogue today or make a behavior-
change request of someone in your life.*

**It is my prayer and commitment today to accept my reality as a
changing organism and to allow the natural processes built into me
to unfold. As I meditate on this reality, I hold these words: "I owe it
to myself to become myself."**

Consider the case of the *chronic* single—the bachelor who never settles down, the woman who dates constantly yet avoids any real intimacy. Even people who have been through a series of failed marriages may, in a way, be chronic singles, doing intermittent stints in relationships while remaining fundamentally self-absorbed.

A common denominator among many of these chronic singles is that they're waiting for a clear-cut Mr. or Ms. Right: someone whom they can recognize instantly as the ideal mate, the best possible life partner for them. Their fear of commitment is similar to any "shopper's doubt." They worry that they'll commit themselves only to find a "new and improved" partner later on down the line. And partnership doesn't come with a money-back warranty!

What these singles don't understand is that their problem rests within themselves, not in the outside world of the mate market. Many people hold very real potential to be a loving partner. We are the ones who need to develop the self-awareness and cultivate the skills so that we can relate intimately with others. Once this awareness and skill is learned and as it is being mastered, we will find a plethora of opportunities waiting in the wings.

❧ *Try to recall and write down at least one time in the past when you rejected someone as not meeting your qualifications as a date or even a mate, only to realize later that your judgment was faulty.*

Today in silence I decide to become someone worthy of being loved rather than looking for someone worthy to love.

How many times do we find ourselves wishing that *others* would speak up about something that's on *our* mind: "Did my joke offend her?" "Is he going to call me before the weekend?" "Does she realize how much I like her?" We wonder and wonder, sometimes very anxiously, but we never ask. Maybe we're too shy, embarrassed, or afraid of seeming nosy. Maybe we're engaging in a kind of power struggle: wanting them to take the responsibility of speaking first. Whatever our reason for silence may be, we're putting ourselves through needless suffering; and human nature being what it is, we'll probably make others suffer in return, directly or indirectly, somewhere down the line.

When there is something on our mind that is bothering us, it's always best to speak up right away, either asking the question point-blank or stimulating a conversation that will elicit some sort of relevant response. People who share an emotional bond need to communicate openly and honestly, instead of second-guessing each other in silence or playing communication games.

⮞ *Today, intentionally speak up to someone during a conversation, either on the phone or in person. You can choose to talk about something that has been on your mind for a while or something that just comes up naturally. Whatever your choice, don't walk away from the conversation wondering.*

Relaxing into my quiet space today, I become aware that connecting with others is the only path to intimacy. I make this vow: "I will risk intimacy by making contact."

Every step we make toward self-awareness, and consequently, toward relating more consciously with others, raises us to a higher level of being. As we continue up our mountain and become conscious and aware, we lose more and more of our narrow, day-to-day concerns. The higher we climb, the greater our perspective becomes in regard to the universal glories of life. It is this perspective that opens the door to finding a real and lasting love. It also inspires us to engage in that love with everything that is in us.

Love calls us to rise above our worldly selves so that we may catch glimpses of eternity. It's often an uphill journey, and we may stumble and fall back a few paces on the rocky slopes. Occasionally, our spirits will slump, and we'll be sorely tempted to ignore the call to move forward. At these moments, we need to remind ourselves that our fulfillment as individuals and as partners in a self-transcendent love depends on our willingness to stay on the path, no matter how difficult. Our reward, as we near the top of the mountain, is an awe-inspiring 360-degree view!

• *Think of a specific way in which you have grown as a person over the past few months by doing the work in this book. Pat yourself on the back for this progress, and let it inspire you to climb even further.*

I take time today for the renewal of my spirit. As I close my eyes, I allow myself to relax into the awareness that I am on the path that will lead me to full aliveness and real love.

Be kind; everyone you meet is fighting a hard battle.
—JOHN WATSON

It's impossible for a human being to move through life without suffering hurts, injustices, disappointments, and setbacks as he or she goes along. And it's impossible for a human being to get over all of these painful experiences right away. Indeed, we can't help feeling certain wounds for many years after they were inflicted—perhaps for most of our life.

In our single state, we can easily forget that suffering is an intrinsic part of everyone's day-to-day experience, not just our own. Looking only superficially at the people we encounter each day, we may not be able to discern the painful struggles that are taking place within. In fact, the people we encounter are probably doing their best to conceal those struggles—not only from others, but also from their own conscious minds. In order to make positive connections with other human beings, as well as to express what is noblest in our own human nature, we need to exercise charity with everyone we meet. This means acknowledging that other people, too, have problems that are deserving of compassion and that they are just as entitled as we are to comfort, happiness, and self-fulfillment.

❧ *In the coming day, practice being more charitable to two persons you encounter. Try to envision them as people who are suffering from their own very pressing problems. See them as wounded children, whether or not they are by outward appearance adults.*

I sometimes forget that I am not the only person in the world with troubles. In my time of contemplation today, I deepen my awareness of the suffering of others and access my capacity for empathy and acceptance.

A major piece of the Imago puzzle is the age-old notion that opposites attract, and so we find two people falling in love because of the complementary ways they have been socialized. For example, a person who was always encouraged as a child to play football and discouraged from drawing cartoons might fall in love with an illustrator who was discouraged as a child from playing rough sports, etc. What's going on here? Nature is up to her old tricks again, that's what, drawing us into relationships that have the potential to heal our wounds and help us grow. With her sly wisdom, nature seduces each individual to pair off with a seemingly incompatible partner in order to create the right chemistry for growth. Thus, we see our cool, left-brain mathematician dating a series of emotional, right-brain poets. Or we learn that two friends who are living together are constantly having sexual conflicts: she enjoys a lot of sensual massage and foreplay, while he seems to recoil from showing affection or being touched.

Today, think about three people you know. In what ways are they or have they been attracted to romantic partners who are not like them at all?

In this time of reflection and peace, I acknowledge the aspects that are underdeveloped in me in preparation for the partner I will one day have.

There are toys for all ages.

— ENGLISH PROVERB

What were your favorite toys as a kid? Balls? Cards? Marbles? Dolls? Building blocks? Jump ropes? Stuffed animals? Puzzles? Model trains? Finger paints? Paper cutouts? To recapture our core sense of aliveness, nothing works better than tapping into our childhood for inspiration. As adults, we may not be able to relive the exact same thrills in the exact same ways. However, recalling in detail the things that delighted us long ago *can* yield extremely valuable grist for our pleasure-seeking mill.

In some cases, we can simply look for grown-up versions of favorite childhood toys: for example, jigsaw puzzles of 1,000 pieces instead of 50, a set of oil paints instead of a box of crayons, or a board game that challenges our strategy-planning skills, instead of the old, beloved board game that only called for following the bunny's footsteps.

In other cases, we can use our imagination to recast the childhood, toy-related experience into something more compatible with our adult status, such as building an ornamental birdhouse instead of constructing a miniature castle with blocks, or going on a camping trip instead of pitching a bedsheet tent in the living room. Many people even get a kick out of simply collecting old toys—especially the same ones they most cherished as children. Or taking an afternoon at a toy store, or renting a cartoon movie.

Just living among toys can make our world livelier and more open to play. There are many ways to set free the enthusiasm and vibrancy of our lost child!

❧ *Identify at least three toys that you enjoyed as a child. For each toy, what is an adult equivalent? Make it a point to "play" with at least one of these toys this week.*

In joyful contemplation today, I recall the joy and aliveness of my childhood. Holding this experience in my mind, I let myself feel the aliveness of unrestrained play and vow to experience my core aliveness daily.

Self-reflection is the school of wisdom.

—BALTASAR GRACIÁN

What do we want from a relationship? What kind of partner is best for us? What kind of relationship are we most likely to have?

To answer these questions and, in so doing, prepare ourselves for the journey of an intimate love partnership, we must examine more closely what happened to us as children. This means repeatedly looking back over our childhood and asking the same questions. This may seem a monotonous task, similar to those detective stories where the victims of a crime are asked the same question eight and ten times. Yet, if you watch closely, you'll see that the answers gain added depth each time the question is asked. It takes repeat sweeps over old material to unearth new gems of insight. Among the most important questions to ask ourselves again and again are those involving our childhood wounds.

What kind of nurturing did we receive at each different period in our childhood?
What negative feeling did we have as a result?
What character defense did we develop to cope with that feeling?

Our childhood wounds have affected all of our major thoughts, behaviors, and life choices since then, especially in the arena of relationships. Consciously or not, we seek to heal our childhood wounds within our committed partnerships. This may not mean we'll get the "perfect" mate or the "perfect" relationship from Hollywood's point of view, but we're literally, albeit unconsciously, programmed to get the best mate from our deepest self's point of view, and we may as well make the most of it!

❧ *Review once more the list "My Childhood Wounds" that you made on Days 171–178.*

Today I breathe deeply, accessing the courage that will enable me to see and understand the woundings of my childhood.

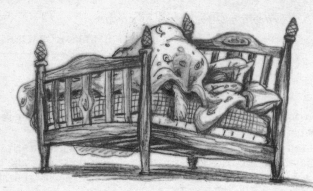

Far back in our childhood, we start hiding aspects of ourself from others. If Mom scolds us when we sing songs with naughty noises, we learn to sing them softly, so no one can hear. After big brother teases us about playing with our genitals, we make sure to play with them only in private. We steal chocolate chips from the kitchen cabinet since we're not allowed to eat them, and we conceal our fear of our uncle's beard because no one else seems to have the same feeling. Over time, we develop a "hidden self"—a secret sharer in our day-to-day lives that thinks, behaves, and reacts in ways that we keep secret from others.

As adults, we get over some of our childhood guilt and shame and find "safe" situations in which to let some of our secrets out, but we still relegate many aspects of our personal identity to our hidden self. Sometimes, our hidden self prompts unconscious reactions that often don't make sense, even to ourselves. Only when we begin to unearth the roots of our hidden self do we begin to understand our motivations. In this unit, you will take a closer look at your own hidden self to see if its secrets are helping or hindering your ability to be whole.

&ₐ *Title a new page in your notebook "My Hidden Self." On this page, list traits and activities that you keep hidden from others. Write each item as if you were completing the following sentence: "What would people think if they knew . . ."*

I recognize those parts of me that I am afraid or ashamed to share with others, as those parts most in need of my love and nurturing. Drawing upon a Power within, I commit to full self-acceptance.

What other dungeon is so dark as one's own heart!
What jailer so inexorable as one's self!

—NATHANIEL HAWTHORNE

While we tend to blame society for forcing us to conceal and confine our hidden self, we as individuals also play a role. We keep parts of ourselves confined because we are ashamed of those parts and what they say about who we are. We may even become neurotic, worried that we might be ridiculed or rejected if we become too self-revealing.

We must learn to cherish our hidden self. True, many behaviors are best kept private: from masturbation to nail biting to wolfing down a quart of double-chocolate-chip ice cream at 2:00 A.M. However, we all harbor personal habits, tastes, and idiosyncracies that are perfectly acceptable and even engaging in the right context, and we alone possess the key to set them free.

The first step toward emancipating our hidden self involves viewing it with more tolerance, respect, and understanding. After all, it is a very human and resourceful self that contains much of what is most authentic about us as individuals. Then, we need to forgive ourselves for keeping it hidden. If we've so far lacked the confidence to be who we really are, thanks to the way we responded to our childhood upbringing, we need to accept this fact, rather than bemoan it. We can still regain that confidence in a more conscious and tolerant environment.

᷄ *Today, review the list of traits and behaviors that you made yesterday. Underline the ones that you feel are not too difficult for you to view more tolerantly—accepting them, respecting them, and possibly even revealing them to others.*

During a time of quiet, I move into a spiritual safety that resides at my core. From this deep place, I pledge to honor those hidden aspects of myself.

We tend to think of our hidden self as an undesirable alien; and, indeed, many of the traits and behaviors that we hide from others might provoke criticism, laughter, or disgust. "I often eat potato chips and ketchup for dinner." "I cheat on my income tax." "I sometimes go three or four days without a shower." But our hidden self also contains treasures: authentic expressions of our unique personality that are potentially endearing, admirable, and even valuable to others. For example, you may love to slip outside at night and whisper wishes to the stars—a very poetic and emotionally satisfying ritual that could be inspirational to someone else. Or you may love to laugh at the Saturday morning cartoons, to write corny song lyrics, or to daydream about wilderness adventures, which are all activities that another person might appreciate or help you to enjoy more wholeheartedly. Some secrets of the hidden self quickly shed their shadowy nature once they're exposed to the light. A few actually manage to shine with a special luster—gifts of ourselves not only to ourselves, but also to others. It's time to gift your hidden self with a green card!

❦ *Review the list of traits and behaviors that you made two days ago (Day 202). Decide which should remain private and which could go public. Select one trait or behavior in particular that stands a good chance of being accepted in a supportive environment.*

Today I relax deeply into a meditative space and visualize myself opening toward others and then being positively received. I acknowledge this truth: "There is beauty to be found in my hidden self."

Sharing is sometimes more demanding than giving.
— MARY CATHERINE BATESON

In order to realize the spiritual and emotional wholeness that we crave as individuals, we need to start bringing our hidden self out into the light. This means sharing it with others. We can experiment with this coming-out process by being more open with close friends. If we're especially motivated, we can also try revealing more of our hidden self to people we are just beginning to date. A newcomer to our private life gives us a fresh chance to be more honest with another human being right from the start.

Sharing our hidden self means overcoming our worries about what another person would think, if they knew, for example, that "I have mystical helpers," "I dream about being a celebrity," "I like listening to old Supremes albums," or "I like to play make-believe roles during sex." Clearly some characteristics or activities of our hidden self are going to be easier to disclose than others. We may not be willing to tell *anybody,* at least right now, that we occasionally steal small items from the grocery store, that we keep a stash of pornography under the bed, or that we sometimes confess our innermost thoughts to a ceramic coyote. But that shouldn't keep us from telling any of our secrets at all! The more genuine and authentic we learn to be with people, the more trust we can begin to build in ourselves and others.

❧ *Today, identify one, or several, people in your life with whom you can begin to share some of the aspects of your hidden self. Make a promise to your hidden self that you will work toward being more open with them in the future.*

During a time of deep reflection, I visualize myself lighting a candle and acknowledging this truth: "I am the one who can shed light on my shadowed places."

> *We accept the verdict of the past until the need for*
> *change cries out loudly enough to force upon us a*
> *choice between the comforts of further inertia and the*
> *irksomeness of action.*
>
> —LEARNED HAND

Past habits are hard to break, and one of the hardest is the struggle to hide from others anything about ourselves that we think may provoke scorn or ridicule. Sadly, we wind up depleting our life force by expending huge amounts of energy to keep our hidden self under wraps.

Why not use that energy more positively, to unshackle our hidden self and release our life force? We can begin now, with the people in our lives who seem the most receptive. These initial efforts will prepare us for the ideal situation in which to experience self-liberation: the safe haven of a conscious relationship with a partner who loves and accepts us unconditionally. Within a loving partnership, protected from the judgments and censures of society, we can restore life to parts of ourselves that we used to feel we had to hide. We can feel free to dance like an animal, to lick icing off our Oreos, to discuss our belief in UFOs, or to spend two hours at a stretch watching *Honeymooners* reruns on TV. And we can work on transforming the darker aspects of our hidden self into more positive and creative expressions.

❧ *Resolve to share one of the secrets of your hidden self with someone else within the coming week. You might choose the one particular trait or behavior that you identified the day before yesterday (Day 204).*

As I relax and breathe deeply, I picture the rich growth my shadows have to offer me as I work toward creating wholeness in my life.

Because of the Imago dynamic, minimizers and maximizers tend to pair off. One of the issues that causes the most problems between them involves *boundaries*—that is, knowing where one person leaves off and the other begins and how much freedom one has to invade the other person's privacy or territory. Maximizers have very few boundaries, which tend to be thin and flexible. They invite everyone into their emotional experiences, and they have a hard time distinguishing their own thoughts from those of others. Malleable, and anxious to merge, they don't have a clear self-image and don't understand others' needs for clear boundaries. They feel free to interrupt their partners with phone calls at work and to chatter away about where *both* of them should go on vacation. Minimizers, on the other hand, have many rigid boundaries defining who they are and what belongs to them, and they don't understand the maximizer's need to share. As a result, minimizers are very slow to show sympathy or even affection. They resist contact and are fearful when their partners start moving personal items into *their* home territory.

❧ *Today, think of a past (or present) romantic relationship with a person having the opposite style of response: that is, if you're a minimizer, think of a maximizing romantic partner, or vice versa. Identify at least two ways in which the other person's sense of boundaries was (or is) problematic for you. Then, identify at least two ways in which your sense of boundaries was (or is) problematic for the other person.*

Descending into the sacred space within, I see myself in a dance, locked into a rigid pattern that I repeat over and over again. Watching myself on the screen in my mind, I begin to dance a new step, clumsily at first, then with grace. I say to myself: "I am as free as I choose to be."

I know that you cannot hate other people without hating yourself.

—OPRAH WINFREY

Hatred is like a wall. It limits our freedom, it cuts off our view, it casts a shadow over our lives. When we build a wall of hatred against another person, the wall acts as a springboard until we ultimately feel the backlash in the form of self-hatred. And when we build a wall of hatred against ourselves, it blocks the light and love coming from other people, so we wind up hating them as well. In order to let love into our lives, we need to break down the walls of hatred we've built: especially the walls of self-hatred, which are the most confining. This means loving the parts of ourselves that we rejected during our socialization—the parts that invite our most intense hatred when we see them reflected in other people and the parts that we tend to project onto our romantic partners.

At first, we'll be very reluctant to do this kind of demolition. We don't want to love, for example, the sensuality or sentimentality that we suppressed, for it feels like a betrayal of those who caused us to reject those parts in the first place. What's more, by allowing these once-scorned parts more freedom, we'd be opening ourselves up to being rejected all over again. Because of the fear we have, it's important that we don't simply blast through the walls with all the emotional dynamite we possess. Instead, we must gently dismantle the wall brick by brick. There's no getting around it: breaking the walls of self-hatred is hard work, but unless we do it, love can't get in or out.

🍃 *Make a list of five traits you hate in others. Identify one trait that others have also seen in you. For the moment, accept it as a trait in you. Then, think of at least two ways that you could exercise that trait more freely, so that you might become more tolerant of it.*

Moving into a place of inner calm, I visualize myself dismantling my wall of hatred, brick by brick. As the bricks tumble, I begin to see the sunlight and beautiful scenery on the other side.

*Men and women, women and men. It will never
work.*

—ERICA JONG

Men and women have endless lists that chronicle the complaints one
group harbors against the other. These lists are the fodder for
countless books and articles, TV sitcoms, sociological studies, and
therapy sessions. "What's wrong" with the opposite sex is the lingua
franca of the locker room and beauty parlor.

Women accuse men of a number of perceived failings: they don't
listen or communicate; they won't express their feelings; they are
condescending, domineering; and all they care about in women is
looks. What's more, they are sexually demanding, sloppy, unreliable,
and insensitive.

It's small wonder that many of the most common gripes that men
have about women are the flip side of the women's complaints about
men: women are too emotional; they talk too much; they're sexually
skittish, too sensitive, and overly concerned with their appearance.

The bottom line seems to be: Why can't a woman be more like a
man, and a man be more like a woman? This can be translated into
"Why can't someone be more like me?" It's an inevitable complaint,
and that bottom-line complaint gives rise to all the other complaints.
Implicit in them is a value judgment: From the men's point of view,
men are better (i.e., more understandable) than women; from the
women's point of view, women are better (i.e., more understandable)
than men. The battle lines are drawn.

☙ *Today, think about and write down the "inevitable" complaints
that you've heard, read, or made regarding the opposite gender.
Looking at each complaint more closely, ask yourself, is this really
a valid complaint, or simply a prejudice based on a value
judgment?*

**In solitude today, I confess my tendency to see the world as an
extension of myself. Accessing the courage of my deep self, I release
this perception and allow the world of others to appear in all its
unique splendor.**

The quest for real love does not depend on looking *outside* ourselves for someone who is perfect. Quite the contrary! To realize a lasting and fulfilling partnership, we need to look *inside* and open our heart, following its lead wherever it takes us. The search for perfection is a demanding process. As a result, we build an obstacle course to weed out all but the most desirable candidates, creating a nearly impossible scenario.

First, our minds are supposed to *objectively* select the prospect who has the best superficial attributes—a pleasing personality, good looks, intelligence, an attractive lifestyle—before we grant our heart the freedom to function *subjectively* by falling in love. Our objective and subjective viewpoints are radically separate, which drastically limits our ability to act and find a winner. Far too often, a person stumbles within the first two or three obstacles of the course.

If we're sincerely looking for a lasting love, we must allow these two separate perspectives to cooperate to their full capacities. Both our minds and our hearts must be fully receptive from the start, so that we can love the people we find and find the people we love. To do this we must tear down the obstacle course and perhaps build a playground where all future relationships can play in safety and love.

ᕪ *Today practice opening up your heart. Whenever you're tempted to critique someone negatively, try, instead, to identify something good about him or her. Mark down in your notebook the number of times today you were drawn to critiques.*

I realize that I too often live my life by objective standards and restrictive rules that make me critical instead of accepting. In this quiet time today, I imagine myself accepting and receptive and feel the invigoration of my life force as I drop my defenses.

For weeks, months, or even years, we can swim through life thinking that we've escaped the emotional clutches of an old love relationship; and then suddenly, like an octopus springing out of the depths of the ocean, a tentacle from that old relationship reaches up from the depths and snags us again. Once more we're trapped in the clutches of unresolved feelings about that relationship: the failed hopes, the unanswered complaints, the undying grudges, and the lingering affections.

Why can't we be free from this octopus once and for all? The problem doesn't lie in the octopus's power but, rather, in our own power. An octopus confines itself to a relatively small area of water. If it continues to snag us time and again, it's because we have yet to swim out of its domain. To be free, we simply need to swim straight ahead, until we've put it far behind us.

🥭 *Today, think of something that still "grabs" you about an old relationship—something that you wish you could leave behind you. Then, use the "Saying Good-bye" process (Days 104–108) to do just that.*

Today I visualize the tentacles that still hold me to old relationships and old modes of behavior. Breathing calmly during this twenty minutes of stillness, I acknowledge that I have the power to swim to clearer waters.

The best way to hold a man is in your arms.

— MAE WEST

In any romantic relationship, touch plays a crucial role. Satisfactory person-to-person communication includes physical contact. Physical intimacy is not just a matter of having sex, despite the fact that we so commonly refer to sex as "making love." Besides aiming for sexual compatibility, physical intimacy involves developing an active and responsive repertoire of friendly hand-holdings, warm hugs, loving kisses, tender cuddles, affectionate pats, consoling embraces, and healing massages.

Some of us have good, general "body" sense, so touching in a loving and responsible manner comes naturally. The rest of us have lost, to various degrees, our "body" sense through socialization: we're inhibited about touching or being touched because we were taught that the body in general is "nasty" or that our body in particular is clumsy, ugly, or something to be kept to ourselves. Tragically, many people are alienated from their own body and other bodies because they were physically abused as children.

Love relationships offer people a unique opportunity to express their body sense more fully as well as to regain any body sense they may have lost. Because of the way the Imago works, it's very likely a "toucher" and a "nontoucher" will wind up as a couple. What better chance for both of them to gain hands-on experience!

❧ *Today, review your current relationships with dates, friends, family, coworkers. Are you a "toucher" or a "don't-toucher"? Do you feel comfortable with the ways you show affection or make contact with others? Reach out and touch someone today.*

In my twenty minutes in silence today, I relax and breathe deeply, experiencing my breathing, the beating of my heart, the sensations of my body, the feeling of my clothes on my skin. I commit to becoming fully alive in my body, and I honor this truth: "My body is holy."

As we grew up, we were inevitably given "hand-me-down" ideas about life: attitudes and platitudes that our parents wore for years. Usually, these hand-me-downs were overly large and loose: "Without a steady job, you're worthless." "Don't get too uppity." "You have to let the man do the chasing." "In a marriage, respect means a lot more than love." "If you can't say something nice, don't say anything at all."

Dependent children that we were, we used these hand-me-downs even if we didn't particularly like them. Even if they didn't really fit us, our parents insisted, and we couldn't just run around naked! After a while, we grew to fit the hand-me-downs, instead of growing into our own natural shapes. They became ours at that point, whether we realized it or not. Now that we're adults, we *do* have a choice. We don't have to keep wearing these hand-me-downs. In fact, we should take a good look at our wardrobe of general ideas and throw out everything old that's too big, too small, too ugly, or too uncomfortable. Get rid of them and get to work on creating a wardrobe that fits the kind of person you really are.

&. *Today, identify at least three ideas about life, love, sex, or gender that your parents gave you as "hand-me-downs." Are you still wearing them to some degree? How well do these ideas really fit you now?*

During this time of quiet reflection, I go through the closet that houses the wardrobe of my ideas and carefully remove those clothes that don't fit the core of who I am. I recognize this truth: "I can choose the clothes that allow my core self to shine!"

*The human heart, at whatever age, opens only to
the heart that opens in return.*
             —MARIA EDGEWORTH

A love relationship develops in stages that parallel those of our childhood development. The earliest stage, *attachment,* is the romantic stage, when the partners first unite with each other, like the infant bonding to its mother. Then comes the stage of *exploration* when the baby realizes its separate identity and when couples begin to differentiate from each other. Next are the stormy stages of *identity* and *competence.* In childhood, these stages cover testing one's powers, to acquiring basic academic and social skills in schools. In the context of adult love, this is the "power struggle" period, with each person probing the limits of the other and developing corresponding roles and strategies. If this work is successful, the relationship evolves into a stage of *concern,* in which each partner genuinely cares for the other's welfare, analogous to the period in "middle" childhood when we learn to have compassion for our peers. Finally, there's the *intimacy* stage, when the couple realizes the dream of togetherness that only tantalized them during the romantic "attachment" stage. It's like that time around puberty when children first begin to share their innermost self with another, except that more fully evolved lovers can perform this sharing expertly, with their total mind, heart, and soul.

In a specific relationship these stages can go in cycles. The secret to making steady progress ahead lies in staying conscious of where we are, and where we want to be.

❧ *Today, think about a serious, relatively long-term relationship in your romantic past. Try to identify and write down the stages that this relationship went through. How far did you and your partner get? Did you go back and forth a lot? What kept you from reaching—or remaining in—more advanced stages?*

Sometimes in my serious relationships, I feel like an adult, at other times like a child. In my time of contemplation today, I accept the fact that changes can herald growth or indicate regression. I choose growth.

Some parts of our inner nature are hidden not only from other people *(the hidden self)* but also from ourselves. These are parts of *the lost self,* forgotten aspects of our identity that we left behind in our drive to become more socially acceptable. Maybe we once loved to dance like the wind or drew maps of fantastical islands, but these activities didn't fit into what others saw as our own best interests. Those parts of ourselves simply became so buried, they virtually disappeared.

While socialization is necessary for people to live together in harmony, its rules often contort our natural self-expression. Our caretakers—representatives of society who are already compromised by their own conformity to the rules—want us to conform as well. Consequently, instead of growing straight, tall and unhindered, the socialization we experience can create twisted limbs and gnarled trunks.

By the time we're adults, we've lost track of many things that make us unique, happy, and most truly attractive to others. In this unit, you will be assisted in finding your lost self.

❦ *In your mind's eye, explore where you lived as a child. Walk around your home, your neighborhood, and your school. In each place, attempt to relive the times you spent there. Notice details that might be clues to identities you lost: What different things did you do? What daydreams did you have? How did other people—especially your caretakers—respond? Be alert for the specific messages that encouraged you to abandon certain parts of yourself.*

Without fear I visit my past, and in this twenty minutes of silence, I pledge to become the sleuth that can discover the clues that will lead me to my lost self.

*Not everyone's life is what they make it. Some
people's life is what other people make it.*

— ALICE WALKER

To find our lost selves, it helps to take a separate look at each of the
ways we went about connecting with the outside world as children,
that is, the four functions of socialization: thinking, feeling, acting,
and sensing. Today, we will consider how our *thinking* might have
been influenced by others or society.

Maybe you once had an imaginary playmate to whom you regularly
confided your innermost thoughts, until you were pressured to banish
this playmate from your life. If so, what "self" did this playmate
know, a self that is now lost to you as an adult? Perhaps you told
other people opinions, problem-solving strategies, or decisions that
were quickly shot down or that you were soon persuaded to reject.
What were they? Did you apply your mind to particular hobbies or
interests that were discouraged by others, until you finally gave them
up? Try to recall what it was like to have these mental outlets. Did
you nurse special fantasies and ambitions that you were ultimately
encouraged to forfeit? What were they, and what made you lose
them?

❧ *Title a new page in your notebook "My Lost Self: Thinking."
On this page, list significant aspects of yourself as a "thinking"
child that you lost by the time you became an adult. After writing
each aspect, briefly state what outside pressure helped cause you
to lose it.*

**Breathing naturally, I visualize myself resting gently in my place of
safety. From this place, I breathe in those special thoughts I once
enjoyed and are now no longer part of me.**

*I did not lose myself all at once. I rubbed out my
face over the years washing away my pain, the same
way carvings on stone are worn down by water.*

—AMY TAN

As children, much of our life force was invested in *feelings*. Through
our emotions, we experienced the outside world profoundly. Our
laughter originated deep in our bellies and our tears overflowed from
the furthest corners of our hearts. We burned with anger, sweated
with fear, and shook with excitement. For days on end, we were blue
with sadness, green with jealousy, or purple with indignation. Many
of these passionate feelings were just too much for the society around
us. Time after melancholy time, we were told by our parents that we
shouldn't be sad, but happy. Anger, jealousy, and indignation were
frowned upon, and no one seemed to like us—or even look at
us—when we were giddy, goofy, or giggly.

Certain limits on our feeling self are, of course, necessary. But
most of us have had to alter ourselves so much to fit in with society
that we have forgotten that we ever had a raucous laugh or boundless
enthusiasm or a deep capacity for rage. Having to disown our
feelings, we lost some of our spiritual essence. Those parts of
ourselves that were capable of feeling so intensely are now missing,
both to ourselves and to the people who become our romantic
partners.

❧ *Today, title another page in your notebook "The Lost Self:
Feelings." On this page, list times in your childhood and adolescence when you experienced or exhibited feelings in a much
stronger manner than you ever would today, as an adult. For
each experience that you list, briefly explain how you were
influenced to lose that intensity of feeling.*

**In quiet contemplation, I recognize my many feeling states as being
the beautiful and vibrant colors of a prism. I pledge to honor the full
spectrum of my own personal prism.**

*I'd gone through life believing in the strength and
competence of others; never in my own. Now,
dazzled, I discovered that my capacities were real. It
was like finding a fortune in the lining of an old coat.*

— JOAN MILLS

When we were children, it seemed as if our parents and teachers
were forever telling us what we should and shouldn't do. Sometimes,
they were communicating helpful instructions that kept us safe when
we rode our bikes or built a campfire. Other times, they were
expressing judgments. "You shouldn't act so silly in front of the
neighbors." "You're clumsy as a cow." "You look so much nicer when
you dress neatly." Inevitably, these messages influenced our actions,
making us lose contact with our more authentic impulses.

As far as our actions are concerned, our lost self is often revealed
when we complain of some lack in our abilities: "I can't dance; I have
two left feet." "I can't draw a straight line." "I'm no good at sports."
We may feel a certain despair or edginess in our complaint that tells
us, if we're listening closely, that we once possessed this capability,
but lost it along the way. Other revelations occur when someone
else—a romantic partner, a good friend, or a casual acquaintance—
points out something about ourselves that we no longer can see.

🍋 *Title another page in your notebook "My Lost Self: Acting."
List all the activities or capabilities that you remember liking as a
child, but eventually abandoned during the socialization process.
For each activity or capability, try to explain what comment or
influence made you abandon it.*

**In the stillness at my core, I recognize the limitations I've placed on
myself by believing I couldn't do something, and now I recognize that
I have the power to transform the "can'ts" into "cans."**

The only sin passion can commit is to be joyless.
— DOROTHY L. SAYERS

Who said children are innocent? They are, in fact, naturally disposed to sensuality. They love to play with their bodies, they delight in running around naked, and they eagerly flirt with everyone to whom they're attracted by their senses.

It is only socialization that makes us self-conscious about our bodies and our sexuality as we grow up to become adults. We still feel a great deal of the passion associated with sensuality, but we've lost much of the unadulterated joy that once accompanied that passion. In its place is shame, guilt, embarrassment, fear, anger, or—perhaps worst of all—an aching emptiness.

Why is love so often tinged with a sense of bittersweet longing? How did we get so out of sync with our natural drives? What happened to our ability to proceed boldly and spontaneously where our senses lead us? In most cases, we lost that vital part of ourselves bit by bit, as our parents, our teachers, and society in general taught us to become more civilized.

&ও *Title a new page in your notebook "My Lost Self: Sensing." Thinking back to your childhood and adolescence, try to remember various ways in which your early expressions of sexuality or sensuality were discouraged or even punished. List some of these ways on this page.*

I enter my internal place of safety today, and become aware of the wounded places in my sensuality. I offer this prayer: "My sexuality is a divine aspect of being fully alive."

> For every five well-adjusted and smoothly
> functioning Americans, there are two who never had
> the chance to discover themselves. It may well be
> because they have never been alone with themselves.
>
> — MARYA MANNES

Our lost self can be difficult to track down. We long ago buried our belly laugh and gave up our funny walk. We stopped running in the rain, catching snowflakes on our tongues, or wishing for luck on a shooting star: all those wonderful, happy rituals that connected us to the universe.

We have internalized the voices of our parents. So, what our parents used to tell us, we now tell ourselves and believe wholeheartedly: dancers *are* sissies, I *won't* have friends if I show any anger, people *don't* like me because I'm an egghead. We can no longer easily recall that distant time when the things that we now reject were parts of ourselves and it was okay to have those parts. Like our hidden self, our lost self is out of sight; but unlike our hidden self, it's also out of mind.

How do you go about finding *your* lost self? You've already done some of the work in this unit—resurrecting your long-forgotten memories of the person you once were. Another step is to look more closely at your past romantic partners. Your Imago guided you to choose them because they possessed traits that you lack. Some of those traits might have been aspects of your lost self: the guffaw that you later replaced with a quiet laugh, the quickness to express anger that you left behind ages ago. Our lost selves can be found within the mirror of past relationships.

🍃 *Today, review all of the "My Lost Self" entries you've made in your notebook. Then, think of your past romantic partners. In what ways might they have represented parts of yourself that you lost as you grew up?*

I recognize my yearning to find those aspects of myself that have been lost, realizing that I must embrace these lost parts of me in order to become whole.

*We waste time looking for the perfect lover, instead
of creating the perfect love.*
— TOM ROBBINS

When the romantic phase of love starts to fade away, our dream partner starts to disappear, turning into a flesh-and-blood stranger. At times, we cast this new character into the role of our worst enemy. This is precisely when the process of real love begins, if it's ever going to begin. Sooner or later, we must decide to view the other partner's welfare as equally important as our own. From the firm ground of this vantage point, we can begin the healing work.

Now we can see the offending partner's behavior arising—not out of hostility, thoughtlessness, or selfishness aimed against us (although that might be the end result)—but, rather, out of his or her childhood wounds, fears, and defenses. This reframing of the offending partner as a hurt child makes it possible for us to empathize, care, and, eventually, to really love. Who doesn't want to help a child in pain? And who could turn away the forlorn cries of a kitten or puppy in distress? Instead of fighting back, we can then begin to resolve the situation by offering more healing gestures: making our partner feel safe in our presence, using intentional dialogue to support his or her need to communicate, and making behavior-change requests instead of dumping criticism and blame.

🔊 *In the coming week, practice viewing the adults who are close to you as wounded children. Notice how much more sympathetic you can be when you look at them this way.*

During this time of wordless prayer, I move into the reality that those who attack me are only trying to keep themselves safe. I recognize that as I help to heal others' wounds, they will feel safer and I will be attacked less.

In moments of partnership despair, we all remember the time-honored words, "Don't worry, there are plenty of fish in the sea." Most fairy tales lend subtle support to this feeling of despair, because they tell us that there is only one person for us—our fated prince or princess. Finding that person, according to the fairy tales, is difficult. In reality, there *are* many fish in the sea. But how on the solid earth do we find our particular Imago match? We need not be concerned. Among that plenitude of fish in the sea of humanity, there are many that could fit our Imago portrait. This fact accounts for why so many people keep really and truly falling in love with the same kind of person again and again.

The secret to a lasting love lies not so much in finding just the right person as it does in staying with a likely person through the rough times. Falling in love is easy—it's the happily ever after part that takes perseverance. Only by working consciously with the tools that will build a firm and trusting relationship can we gain the insights and develop the skills that are necessary for building a real and enduring love.

꒰ *Today it's time to recheck your Imago "radar" system. How do you know when you've fallen in love? Do you experience sleeplessness, loss of appetite, giddiness? Do you want to merge with that person—physically, emotionally, and mentally? Do you get all tongue-tied, or talkative, whenever they're near? Identify at least three of your most reliable love symptoms.*

As I relax today, I revel in the thought that the way I am designed is so perfect that if I follow my heart, I will meet the person whose needs will call me to my wholeness.

I recognize no rights but human *rights — I know
nothing of men's rights and women's rights.*

— ANGELINA GRIMKÉ

Let's face it, for all the recent progress toward achieving equal
gender rights, it is still, in many respects, a man's world. In business,
government, science, education, religion, the arts, sports, and entertainment, men continue to hold the vast majority of the dominant
positions. The result is a patriarchy that sets the standards for male
and female roles and behavior. On the surface, it would seem that
men would thrive under these conditions, with women being the
victims. But the truth is even gloomier. Both men *and* women suffer
a loss of wholeness under such a one-sided system. Men are not
encouraged to be emotionally sensitive, nurturing, and able to enjoy
passive roles. Women, disadvantaged from the start, wind up suppressing their natural, so-called "masculine" abilities. They are not
expected to command, compete, and savor more active roles in life.

As individuals, we have to work against this patriarchal conditioning
and develop a more flexible concept of gender—one that allows us
and our partner the freedom to become whole and fully realized
human beings. For it is only in uniting the incomplete qualities of each
gender that we achieve the total balance of who we can become.

&b *Today, give your contrasexual self more freedom. If you're a
man used to being rough and macho, try doing something softer
and more "feminine," such as admiring the flowers in a local rose
garden or florist. If you're a woman who's usually passive,
experiment with doing something more assertive and "masculine":
invite someone out to a movie, or ask your boss for a raise.*

**In contemplation today, I allow myself to feel the deep wounding
that our society has suffered through the dominance of the patriarchy
and recognize that wholeness can only be achieved through a full
honoring and integration of the opposites in all of us.**

The single life exists within a limited framework. While we would like to think that socialization alone primes us for a committed partnership, there is a deeper reality at work. To be human is to crave wholeness and connectedness and, specifically, a safe, intimate, enlivening partnership. As children, we were utterly dependent on our close relationships for physical, emotional, and spiritual sustenance. Now, as more independent adults, we are driven by nature to seek an equal partner who can heal our childhood wounds and connect us to something greater.

If this seems overstated, just think about how we commonly refer to people who are "single." We seldom use the term literally, as in "a solitaire," "an isolato," or "a person unto him- or herself." Instead, we tend to define singles *in relationship to their relationships:* divorced, widowed, separated, bachelor, or spinster—some version of *not married.* On the surface, this may seem to reflect our society's bias toward marriage; in fact, it reveals our unconscious acknowledgment of our essential relational nature. To see the truth of this, we have only to recall how alive and at peace with the world we feel when we're in love and united with another.

🍂 *Today, review the childhood wounds you identified on Days 171–178. Then spend a few minutes thinking about at least three ways in which you can grow as a person through participating in a committed relationship. For example: "I can learn to be less critical." "I can learn to follow up on my promises."*

Today, as I enter my deep core, I ponder this powerful truth: "Wholeness comes only in relationship."

> *A false, or misunderstood word may create as much
> disaster as a sudden thoughtless act.*
>
> — JAMES THURBER

In the heat of an argument, we say words we don't mean and hear
words in ways they were not meant. Like cornered animals, we lash
out with claw and fang whenever we are feeling in danger. And
being the recipient of someone else's anger certainly constitutes a
dangerous feeling! The cold silence that often follows an argument
becomes a wide open chasm. Remembered words bounce off the
canyon walls to reverberate in distorted ways. Perhaps we also hear
the echoes of other angry exchanges from our past. With all the
reverb and echo, the possibilities of misunderstanding the other
person, and being misunderstood by that person, are enormous!

Intentional dialogue brings clarity into this type of situation. It
gives two people a unique tool for untangling misconceptions, expressing true feelings, and maintaining an even temperature. By
taking the time to reflect what we hear *when* we hear it, we make
sure that we interpret it, and remember it, accurately. And by
validating what we've heard and empathizing with it, we not only
process it in the most accurate and constructive manner, but also
assure the other person that we have understood what they were
trying to say. We're acting creatively, instead of reacting destruc-
tively. And suddenly, the words that once led to misunderstandings
amplify the work we are doing to achieve mutual understanding.

❧ *Today, make a special effort to practice your intentional dialogue skills in at least two conversations with other people.
Remember, any type of conversation can be used to practice these
skills so that they will come more naturally when you really need
them. Remember, any relationship you have can be used as a
training ground for a committed relationship.*

**In my twenty minutes of quiet today, I allow myself to become aware
of the power of words. I make this resolution: "My words will always
be healing."**

When meditation became popular in America during the 1960s, many people thought of it merely as a drug-free way of inducing an altered state of consciousness developed by Indian gurus who had been doing it on lonely mountaintops for centuries, unbeknownst to Westerners until technology made the world much smaller. There's a kernel of truth in this scenario. Although meditative practices have always been part of the West's Judeo-Christian religious tradition, it was the popularization of Eastern religious philosophies during the 1960s that prompted the average Westerner to "rediscover" meditation's day-to-day benefits.

Now meditation is widely appreciated as a unique means of breaking through our everyday consciousness to a type of awareness that is both mentally and spiritually liberating. By meditating, we can free our minds from all our worldly entanglements and attend to the things that have special value to us: our deepest feelings, our most significant experiences, and our most important relationships. As American poet and Zen practitioner Gary Snyder once said, "Meditation is the art of learning to do one thing at a time, and doing it supremely well."

❧ *Today, as a means of enhancing your meditative practice, give special attention to the meditation offered below.*

Today I focus on a point of light on my forehead, centered between my eyes. As I hold my attention there, I see rays of light streaming from my eyes, bathing the world with love.

In losing parts of ourself through socialization, we have become less natural—the person we were meant to be—and more artificial—a person that others wanted us to be. As a result, we have grown estranged from the natural world. No longer do we experience that sense of joyful oneness with the universe that we did as children. We've ceased to feel like a vital node in the great tapestry of being. Instead, we feel like an isolated speck in a vast emptiness.

The world of nature strikes us as exotic and foreign—an uncivilized realm that we do our best to tame or keep at bay. We carry on the business of life inside buildings, cities, and nations, cutting ourselves off from nature. What we need to remember is that what we reject externally is something that has been internally buried and disowned. To recapture our original wholeness, we need to reconnect with nature. We must learn again to see its mysteries as marvelous wonders, rather than frightening unknowns. We must reach out to nature as a child would, with fresh, unfettered senses, an active imagination, and a thriving conviction that we are a part of all that we encounter and it is part of us. In this way, we can rediscover and put into use the wild, untamed parts of ourselves that can offer us so much vibrancy and life!

❧ *In the coming week, seize every opportunity to embrace nature as you did when you were a child. Run with the wind, waving your arms. Roll in a meadow of wildflowers. Watch your face ripple in a windblown puddle.*

Taking time for prayerful solitude, I visualize the world as it would be seen from the moon. From this perspective, it is small enough to hold in my hand, and I can easily see how connected all forms of life must be.

Too many times, a mechanical "thanks" is the only response we give to those who do nice things for us. Sometimes, we don't do anything at all. How much nicer it would be if we would surprise them with a small gift as a token of acknowledgment, praise them for their support in front of others, or write them a short note telling them just how much we value their action on our behalf. Our failure to be demonstrative in this way is usually not because we don't sincerely appreciate the other person's kindness. Instead, it's because of some more complicated inner conflict on our part. Maybe we're shy about expressing ourselves. Maybe we do not feel worthy and it is difficult for us to accept loving kindness and support from others. Maybe we have trouble admitting, so overtly, that we did, in fact, need their help. Or maybe we're so self-absorbed that we assume the other person already knows how grateful we are.

We need to make sure that we expend the time and effort to convey our gratitude to others in an appropriate manner, or we may wind up losing them as helpers. It won't necessarily be because they've turned sour on us. Faced with our somewhat tepid response to their past kindnesses, they may justifiably (and nonjudgmentally) feel that we didn't need them as much as we do.

Today, identify at least one close person in your life who recently did you a favor, but whom you may not have sufficiently thanked. Then, think of a specific way you could express your gratitude beyond simply saying "thanks."

In these next few moments of prayer, I hold all gifts received from others in mind and experience the blessing of love.

Many people go right through life in the grip of an idea which has been impressed on them in very tender years.

—AGATHA CHRISTIE

Sometimes, the smarter and more sensitive we are as children, the more quickly and completely we capitulate to society's plan for us. We're too smart for our own good! Once we figure out the appropriate camouflage, we busily get to work creating a jungle suit that will carefully allow us to blend in seamlessly. Clever at figuring out how to thrive in the world, we succeed all too well at getting rid of traits that aren't well-received or approved of. Soon, we have so successfully digested the incoming messages of socialization that they become part of us. We not only adopt the "best," most-recommended behaviors, we actually internalize the beliefs and values behind those behaviors.

In psychological language, we have *introjected* society's lessons. No longer do we need parents, teachers, coaches, or clergypeople to tell us that we shouldn't cry or that we're not talented enough to get the job we want or that good girls aren't supposed to be sexy. There's a voice deep inside us that does the job just fine!

ã» *Today, review the pages in your notebook that you wrote during the socialization unit (Days 187–193). Have you had any insights since then about the lessons you were socialized to learn or how deeply you "introjected" those lessons?*

Taking time in my chosen place of reflection, I identify the ways in which I've internalized the values and judgments of others. As I do so, I feel those voices losing power to sway me.

> *The test of a civilized person is first self-awareness,*
> *and then depth after depth of sincerity in self-*
> *confrontation.*
>
> —CLARENCE DAY

Have you ever made this type of indignant complaint after someone has criticized you: "Me? Insensitive?" "Are you trying to tell me I'm jealous?" "I am *not* being intolerant!"

Our denied self consists of all those personal qualities that *we* don't see—or acknowledge—but that *others* are well aware of. The traits we deny having are usually ones that are too painful for us to accept. We become aware of them only as we become sensitive to how forcefully we respond when certain "buttons" are pushed. Often these "buttons" point to specific aspects of our parents (technically called "introjects") that we've picked up unconsciously and that we particularly despise: the refusal to admit we're wrong, the overindulgence in food or drink when we're feeling insecure, the smirking laugh that uncontrollably pops out whenever someone else is blundering. To realize that we do, in fact, possess these traits would be to recognize that we *are* like our parents. For most of us, this is at best discomforting and at worst horrifying!

Over the next three days, you will be helped to confront your denied self with a minimum of pain, so that you can work toward wholeness. The more you can accept who you really are, the better able you will be to work toward positive change.

🍂 *Title a new page in your notebook "My Denied Self." On the top half of this page, list criticisms that other people have made of you that have surprised you into a shocked denial. Underline those traits that you can now most readily identify as aspects of your denied self.*

I enter an inner place of courage and recognize that I need to know and understand my darker truths as I strive to become conscious.

Our denied self is mainly revealed to us when we get all hot, bothered, and bewildered about someone else's criticism of us. We can't understand how we could possibly be attacked for that particular negative character trait. And yet, part of our pained resentment comes from a nerve being hit. Somewhere, deep in our psyche, that negative self that we've always denied is flinching from a direct blow—and a "button" has been pushed.

There is, however, another very significant way in which our denied self is revealed. It shows up in our criticism of others, for we tend to dislike in others what we dislike most—and, often, deny—in ourselves. We complain to a lover, "You never want to have sex!" when the truth is that *we* never initiate sex. We rant and rave about their failure to take our side, when we're always letting *them* down. Criticism is usually a form of indirect exhibitionism: what we deride so dramatically in others is actually a flagrant display of our own unsavory traits.

❧ *On the bottom half of the notebook page entitled "My Denied Self" that you worked on yesterday, list the traits that you have most hated to see in your close friends and past romantic partners. Underline those traits that you can now most readily recognize as aspects of your denied self.*

During this time of quiet prayer, I confess that my criticisms of others point to areas that I dislike in myself.

Faith is not making religious-sounding noises in the daytime. It is asking your inmost self questions at night—and then getting up and going to work.

—MARY JEAN IRION

It's *undeniably* painful to hear criticisms from people that we care about, especially if those criticisms reflect traits that repulse us. It's no wonder that we so often try to bully others and ourselves into disavowing the criticisms. One tack is to throw the same criticisms back at the people who make them. Unfortunately, the truth is like a boomerang. No matter how hard we throw it away from us, it always winds up landing back at our feet!

But have faith! Accepting the hard, hitherto-denied truths about ourselves can be tremendously liberating. It certainly beats tiring ourselves by constantly deflecting or throwing back the blows we receive from others. Those truths do not exile us from the human race; after all, other people have managed to like us and care for us, despite having observed those traits in us. Once we experience this initial relief and realize that we are now coming face-to-face with our damaging behaviors, we can start stretching to change them and to become whole again.

❧ *Review the notebook page "My Denied Self" that you have worked on during this unit. Are there any other negative traits listed on this page and not yet underlined that you can recognize today as parts of your denied self? If so, underline them. Also, promise yourself that you will keep track of the criticisms you receive—and make—in the future and ponder them to see if they do, in fact, reveal aspects of your denied self.*

No longer afraid to know the truth about myself, I enter the silence today in celebration of my budding self-awareness.

It is better to give and receive.
— BERNARD GUNTHER

Real love—the type of love that is lasting and fulfilling—might also
be called "reality love." It is not based on the illusion of romance or
the fantasy that our partner will anticipate our every desire. Unlike
romantic love, which derives from yearnings and dreams inspired by
our childhood needs, reality love takes its energy from day-to-day
awareness, respect, and commitment. And unlike romantic love,
which is whimsical and dissipates with the first relationship storm,
reality love builds a firm foundation that can withstand the fiercest
gale.

To achieve reality love, we need to know more about ourself, our
partner, and the healing purpose of relationships. We have to become
more accepting of our partner's weaknesses and desires. We must
be prepared to give unconditional love to our partner, so that he or
she can be healed of his or her emotional wounds. And we must be
open to receiving the unconditional love of our partner, so that we
can be made more whole.

Reality love does not create relationships. It is created *within*
relationships, by two individuals who keep in motion a cycle of
nurturing as well as being nurtured.

❧ *Think of a close, nonfamily relationship in your present life.
Identify at least three ways that you give to the other person in
this relationship. Identify at least three ways in which you receive
something from the other person.*

**In deep meditation today, I hold in my mind a vision of selfless love.
Slowly I put myself into the vision as the lover and discover with
shock that the more I love, the more I am loved.**

*If someone listens, or stretches out a hand, or
whispers a kind word of encouragement, or attempts
to understand a lonely person, extraordinary things
begin to happen.*

                                      —LORETTA GIRZARTIS

Any good lover knows that one secret to being a more caring partner—while at the same time having fun—involves turning otherwise ordinary moments into special occasions. When your romantic interest does a favor for you, give him or her a nice card, a small box of candy, or a bouquet of balloons, rather than just saying, "thank you." Instead of leading your dinner date once again to the little Italian restaurant around the corner, surprise him or her with a prepacked picnic in your living room, complete with flowers, fragrant potpourri, and a country-meadow sound effects tape. If the two of you are doing laundry together, bring along a new board game or perhaps even a camera, so that you can make a funny mini-album later on. Even a rose left on the other person's pillow or remembering to have some of their favorite foods in your house tells them that you are thinking of them in a special way. It takes a certain amount of time, effort, and creativity to add a special touch to an otherwise commonplace event, but it's a wonderful way to demonstrate your thoughtfulness and to enliven the relationship.

In the coming week, think of at least one way you can make an ordinary event a bit more special for a lover, a date, a close friend, or a family member.

Every event is pregnant with the divine, each moment can be a moment of real meeting. In my quiet moments today, I allow my eyes to develop this X-ray vision of the sacred in each moment.

When you want to believe in something you also have to believe in everything that's necessary for believing in it.

—UGO BETTI

We must *surrender* ourselves to the process of self-transformation. In our action-oriented culture, the word "surrender" has a faintly distasteful ring to it. It seems related to some sort of religious dogma or an authoritarian rationalization that asks us to submit to the rules without challenging them. Defensive creatures that we are, surrender strikes us as a kind of death or self-annihilation.

Nothing could be further from the truth. By surrendering to the process, we are cooperating with rather than fighting against our unconscious drive to be our whole, true selves, to feel fully alive. It's an act that reflects our trust in our own basic self-worth. It is not surrendering to an outside force, but surrendering into oneself more fully. Seen in this light, surrender is a very courageous step. Far from being suicidal in some way, it is supremely life-affirming.

Acknowledging the wound as well as the health, admitting weaknesses while embracing our strengths, and owning split-off parts as well as presentational parts are the prerequisites for opening up to change. To realize our full potential, we must first stop playing games and start taking full responsibility for who we are now.

❧ *Spend a few moments thinking about and writing down ways in which you refuse to face certain parts of yourself that you don't like or ways in which you refuse to give up certain parts of yourself that cause problems for you and others. How prepared are you to stop refusing and, instead, start surrendering?*

I take time today for the renewal of my spirit, and visualize a deep, clear pool of sapphire water. I imagine surrender being akin to diving into this pool so that I may heal and become whole.

As we were growing up, we received the message that anger isn't "nice"; we may have even been taught that anger is dangerous. Many parents made attempts at cajolement: "Oh, come on now, what's the matter? It's nothing to be upset about! Let's go out and play in the yard." If this didn't work or if our parents didn't have the patience to try it out, we were ignored, threatened, spanked, denied privileges, or sent to our rooms. Very rarely were we permitted to express our feelings with a sympathetic, "I understand that you're angry, and you need to go ahead and let it out."

Is it any wonder that television, movies, video games, comics, rap songs, rock music, and contact sports seethe with a violence that is so incongruent with our "nice," polite social codes? We have to process our anger somehow, and so we conceptualize, compartmentalize, and ritualize it so that we can cope with it in the safest way possible. But this is secondhand anger. It is not original to us.

❧ *Take out your notebook and think for a few minutes about your angry moments as a child. How were you treated? Also think about how your parents expressed their anger—did they scream at each other or withdraw and become moody? Now, think about the present: How do you usually go about coping, or not coping, with your anger? Do you ever find other ways of releasing it? For example, through going to an action movie or becoming righteously indignant at a perceived political enemy or putting on an old rock-and-roll album and turning the volume up until the walls shake?*

In this time of reflection, I reach into the depths of my courage, recognizing my divine right to feel, experience, and express my anger in ways that will not harm myself or others.

He that will not sail till all dangers are over must never put to sea.

— THOMAS FULLER

It's understandable that when we're in love we want our partner to do all the changing necessary for us to get along together. The truth is much harder to accept: In order to have a healing relationship—the only kind of relationship that stays alive—*we* must change and become the kind of person that our partner needs in order to heal. This kind of person is someone who can "parent" his or her partner's inner child more effectively than the partner's real parents did. In order for us to become this kind of person, we need to change the negative traits we have that are similar to the negative traits possessed by our partner's parents—the very traits that unconsciously drew our partner to us because of his or her Imago.

This is a daunting task. It is not simply obstinancy that paralyzes relationships, although it often feels like it. It is fear of change. We are afraid to grapple with our lost and denied selves. It means facing our own internalized self-hatred and accepting the responsibility for feeling unsettled and unlovable. Indeed, change can feel downright dangerous! Our lost and denied selves are survival mechanisms. We fear that if we reclaim in ourselves what was once deemed unacceptable, we will die. And on top of that fear, we feel hampered by a lack of partnership skills.

The ideas and skills that you are learning in this book are intended to help you feel less fearful about taking the initiative to change.

Today, lie back and do something relaxing for a change. Take a nap or a long bath. Watch the sun go down. Listen to some music that you haven't heard for a while.

Today in quiet, I make this my prayer: "Help me to change the things I can change, to accept the things I cannot change, and give me the wisdom to know the difference."

> *Alternatives, and particularly desirable alternatives,*
> *grow only on imaginary trees.*
>
> — SAUL BELLOW

Fantasies are fun. When life gets tough, or when we feel all alone, unappreciated, or bored, it helps to lie back and envision some paragon of sexiness and sensitivity catering to our every desire and lifting us to new heights of ecstasy. The more we suspend reality, the more exciting the fantasy gets. Our supremely well-endowed and sensually gifted love partner not only defies all logic by being totally enthralled with us, but transcends the laws of nature: maintaining a superhuman level of energy, stamina, and attentiveness, assuming postures that are inconceivable in real life and inspiring orgasmic delights far beyond any we've ever imagined possible.

How can flesh-and-blood partners compete with this fantasy? They cannot. We must be very clear in our minds about what is fantasy and what is reality. We must never confuse them with each other; and for any amount of time that we devote to enjoying fantasy, we must devote *at least* equal time to enjoying reality.

❧ *Today, lie back for a few moments and fantasize about some ideal lover. When you've finished, say to yourself, "I just had a fantasy — something that is, and should be, very distinct from reality. Why did I need this?"*

Entering my place of silence today, I make this vow: "I will live in the real world and use my fantasy as a guide to what I need."

If we're not careful, conversations can degenerate into interrogations. A playful mood suddenly shifts, and we feel as though we are sitting across from a detective—or becoming one ourselves—as we fire one question after another at the person we're with. When we're nervous and curious on a first date, we may find ourselves acting like an interviewer: "Where were you born? Do you have any brothers or sisters? Do you like rap music? Have you ever been to Europe?" When we're angry, we may grill the other person as if we were a prosecuting attorney: "Where were you last night? Why didn't you phone? How do you think I felt? What's wrong with you?"

Too many questions make a dialogue seem oppositional: they challenge the other person to keep on giving up information, while we keep on taking it from them. Intentional dialogue, by contrast, is a means of gently assisting someone to talk about what they want to talk about. Not only is this approach much more likely to make the conversation comfortable for the other person, it's also more likely to provide us with insights into what this person really thinks and feels.

 In the coming day, practice your intentional dialogue skills in all conversations. Whenever you're tempted to break into the natural flow of the other person's remarks with your own questions, try instead to encourage the other person to continue talking, by reflecting, validating, and empathizing.

I am aware that I have many ways of keeping myself safe while asking others to expose themselves. In the silence today, I vow to keep others safe in my presence.

The weight of the centuries lies on children.

Ironically, much of the psychic damage we experienced as children was done at the hands of those who most wanted to protect us—our caretakers. Even exceptionally well-intentioned and hard-working parents wind up doing things that can hurt their children. They can't help it. After all, parents carry wounds from *their* childhoods—reinforced by many years of suffering negative feelings and exercising problematic character defenses. And their parents—our grandparents—had childhood wounds too, which influenced *their* parenting, and so on, as far back as human life goes.

Even assuming that both parents have resolved many of their childhood wounds through their own loving partnership *before* they have a child, they will still wind up wounding that child. Each child is a unique human being with his or her own innate temperament. For wounding *not* to happen, both parents would have to be thoroughly adept at instantaneously correctly assessing their child's moment-by-moment feelings and respond correctly to that feeling state based on the child's inborn needs. No parent in recorded history has ever been quite so talented or well equipped!

❧ *Today, if you know, think back to how your parents were raised. How might they have been wounded as children? How might that wounding have affected the way they raised you and your own childhood wounding?*

Today, in reverential stillness, I acknowledge the deep woundings that my parents have experienced as children and open my heart to the hurt parts that they hide.

Loving, like prayer, is a power as well as a process.
It's curative. It is creative.

—ZONA GALE

There is no path to salvation except love. It is not in seeking love or in finding love, but in loving itself. This is the lesson of evolution and history. This is nature's plan. When we meet our Imago-match partner—as incompatible as this person may seem—nature has arranged for a biochemical reaction to occur that will bind the two of us together, at least temporarily. We must make an effort to go with this person as far as we can. In other words, we must follow our heart's lead. We need to stretch to meet this special person's needs: not giving the love that *we* want to give, but, rather, offering the love that our partner needs to be healed. For it is through what seems to be a roundabout way of taking care of our partner that we create the safety and trust within a relationship that will enable our partner to heal our own childhood wounds.

Nature does not care if we are comfortable; it only cares that we eventually evolve to enjoy a fuller, more soul-stirring life. Nature itself is in travail as long as we remain blocked and incomplete. Our defenses disrupt its pulsation and partially impede the flow of energy in the universe. Learning to love is not just a personal challenge, but an appeal from nature. When we answer that appeal, and follow nature's law, we—and nature—are healed.

❧ *Today, extend your love out into the natural world. Do something that will help heal your local environment and, in the process, make your personal world a little better. Clean up a pile of debris, water a starving tree on the street, plant some herbs in a windowsill pot or a bare spot in your garden.*

In this time of wordless prayer, I dwell on the beauty of spiritual healing that is a potential through partnership.

Early in this century, the Russian physiologist Ivan Pavlov conducted a famous experiment in behavioral science with dogs. For weeks, at the dogs' scheduled mealtimes, he rang a bell before feeding time. Eventually, the dogs were conditioned to salivate every time they heard a bell, whether or not it was their mealtime or any food was provided. Because of our early socialization, we, too, are conditioned to respond mechanically—and inappropriately—in certain types of situations. Each person bears the unique burden of his or her particular conditioning.

For example, a young girl may become so sensitive to her friends and relatives cruelly laughing at her awkward behavior that now, as a woman, she immediately flinches with anger whenever anyone laughs over something she did, even if it's meant to be a shared laugh of delight. Or a teenage boy may be conditioned so rigorously by his peers and by movies on how to make the moves on teenage girls that later, as a man, he automatically forces himself on women in the same crude, doltish way. Luckily, we are not dogs but human beings. With time, patience, and self-education we *can* overcome the bad conditioning that we received as children and adolescents.

ı❧ *Identify at least three different, bothersome ways that you still act—or react—the way you did when you were a child or adolescent.*

I move into this quiet time and access my courage for the journey ahead. This truth is a beacon before me: "The parts that I dislike most about myself are the parts most in need of healing."

Love is not enough. It must be the foundation, the cornerstone—but not the complete structure.

—BETTE DAVIS

Thanks to our Imago, we really don't have much of a choice when it comes to selecting our mate. Marriage is, by default, the final catchall for the ravages of childhood—the only state in which these ravages can be clearly manifested and completely healed. It shouldn't surprise us, therefore, that marriage has such dramatic ups and downs. All too often the person we idolized and were madly in love with quickly becomes the person we may wind up bitterly divorcing. We just can't stand their negative traits, although it is precisely these Imago-based traits that we must sooner or later learn to handle if we are ever to realize our full potential as individuals and love partners.

Fortunately, we *do* have a choice about what kind of marriage we have. Most marriages fail because of the persistence of the unconscious aspects of the relationship—the struggles that keep repeating themselves without our knowing why. As singles, part of our preparation for a more conscious marriage, one that will stand a far better chance of succeeding, is to become more aware of the hidden needs that drive our intimate relationships and to learn the skills we need to address or express those needs effectively.

❧ *Today, think of a marriage (yours or someone else's) that ended in divorce. Try to identify at least one struggle in the relationship that repeated itself over and over again without getting resolved—a struggle that seemed to baffle and torment both parties. Now, identify at least one skill you've learned so far in this book that might have helped to resolve this struggle.*

Today, in the private space in my mind, I review my past failed relationships. Seeing all closed doors as opportunities, I open my heart and mind to new knowledge and skills for the journey to love.

To say something nice about themselves, this is the hardest thing in the world for people to do. They'd rather take their clothes off.

—NANCY FRIDAY

Have you ever dismissed a compliment with this type of self-deprecating remark: "Me? Foxy? You're kidding!" "I'm not really an artist." "I could never have done it without help." "Please! It's nothing to fuss over!" "I'm sure anyone else would have been just as good or better."

Many of us have positive traits that are obvious to others but that we ourselves never acknowledge or, in some cases, fail to even recognize. When these traits are pointed out to us, we're being introduced to our *disowned self.* Even though the traits of our disowned self are not in themselves negative, we refuse to accept them because they don't fit our preferred self-image. For example, a woman who sees herself as sensitive, poetic, and free-spirited (qualities that society values in a woman) may not want to acknowledge that she can also be aggressive and businesslike. A man who wants to appear macho may deliberately downplay his skill in cooking. A shy, self-effacing person may not even realize that s/he is attractive, funny, and fully capable of commanding the center of attention. To reclaim our wholeness as individuals, we need to own up to all our fine qualities, as well as all our rough ones.

❧ *On a new page in your notebook entitled "My Disowned Self," list the positive traits that others appear to recognize in you—or even compliment you for—but that you have a hard time believing or accepting. Look over this list and see how each trait might actually describe you.*

Moving into my inner sanctuary, I breathe deeply, allowing my lungs to swell, not only with air, but with pride in myself for all aspects of who I am.

Why do we often hide our light? Why do we sometimes get embarrassed or even fearful when others compliment us? Many of us have been conditioned to suppress certain qualities that seem inappropriate given our job, our role in the family, or our professed goals in life. And we've all been taught not to brag about ourselves.

How much easier it is to develop a blindness toward our own embarrassing virtues and, instead, to admire and even envy the virtues of others. We notice the magnetism that always makes one of our friends the life of the party, another friend's ability to articulate his thoughts and feelings so eloquently, a relative's sense of inner peace and ability to commune with nature. The strange thing is, what we admire in others is often present but disowned in ourselves. Just as we must learn to accept in other people the qualities that most frustrate us in order to accept these qualities in ourselves, so too must we respect *in ourselves* the qualities that we now admire only in other people. It's okay to see and praise the virtues of others, but we must learn not to put ourselves down as we're doing this. We must try to see and praise those same virtues in ourselves.

&. *Recall specific positive qualities that you have admired in other people. For each quality, ask yourself, "How do I, too, possess this quality?" Think of specific incidents that reveal that you ∂o, in fact, also have this quality.*

In my time of sacred solitude today, I visualize those beautiful aspects of myself shining outward from my core, like the warming rays of the sun.

We may be on the mark and set to undergo magical transformations, but we must be very careful not to expect—or provoke—sudden change. In our quick-fix culture, we are addicted to fast, dramatic results, especially if we are frustrated and discouraged with our present position.

But real and lasting change takes time. Change, in and of itself, is frightening to contemplate—or even live through. Rushing headlong into a dramatic makeover can cause tremendous upheaval in our relationships and can also be incredibly disorienting from a personal perspective. To rush into change before we've fully prepared ourselves is like purchasing the most updated software for a computer that is ten to fifteen years old. The old computer does not have the capacity to run the new software. Change simply will not take hold in one's life until the psyche has had some time to adjust. In other words, we have to update our computers and make sure they are running smoothly before we load in any new information, or software. In matters of self-development, slow and steady definitely wins the race.

🔊 *Today, take some time to assess your progress so far in mastering new relationship skills. Congratulate yourself on the long-term effort you've been making. Reassure yourself that there's no rush to be a paragon of good behavior. Instead, the "new" you will emerge in its own, natural time as long as you continue to encourage it.*

Relaxing and breathing deeply, I acknowledge the importance of moving slowly on this self-prescribed journey. I offer this prayer: "Whatever is worth having is worth taking the time to cultivate."

In every pardon there is love.

—WELSH PROVERB

How can we move freely into a more open, self-liberating future if we're still lugging around heavy and useless baggage from the past? What good does it do us to bear grudges against family members who hurt us long ago, to replay painful arguments with past lovers in the hope that we will finally come up with the right "last words," or to fantasize revenge against turncoat friends who are no longer part of our lives? Worse than doing us no good at all, these obsessive thought processes actually harm us. They keep old wounds—and old antagonists—alive, and most troublesome of all, they distract us from concentrating on our positive goals of becoming more skilled in our relationships with others and more complete as individuals.

The work of self-healing won't begin until we can forgive the people who hurt us. In doing so, we are reorienting ourselves from a negative frame of mind to a more positive one. Having this new perspective, we can reconnect with the universe and feel, once again, faith, hope, optimism, and goodwill.

🐾 *Today, practice forgiving at least three people who have hurt you in the recent or distant past. Speak your forgiveness aloud, stating the specific thing(s) you are forgiving. If appropriate, use the process for saying good-bye that you learned on Days 104– 108. Then consider expressing your forgiveness directly to them in person.*

Today, I consider the possibility that holding on to past hurts involves the whimsical belief that if I hold on to them long enough, ultimately the offending person will confess their wrongdoing. In my time of creative quiet, I surrender that belief.

*You can have anything you want if you want it
desperately enough. You must want it with an inner
exuberance that erupts through the skin and joins
the energy that created the world.*
                              —SHEILA GRAHAM

Socialization is essentially a process of mutilation: chipping away at
our wholeness as individuals, suppressing whatever we can't chip off,
then adding on whatever is needed to fill in the holes. In the process,
we lose contact with the exquisite pleasure of our own, pulsating life
energy. Restricted, admonished, rejected, and punished for being
ourselves, we shatter our essential unity and give up our intrinsic
spirituality.

And yet, we are still driven by our innate human yearning to realize
happiness and fulfillment. Looking again to our social culture for
guidance, we try to purchase our aliveness in the form of goods that
are marketed as "love," or "sex," or "success." This covers a huge
range of ultimately unsatisfying products—from soft drinks and fine
wines to sleek cars and trendy clothes, from making a big business
deal to honing a sure-win video game technique. We become addicted
to anything that promises to numb the pain or stimulate the senses
of our chipped-away existence. To restore our sense of full aliveness,
we must come home again to our lost self; and we can only do this
through building a conscious, loving relationship with someone who
can mirror and guide us along the way. If we truly want to make this
journey, we can.

🐾 *Today, identify at least three products or pastimes you substitute for your innate feelings of aliveness. Promise yourself that
you will work even more intensely on the relationship skills
presented in this book.*

**In a twenty-minute period to honor my inner process, I visualize
myself looking into a clear, deep pool of water. The face I see is
radiating with love and acceptance for the totality of who I am.**

The childhood development stages are not confined to childhood. The cycles repeat themselves throughout our adult lives: beginning with attachment when we're infants and proceeding, as we mature, through exploration, identity, competence, concern, and intimacy. The cycles tend to reappear as we enter new situations and circumstances. We are repeatedly reexperiencing the need to bond with someone who attracts us, to achieve competence in a particular endeavor, to develop more intimate ways of relating to one very special person.

Sometimes, when we're recycling through a certain stage of development as an adult, we regress to the way we were as a child during that same stage. For example, we may have feared abandonment when we were attachment-stage infants and responded by clinging to our parents. If so, we're likely to behave the same way in the infancy of a relationship, clinging to the other person in order to keep him or her from getting away. We may not always regress fully, but we should not underestimate the hold these cycles have on us. Because often, once we unconsciously slip back into a cycle, we are bound to that cycle until we play out the full rotation. Our salvation lies in *conscious* attention. The more we know about our unconscious patterns, the more we can work to effect intentional change.

❧ *Today, review the childhood wounds that you identified during Days 171–178 and underline those that still feel the most active to you.*

In quiet prayer today, I recognize that the pull of old behaviors are the brambles along my current path. I celebrate with this wisdom: "Consciousness can steer me away from the brambles."

The unexamined life is not worth living.

—PLATO

At regular intervals, we all need to step aside of our busy lives and assess where we've been, where we are, and where we're going. We do this as a culture on New Year's Eve and, on a more personal level, when we reach the milestone of our birthday each year. Only from this detached perspective can we begin to achieve a bit more objectivity about the way we go about living our day-to-day lives. Only by taking a more comprehensive and analytical look at our past, present, and future can we determine if we're simply muddling through from one event to another or really heading somewhere, consciously and purposefully. It is important to do these mini self-reviews more often than once a year on our birthday!

In doing the work in this book, you are taking that step aside each and every day. You have seen how the troublesome heat of the moment can be cooled later by a few moments of withdrawal and how the embers of inspiration, almost extinguished by the daily grind, can be fanned into flame by a few moments of reflection. So, imagine what this kind of reflection can offer your process as a whole! The brief time that you spend each day to review past experiences, evaluate present activities, and project future possibilities is time that helps improve the quality of your entire life.

𝕒 *Today, look back for a moment and consider how much you've learned—and grown—over the past 250 Days. Then, renew your commitment to do the work in this book.*

I imagine myself at the top of a mountain, looking down at a valley with a winding road flanked with mileage markers. I see myself moving on the road, passing the markers, and chart my progress in preparation for a loving, committed partnership.

Whether we know it or not, our intimate others—family members, romantic partners, close friends, and colleagues—know about the traits that we deny to ourselves. They can see that we're inclined to be melancholy, depressed, irresponsible, or self-absorbed, even if we can't. In time, their presence in our life forces us to see what they see, and we flinch at the sight. We realize that we can't really fool the people who are near to us, even if we can still fool the people at large.

Our denied qualities are part of us and, to become whole, we must face up to them and integrate them into our conscious personalities. The psychologist Carl Jung called this aspect of our identity our "shadow." No matter how much we try to ignore or avoid looking at our shadow, the people who bring the most light to our lives are bound to make it all the more visible. It may seem frightening at first to think about stepping into this shaded area of our existence. But until we own our shadow we will forever find ourselves at the mercy of our denied self. And our shadow grows with each day that we do not embrace it.

❧ *Review again the list of denied self traits you made on Days 230–232. Choose one trait and, in the coming week, watch with special care to see if it appears—or if someone close to you points it out.*

In a place of honest prayer, I ponder the uncomfortable truth that my wholeness depends upon my courage to bring what is "dark" in me into the light.

*One must learn to love oneself . . . with a wholesome
and healthy love, so that one can bear to be with
oneself and need not roam.*
— FRIEDRICH NIETZSCHE

"**A**tonement" is not a common word in the popular vocabulary. Most people think of it strictly as a religious term, associated with the concept of making amends for past wrongs. As such, it smacks of punishment or reparation. Actually, atonement literally means "at-one-ment," referring to a state of unity or completeness. Taken this way, it deserves to be much more prevalent in our language, for it describes the condition to which we all secretly or not-so-secretly aspire.

Each one of us began life intimately connected with the entire universe around us. Growing up in our families and in society meant sacrificing some of this aliveness and connection in order to "fit in." The birthing process alone separates us from our warm, safe, and fully connected environment, hurtling us into a cold, new reality. Now we're left with a yearning to be restored to our original self, to be "at one" again, instead of being fragmented, partly alive, and lonely. Atonement is a restoration to wholeness. It's the natural and personally sacred outcome of recognizing, accepting, and transforming *all* of ourselves.

❧ *Today, in order to gain a better appreciation of what atonement can mean for you, review your lost self parts that you identified on Days 215–220. These are the parts that you must reintegrate into your identity.*

A time of gentle, slow breathing connects me to my deeper self; I allow the quiet of this meditative time, and it imbues me with a sense of peace. Acknowledging my original connection to God and to others, I visualize myself as a person who has reached at-one-ment.

See there within the flesh
Like a bright wick, englazed
The soul God's finger lit.

—MECHTHILD VON MAGDEBURG

Whenever we feel angry or discouraged at the whole human race, or even when we single out one person as alien, contemptible, or worthless, we're in danger of succumbing to selfishness. We need to recognize that our point of view at these times is far too narrowly restricted to do us any good. Those who live in glass houses are the first to throw stones. AND we're seeing only superficial distinctions: what *we* want, think, or feel at the moment, and how that appears to be threatened by what others want, think, or feel at the moment. We must pause and look beyond our own point of view to a vision that is much greater and much more profoundly true.

No one person is, by nature, superior or inferior to another. Each of us holds a unique place in the great tapestry of being, and each of us has special insights into the wonders and beauties of life. But for all this singularity, we are not unrelated beings. We are members of the human family and children of the universe. Though we may appear to be strangers to each other on the surface, underneath we are all illuminated and invigorated by the same eternal flame. So, it's time to put those stones away and instead marvel at the similarities that lie within our glass structures!

In the coming day, make a concerted effort to see the divine spirit within everyone you encounter. Seeing the divine could be a special sparkle in a person's eye, a kind gesture. Anything that shows that the person you are seeing is doing something for the larger good, a selfless act.

In the holy place of quiet today, I visualize the universe as one pulsation and I participate as one pulse within the whole.

The way we are socialized as children differs markedly depending on our community and demographic group. Children growing up in farmlands where animals are mated and bred may receive very little negative conditioning about sex, compared to children growing up in cities. A son of laborers living in a working-class neighborhood may be chided for his intellectual "pretensions," while a daughter of Ivy League graduates may be called to account if she fails to get all "A's" in her schoolwork.

As we mature, it's difficult to hold on to a sense of self in a society that bombards us with messages to conform and inevitably devalues huge chunks of our identity. Being anonymous within a group always feels safer at first. And it becomes even more difficult to establish intimate relationships with other people without devaluing parts of *them* or insisting that *they* conform to *our* feelings, attitudes, and ambitions. We need to remember that the more secure we feel about ourselves, the less we will need the external validation of others.

🍂 *Today, try to recall various ways that you had to struggle to be yourself against community or group pressures during adolescence. Then, thinking about your past intimate relationships, try to recall ways in which you may have applied pressure on other people to be more like you.*

In mindful prayer I honor the unique beauty that lies within the core of my being. Breathing deeply, I focus on this thought: "The more secure I am with myself, the more I can embrace and celebrate diversity."

Self-expression must pass into communication for its fulfillment.

—PEARL S. BUCK

Change can be awkward, embarrassing, and even discouraging at times. The people around us may easily—and understandably—become uncomfortable when we step out of the roles that *they* have become dependent on, whether these roles are healthy or unhealthy. To them, we have overstepped the bounds of polite, socialized familiarity. In venturing into unfamiliar ground, we ourselves may be so preoccupied with our own sense of vulnerability that we can't read the "different" reactions of our friends. Even though these reactions may well be positive, we only see them as confusing, uncertain, and possibly "unsafe." There is also the problem of reciprocity. We have to have the courage to practice new skills and behaviors in a one-sided fashion, without letting others know what we're up to (at least for a while).

Nevertheless, we must persevere in practicing what we learn among the people who are important in our lives: our family members, close friends, colleagues, and romantic partners. Making changes always means taking risks. It is impossible to master relationship skills in the privacy of our own home. They must be learned in context with others—our training buddies, unwitting or not. And we cannot achieve wholeness without taking risks!

❧ *Today, choose one particular relationship skill—for example, intentional dialogue or behavior-change request—and plan to practice it with someone close to you within the next week.*

During this time of self-restoration, I hold this truth: "Change means taking risks and understanding that the healing I am doing is worth the risk I'm taking."

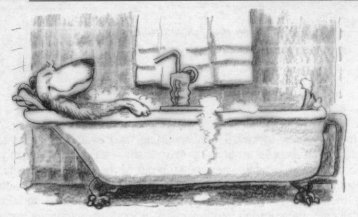

We may feel the most sensual when we are having sex, but sensuality and sexuality are *not* the same thing. Pleasures that appeal to the senses come from many different kinds of activities. We can be ravished by fine paintings or brought to a peak of ecstasy with music. Cappuccino can enrapture our senses of smell and taste, and our whole being can become newly invigorated by breathing in the fresh autumn air. Our sense of touch, which we associate so single-mindedly with sexual arousal, can also be blissfully stimulated by a silk shirt, a toasty fire, or a bracing shower.

The energy we derive from consciously experiencing sensual activities can be stored. We can build up a reservoir of sensuality to help us feel fully alive when we need to. If we do not currently have a sexual partner, we can indulge our sensuality by taking a long, hot, aromatic and sudsy bath. Or we can treat a friend to an exquisite gourmet meal—or even go and have one by ourself! The more creative, comprehensive, and persistent we are in seeking sensual delight, the more fully alive we will feel.

❧ *Today, do something sensual that you haven't done for a while. Here are some suggestions:*
- *Take a long bath in some fragrant oil.*
- *Get a professional massage, or have someone you love give you one.*
- *Prepare a candlelit meal with several of your favorite foods.*
- *Take a leisurely walk in a beautiful woods or park.*

In the serenity of this time alone, I move into the sensuality that is alive within my core and hold this truth: "Sensuality is a quality that lies within me, not within the sexuality I share with a partner."

Remember that moment in L. Frank Baum's *The Wonderful Wizard of Oz* when Dorothy and her traveling companions come face-to-gigantic-face with the mighty, superhuman Wizard of Oz? Toto the dog pulls back a curtain and reveals the small, frail human being who is manufacturing that face to appear powerful and wizardlike.

As we hide, lose, deny, or disown various aspects of ourself, there isn't much left of our original core self. To replace it, we fashion a new substitute self to give the appearance of wholeness and strength. This public persona is the one we use to gain approval, exercise power, and win love. It is called the *presentational self*. We don a mask of assuredness and composure, while inside we feel insecure and afraid. But every facade eventually cracks under pressure, or is caught off-guard. We must never forget that the artificial self we present to others is only a poor substitute for the real, human, spiritually endowed individual underneath. In peeling away our presentational-self traits and behaviors, our true identity reemerges.

꒰ *Title a new page in your notebook "The Presentational Self." Make a list of your presentational-self qualities: the traits and behaviors that you use to cover up or replace your hidden-self qualities (listed Days 202–206), your lost-self qualities (listed Days 215–220), your denied-self qualities (listed Days 230–232), and your disowned-self qualities (listed Days 244–245).*

As I settle into this time of quiet, I acknowledge the restrictive quality of the masks I've adopted. I recognize that these masks were created for protection and safety, but I open myself to the vitality beneath.

There is as much difference between us and ourselves
as between us and others.

— MICHEL MONTAIGNE

Our presentational face increasingly estranges us from our original, inner self. We get confused about what's real. Is our "self" the presentational image that we've so carefully constructed to make our way through life, or is our "self" actually our core identity deep inside?

When we enter into a conscious love relationship, we learn to appreciate that our real self is, in fact, our core self. This type of relationship demands the participation of our core self. At first, the demand makes us squirm. We're far more comfortable with our presentational self. But the demand is an indirect gift. Through revealing our authentic self to our romantic partners, and seeing that they love us as we truly are, we can step out of the stifling limitations imposed upon us by our presentational selves. Only then can we begin to restore our inner self to its original wholeness, thereby reconnecting it with the universe.

Preparing for a conscious love relationship in the future means beginning now to recognize the traits of our presentational self and to work on shedding those traits whenever we have the chance. Outgrowing our presentational self is a liberating process that allows us to be who we really are.

🥦 *Today, look over the list of presentational traits you made yesterday. Choose one trait in particular that you think you can now begin to shed. Identify situations when that trait typically emerges and think about how you might behave more authentically in such situations. Then, promise yourself that you'll work on shedding this trait from now on.*

In wordless prayer, I allow myself to slowly peel away the masks I've created, just as a snake must shed its skin in order to make room to grow.

Oh, how hard it is to find
The one just suited to our mind!
                              —THOMAS CAMPBELL

As a means of getting through the single life, the mating game is a losing game. If we play it addictively, we'll be too busy auditioning potential life partners to develop real-life relationships with anyone. The single state offers us an invaluable chance to get to know ourselves better and to experience a variety of temporary, noncommitted attachments with a number of people, so that we can learn more about life, love, and togetherness. A relentless search for Mr. or Ms. Right is a waste of this unique growth opportunity. It's far more productive to prepare ourselves for real love so that we'll be ready when it evolves naturally from the way we are living. It *will* happen, if we allow it to. And when it does, we're in for a surprise. Heaven knows, our Imago match is not likely to be someone who matches our mental fantasy of Mr. or Ms. Right, given all the resemblances this person will have to the early caretakers who wounded us. But this is the person with whom nature intended us to be, so that our wounds can finally be healed.

🍃 *Today, renew your commitment to withdraw from the mating game while you're doing the work in this book.*

Opening myself to a greater Power, I commit myself to self-completion, to finishing my own creation, and surrender all my attempts to avoid my own evolution.

> *Even the most exalted states and the most*
> *exceptional spiritual accomplishments are*
> *unimportant . . . if we cannot touch one another and*
> *the life we have been given with our hearts.*
>
> —JACK KORNFIELD

The need to give and receive love is our most fundamental need. As individual bearers of the life force, our ultimate happiness depends upon joining with others in a positive, joyful, and healing way. The most intense and rewarding form this love can take is an enduring union of body, mind, and soul with another human being; but our ever-present drive to create love, or be recreated by it, can find expression in *everything* we do. Offering a smile as you pass by someone, complimenting a stranger, and helping someone with heavy bags are some ways to express this feeling. When we apply loving kindness to ourselves and others as we perform day-to-day tasks and live through our day-to-day experiences, these tasks and experiences become far more pleasant and enriching. Instead of seeing them as insignificant, annoying, or burdensome events, we start looking upon them as opportunities for making our lives more vital, and the world around us more satisfying and meaningful.

&▸ *Today, try approaching each person you meet, each task you perform, or each experience you encounter with an extra amount of loving kindness. Keeping the words "loving kindness" in your mind, ask yourself, what can I do to make this moment more joyful and alive? What attitude or behavior on my part will be the most nourishing to myself and to those around me? A clear answer won't always spring to mind, but the fact that your intention is so positive will probably work wonders.*

Today in silence, I hold this powerful truth: "The world in itself is neutral until I color it with my perceptions."

*There's folks 'ud stand on their heads and then say
the fault was i' their boots.*

—GEORGE ELIOT

Blame and criticism are characteristic strategies of the power-struggle stage of a relationship. What happens represents the flip side of the romance stage: same agenda, opposite tactics. We are still interested in having our romantic partner meet all of our needs; however, as reality bursts the bubble of romantic love, our partners become less willing to cater to our every whim. In turn, we no longer try to charm and woo our partners into meeting our needs and making us whole. Instead, we try to coerce and browbeat them into doing so.

In the heat of the power-struggle moment, we find it very hard to believe that these negative tactics won't work. As infants we learned that when we cried or complained our caretakers would usually attend to us. And, we all know the adage that the squeaky wheel is the one that gets oil. So we wrongly assume that we can use these tactics to get what we want and need from our partner. We figure they will heed our cry, if only to shut us up. What we're much more likely to get, unfortunately, is just the reverse: increasing conflict and an escalating fear that we're never going to receive from our partner what we so desperately need.

& *Recalling a past love relationship, try to remember times when you tried opposite strategies (perhaps separated by a significant period of time) to get the same basic thing: first, recall a nice romantic tactic; later, a down-and-dirty power play.*

As I enter my quiet place today, I meditate on this truth: "I am responsible for what comes to me. Outcome is a direct consequence of input."

I always looked outside of myself to see what I could make the world give me instead of looking within myself to see what was there.
—BELLE LIVINGSTONE

"**W**hat does the outside world have to offer me, if I'm lucky—or hardworking—enough to find it?" When we think about this question, dozens of images immediately leap to our mind, involving love, sex, money, power, a nice car, a great home, a fabulous job. But when the question becomes "What do *I* have to offer *myself?*" our minds tend to go blank. The question strikes us as silly, irrelevant, unnecessary, or—worst of all—unanswerable.

The truth is, we either underestimate ourselves or take ourselves completely for granted, without ever really examining the full range of qualities, skills, and resources we have for self-development and self-fulfillment. We place no value on our intelligence, despite our college degree. We think of ourselves as boring, forgetting our crazy family life and the colorful places we've traveled. We discount our ability to persevere with a difficult assignment until we're successful, even though we've done this time and time again for our employers. And we think of our lives as empty without other people around, when, in fact, there are many things we can enjoy all by ourselves.

❧ *Today, identify at least three ways that you could make your own world better or happier by appreciating or developing what you already possess.*

In this time of restful solitude, I make my world an expression of myself rather than fill myself with expressions of the world.

Many people have a great deal of trouble accepting that their romantic partners do, in fact, love them. Some of us even go to great lengths unconsciously to "test" our partners. We offer them glimpses of ourselves that we feel are less than worthy, assuming that they will walk out the door at the first opportunity. What accounts for this suspicion, disbelief, or denial? We can't believe that others love us because we can't love ourselves. We disparage ourselves for having needs that our childhood caretakers led us to believe were excessive, for having traits that were discouraged as bad, silly, or inappropriate. We downgrade the natural endowments that are behind these needs and traits—our sexuality, our vulnerability, our competitiveness. Because of this self-hatred, we cannot believe that we are lovable.

And this brings us to an even harsher truth: If our self-hatred makes it impossible for us to believe that we are lovable, it is impossible for the love of a partner to heal our wounds. So, when a partner does leave us, it reinforces our belief that we are not lovable. We allow this belief to sink in, instead of recognizing that it may have been our defenses—and not our core self—that pushed our partner away.

❧ *Today, refamiliarize yourself with your particular character defenses—the list you made on Day 160—so that you can work more conscientiously toward letting those defenses down a little.*

In this quiet time of prayer, I allow myself to feel the sadness and pain of my self-hatred. As my breathing deepens, I vow to allow divine love to permeate every corner of my being.

What families have in common the world around is that they are the place where people learn who they are and how to be that way.

— JEAN ILLSLEY CLARKE

The dynamics that draw us to our Imago match and make our Imago-based relationships so tumultuous are complex and paradoxical. One of the most difficult and unappealing ideas for us to grasp is that our Imago match resembles our childhood caretakers. Not only do we tend to *react* to that person as we did to our parents during our childhood, but we also tend to *act* toward him or her as our parents acted toward us.

For example, we may cling to our Imago match, fearing abandonment, just as we once clung to our parents. At the same time, we may also refuse to indulge our partner's weaknesses, just as our parents refused to indulge ours. Meanwhile, our Imago match is also reenacting the relationship with his or her parents through us: perhaps seeking isolation to avoid being engulfed by us, while also counting on us to make up for his/her weaknesses.

The Imago-based relationship is a game of mirrors and mirages that is nevertheless very real and vitally important. To heal our childhood wounds, we need to reconnect with someone like our parents and, this time around, do better.

❧ *Today, take another look at how your personal Imago match reflects your childhood relationship. Review the Imago portrait you made on Day 50.*

As I sit in sacred stillness today, I open my heart to the reality that there are aspects of my caretakers in me. I recognize this truth: "We can only come to terms with those things we acknowledge to be our truths."

*Love knows no limit to its endurance, no end to its
trust, no fading of its hope; it can outlast anything.
It is, in fact, the one thing that still stands when all
else has fallen.*

—ST. PAUL

Romantic love, for all its resemblance to a "peak experience," does
not represent the pinnacle of love. Nor does it give us the greatest
vista of life's wonders. Instead, it offers a mere preview, a fleeting
glimpse of what is possible. Although romantic love is an illusion, it is
not a lie. It is "unreal" only in the sense that it is unstable. We can't
hope to hold on to its giddy delights. But if we remain within that
relationship and work on it diligently, we *can* evolve into a person
who truly possesses the best and most beautiful things that the world
can offer. Working on ourselves is like creating a natural water
spring: once we've carved out real love from the rocks, the water
flows to nourish us endlessly.

Nature knows it has to lure us with ecstasy—romance—to the
portals of transformation first. Its intention is not to leave us with the
dregs of disillusionment that come from failed romance. Nor does
nature have any interest in pain or suffering as our existential
condition. These are meant to be only temporary by-products of the
journey, occurring when the romantic phase starts ending and just
before the next, more turbulent stage of the power struggle begins.
In a committed relationship, the euphoria of romantic love can
become a constant. But it is only available when we reach the other
side of the valley of conflict and fear.

🍃 *Think about relationships in your past that did not survive the
end of the romantic phase. Focusing on one relationship, write
down at least two of the wondrous possibilities you foresaw
during the romantic phase. Did these possibilities eventually seem
impossible? Why? What could have made them possible?*

**In deep relaxation, I allow the wonder and symmetry of the healing
process to wash over me in waves of cleansing hope and joy.**

Committing ourselves to a relationship means giving up certain avoidance activities that we may consciously or unconsciously use to keep the other person at a distance. These activities serve as quick "exits" from the hard work of resolving conflicts or learning to love more caringly.

Some of us have exits that are relatively harmless and easy to close. Maybe we tend to watch TV too much instead of talking or playing cards with our lover. Perhaps we've made a habit out of retreating to our office or garden or workroom whenever we're annoyed at someone close to us—waiting for the whole incident to "blow over" rather than working it out with the other person face-to-face. Others among us have more problematic ways of exiting relationships: creating a smokescreen with cigarettes, distracting the mind with alcohol and other drugs, or seeking physical release through long-term absence, sexual infidelity, or high-risk recreational activities. Many of us abandon the relationship altogether at the very first sign of difficulty. We must agree to say "no" to all these exits and "yes" to the process of making our relationships stronger and more comforting—and safer for both people to do the work of healing each other's wounds.

≈ *Today, thinking of the people who are—and have been—close to you, identify at least two ways in which you tend to "exit" from problems in a relationship.*

One thing I can always learn more about is contact and commitment. Today I take this commitment to my quiet place and nourish it until it is stable: "I surrender my fear of intimacy."

*So long as one is able to pose one has still much to
learn about suffering.*
                                        —ELLEN GLASGOW

If we understand the nature of the missing parts of ourselves, we
can not only predict the kind of partner we will attract and be
attracted to, but we can also foresee some of the problems we will
face. For while we choose partners who possess the *positive* traits
that we have buried, we also pick partners with our denied *negative*
traits. These traits are a deeply internalized group of qualities that
we cannot accept as part of our preferred self-image. Instead, we
unconsciously gravitate toward partners who have these traits, or
seem to have them, if only to a small degree, so that we can project
our denied traits onto them. And our partners unconsciously gravitate
toward us for similar reasons. As the relationship continues, and the
projections keep crisscrossing, the problems compound! Only when
we stop posing as "perfect" people—which means ceasing to deny
these negative qualities as our own—can we start getting rid of
these problems.

❧ *Think of someone you know fairly well who is in some way
blind to one of his or her negative behaviors or personality traits.
Maybe this person has actually denied having this trait. Now take
a closer look at yourself. Is there any way you may be similarly
blind to an aspect of your own behavior or personality?*

**In this time of sacred stillness, I move into a strength that can
enable me to view my negative aspects without judgment. I hold this
important truth: "Only through owning all aspects of myself can I
achieve wholeness."**

During the course of any of our emotionally intense relationships, there are times when we find ourselves in the doghouse. We've done something wrong, and now the other person is punishing us by keeping us at bay. Often, we aren't even sure what the charge is. We haven't been read a statement, and we have become demoted to the point where we feel we have no rights. Even if we do know what we've done to be in the doghouse, we may feel either falsely accused or not the least bit guilty for having done it. In any event, our goal is to get out of the doghouse and back in the other person's good graces. To realize this goal, we need to do what real dogs can't: engage the other person in intentional dialogue. We need to tell them how we feel and then ask them to clarify their feelings: mirroring, validating, and empathizing with whatever they have to say. Only then will we be able to resolve all the hurt on both sides. Barking at our partner out of frustration and anger simply won't do!

🖎 *Today, review the process of intentional dialogue (Days 35–38, 57–59, and 82–85). Is there a situation in your life now where intentional dialogue would help you to avoid, or get out of, a doghouse? Resolve to use these skills the next time there is a conflict in your life.*

Breathing deeply, I enter a state of deep relaxation. Here, I experience my status in relation to all other forms of life and energy. Wherever I feel disconnected, I bring to mind the vision of the Oneness of all things. I hold this truth: "I have the power to remain connected in all circumstances."

Sexuality is a sacrament.

—STARHAWK

Our sexuality is a central and highly personal aspect of our identity. It is also a wondrous gift of nature that we need to honor as well as enjoy. Ultimately, our sexuality enables us to achieve the kind of physical and spiritual ecstasy that can happen only between two people who have committed themselves to each other body *and* soul.

This does not mean that we, as single people, cannot, or should not, express our sexuality in other contexts. It simply means that we need to avoid *abusing* it. We can do this by being conscious, responsible, and, above all, joyful and respectful about how we exercise our sexuality. We can learn to appreciate that genuinely pleasurable sex is an expression of love. Then we can reclaim our full, inborn capacity for sexual pleasure, freeing it from all the inhibitions, distortions, and mythologies that socialization has imposed upon it. Finally, we will arrive at a clearer vision of what will fulfill us sexually and a better knowledge of how to turn that vision into a reality.

During the next few days, you will be focusing more closely on your own sexuality: how it has functioned in your life so far, and how it could serve you better in the future. Think of this unit as your golden opportunity to look at something clearly that so often takes place in the dark!

❧ *Today, think for a few moments about how your sexuality expresses itself in your current life. Let your mind roam freely, without judgment, over the following questions:*
- *What arouses me sexually?*
- *How do I satisfy — or try to satisfy — my sexual urges?*
- *How do I block — or try to block — these urges?*
- *How do I go about attracting — or responding to — the sexual interest of others?*

Moving more fully into myself during this time of serenity, I visualize myself collecting the aspects of my disowned sensuality, as a bee would collect nectar from a flower.

*I consider promiscuity immoral. Not because sex is
evil, but because sex is too good and too important.*

—AYN RAND

Sex without love, or love without sex, is frustrating and incomplete.
The truth is that sex and love nourish each other and, in turn, nourish
the people who blend these activities together.

As any committed couple in a passionate relationship will testify,
fulfilling sex is the product of a strong, lasting emotional commitment.
Yes, we can grab fleeting pleasure from the relatively loveless, if
affectionate, sex that's associated with one-night stands, short-term
partners, or multiple, overlapping affairs. But we always return to
our uncommitted selves in the end: alone once more, still sexually
hungry, and suffering the same emotional bruises and bumps we've
suffered before, time and time again.

The pleasure to be gained from so-called "free" love—sex without
emotional and spiritual bonding—lacks the depth of passion that
results from staying sexually faithful to one special partner. Especially
if we are unconsciously using this kind of sexuality to make up for a
lack of love or nurturing in our lives. The kind of fidelity that comes
from real love encourages a person to be true to his or her innermost
self. The result is a deep personal opening-up that carries with it a
profound sexual release.

ᐤ *Today, think for a few moments about the following questions
relating to sex and love in your* current *life:*
  • *How much value do I place on sex? On love? Do I tend to
    value one more than the other? Why?*
  • *How would I rate my level of "sexual satisfaction" on a scale
    of 1 to 5 (5 being the highest)?*
  • *How would I rate my level of "love satisfaction" on a scale of
    1 to 5 (5 being the highest)?*

**I call upon the reservoir of divine energy at my core, recognizing that
love and sexuality blend together to create a harmonious symphony
of sound.**

The sexual drive is nothing but the motor memory
of previously experienced pleasure.
— WILHELM REICH

Our life as sexual beings did not begin at puberty, but at birth. It was first set on course by the specific erotic experiences we had as children. If, at age six, we engaged in our earliest heterosexual sex-play with a six-year-old neighbor who was also a close buddy, we may now associate sex with cozy and loving companionship. If, instead, our initial partner was an emotionally distant and overbearing person we barely knew, we may now seek sexual thrills in power struggles with strangers or, alternatively, we may fear sex altogether. Perhaps we suffered sexual abuse or rape, incurring pain that can last a lifetime.

Our childhood attitudes toward sex were also shaped by the forces of socialization. If our mother caught us masturbating and told us how disgusting it was, we may have become ashamed to touch our bodies or afraid of being "caught" enjoying sex. Perhaps we were led to believe that "real" males are always aggressive sexually, while "real" females are always passive. Maybe our favorite movies left us with crude models of the erotic-but-"bad" partner as opposed to the decidedly unerotic-but-"good" partner, thereby confusing us about the relationship between sex and virtue. Whatever the case, we must look to our childhood to see the origins of our sex life as adults.

❧ *Title a new page in your notebook "Childhood Sexual Experiences." On this page, list at least three memorable sex-related incidents or influences from early childhood through age twelve: positive ones as well as negative ones. As you list each incident or influence, be sure to describe briefly how it made you feel about sex.*

In reverential stillness, I acknowledge the messages about sex that wounded me, and now choose to envelop the wounding with sensual love.

Those pleasures so lightly called physical.

—COLETTE

Most of us grew up in a family and a social environment that trained us to value work and propriety above sexual fun. Taboos were imposed upon us that imprisoned, rather than liberated, our inborn sexual nature. During our teen years, with hormones surging, some of us broke out of prison for a while to roam freely across the sexual landscape. But most of us scurried back behind bars when we became adults, newly concerned about work and propriety but still without a clue as to how to integrate intimacy and sexuality.

Now, in our "mature" relationships, we try to recapture the intensity of our adolescent sexual feelings and, at the same time, find a haven of emotional security, support, and love. What we generally get, however, is too much of one and not enough of the other, or too little of both, or neither at all. Our sex life consists of ultimately unsatisfying episodes based on old habits and assumptions, rather than a continuum of fulfillment based on sharing a conscious, ever-renewing life with one special partner.

To improve our chances of achieving full and lasting sexual satisfaction with another person, we need to know more precisely what has worked for us and what has *not* worked for us in our past sexual experiences as adolescents and adults. This kind of knowledge can set us free to be the fully alive individuals—and lovers—that nature intended us to be.

&. *Title a page in your notebook "Adolescent and Adult Sexual Experiences." On this page, list at least three memorable sexual experiences since age twelve: both the positive ones and the negative ones. As you list each experience, briefly describe how it made you feel about sex in general.*

I move into my divine space; I realize that I must move through the wounding in order to claim my wholeness.

Woe unto those who don't believe in the unbelievable sweetness of sex love.

—JACK KEROUAC

Whatever trauma, embarrassment, fear, shame, bad luck, or boredom we may have experienced in our sexual histories, we all harbor dreams, fantasies, and hopes of sexual fulfillment. Some are based on actual experiences; others come from what our friends tell us, from what we see in movies, or simply from allowing our imagination to run wild. Perhaps we harbor secret fantasies of a romantic interlude at the beach, with the ocean waves crashing onto the shore in the distance. Or maybe our ultimate fantasy involves down comforters and bunches of pillows in front of a fireplace, with wine and soft music in the background. Maybe we enjoy the thought of being awakened in the middle of the night, to engage in some sexuality. Or perhaps our favorite time would be first thing in the morning. In creating a vision of the type of sexual relationship we want, we need to acknowledge these secret desires and allow room for experimenting with them.

❧ Title a new page in your notebook "My Sexual Relationship Vision: Secret Desires." On this page, list your own, personal dreams, fantasies, and hopes relating to sex. Here are some examples to trigger your imagination:
- *I'd like a two-hour, full body massage by candlelight.*
- *I'd like to make love while watching myself in a mirror.*
- *I'd like to be able to talk about my fear of impotence.*
- *I'd like my lover to be aggressive and seduce me.*
- *I'd like to make love surreptitiously in a public place.*
- *I'd like my lover to join me in acting out a sexual role-play.*
- *I'd like to be less inhibited about playing with sex toys.*
- *I'd like to just kiss for hours without going any further.*
- *I'd like to feel free to talk suggestively as I make love.*

Moving into a relaxed state of prayer, I allow myself to access and feel the deep sensuality pulsating at my core.

We tend to think of the erotic as an easy, tantalizing sexual arousal. I speak of the erotic as the deepest life force, a force which moves us toward living in a fundamental way.

—AUDRE LORDE

Our sexuality is a part of the pulsating energy of life, and our drive for a sexual union arises from our yearning to connect with the universe. In a conscious relationship, we bring all of ourselves to our partner, including the full spectrum of our sexuality. It's a deeply spiritual act that restores our sense of being fully engaged and connected to the passion of life around us. Love between two persons is the incubator of the sacred in life. Vulnerability and honesty between lovers seeking a union of mutual respect and gratification give birth to a sense of wonder and the divine that connects us to the All.

While we are still single, there is much we can do to rediscover our innate sexuality and to increase our potential for sexual intimacy.

❧ *Title a page in your notebook "My Sexual Relationship Vision: Emotional Needs." In the top half, list the feelings you'd like to have about sex, using positive words or phrases, for example: "relaxed," "excited," "that it was special" rather than "unpressured," "not boring," "not dirty."*

On the bottom half, list the main fears that you'd like to overcome, using short words and phrases, for example: "failing to satisfy," "being frigid," "being hurt."

During this time of quiet reverence, I take time to anticipate the full pleasures that await me at the end of this journey, and I offer a prayer for freedom.

When we're struggling to grow through a love relationship, the process of reclaiming our lost and denied selves is bound to be disorienting at times. We don't quite know where we are or where we're going, we're stripped of many of our most important defenses, and we're afraid we may wind up losing our best chance at happiness. As we dismantle our old defense mechanisms, we may find ourselves searching for familiar landmarks in a new and alien land. As many problems as we may have had, at least they were familiar problems! We miss the old-brain strategy of being late for a date just to make the other person worry. We long to throw an out-of-control tantrum when we don't get our way. Once again, we're tantalized by mirages of perfect mates waiting for us somewhere else.

At such bewildering times, we need to do some reorienting. We need to once again set up the new landmarks to live by. This means reminding ourselves that our goal is the only worthwhile goal to have—a relationship that is loving, fulfilling, and lasting. We must also remember that the only way to get there is through building better relationship skills.

&. *Today, review one of your major maps again: the Imago portrait you made on Day 50.*

Breathing deeply today, I allow myself to experience my ambivalence about changing and remaining the same. I am aware I must choose between the tension of remaining the same in a changing context or living in relationship. I choose to be relative to my context.

My wound evokes your healer. Your wound evokes my healer.

—RACHEL NAOMI REMEN

Many spiritual traditions hold to the belief that a person must suffer great wounding in order to be a great healer. Most tribal shamans were—and still are—men and women invested by near-death experiences with special healing insights and powers. Buddha only became a healing teacher after enduring extreme privations as a wandering ascetic. And Jesus, whose career as a healer began only after a forty-day ordeal in the wilderness, achieved his role as Christ the redeemer by passing through the mortal agony of death.

We see a similar kind of dynamic within a committed love relationship. It is our wounded self—the self made vulnerable and defensive through childhood conditioning—that comes to understand, value, and respond to love, so that we, in response, can become more powerful lovers—and healers—of our partners. Even more miraculous, it is our wounded self that helps activate our partner's powers to heal us. The words "heal," "whole," and "holy" all come from the same root. When we participate in healing and being healed, we are creating wholeness, and the work we are doing is holy.

೮ *Today, do something that is healing. Forgive someone who has done you a disservice. Visit someone who is sick. Cheer up someone who is sad. Help someone you don't even know by donating to a charity.*

In deep contemplation today, I hold in mind the mystery of mutual healing as the path to mutual wholeness.

The fairy-tale frog prince was cursed. He knew that a kiss would turn him into a prince, but he couldn't simply ask for it. Instead, he had to wait for the kiss. Who knows how much time that took!

We are not fairy-tale frogs; we are real-life human beings. And yet we often impose a similar curse upon ourselves. Our "reasoning," if it can be called that, goes like this: If we have to tell the other person what we want, it won't mean anything when we get it. They have to *know* what we want without prompting. This may be a good fantasy, but it's very bad logic. And it keeps us in the role of frog prince much longer than is comfortable or useful. The best way to get what we want—and need—from the people around us is to ask as clearly as possible. We may be too embarrassed to admit that we like to be tickled during sex, too proud to ask for help in a crisis, or too insecure to value any personal attention that isn't spontaneous. But unless we leapfrog over these inhibiting feelings, we're stuck in our own, self-created, unfulfilling swamp.

❧ *Today, ask someone for something that you've wanted from them for a while, but have so far failed to request. If appropriate to the situation, use the process for making a behavior-change request (Days 146–151).*

I take twenty minutes today for inner renewal, recognizing that it is unfair to assume that others will know what I want and need. I offer this prayer: "A willingness to hear what I need is an expression of love from another."

You need to claim the events of your life to make yourself yours. When you truly possess all you have been and done, which may take some time, you are fierce with reality.

—FLORIDA SCOTT MAXWELL

Conflict, endemic to all intimate relationships, is the cauldron that transforms raw emotion and instinct into pure gold. It is the chemistry of growth, which is a precondition for entering the paradise of real love. Deep, profound changes in the self must occur, involving very hard work—some of the hardest work we've ever had to do. But the aim of this work is not to make us into someone else. Drawn into the relationship by our inner Imago, we are already not our true self. We sacrificed that self on the altar of fear many years ago, during the socialization process. Now we must make another sacrifice, this time on the altar of love. We must surrender our fear of realizing our full potential as human beings. We must give up our false, presentation self in the name of our more authentic self. If we make this sacrifice and continue working toward change, we will rediscover who we truly are and become whole once again.

🍂 *Thinking about a past relationship, identify at least three ways in which you were* not *your true self during its early, romantic phase. How did each way help to fuel the romance, at least at first? How did each way eventually end the romance?*

During my twenty minutes of meditation, I visualize the cauldron of change that bubbles at my core. I hold this truth: "Transformation, while painful, restores rather than destroys me."

We will know we've almost made it to the paradise of real love when we feel as if we were falling into the pits of hell. The demons that keep our wounds open and sore, those harrowing voices from the past, flock around to frighten us away from the prize. Our defenses begin crumbling to the ground, and our whole character structure starts twisting and turning in the flux of change. As we repeatedly violate the injunctions of our childhood socialization, our worst fears come rising to the surface. And all this upheaval in our psyche makes the problematic issues between us and our partner even more intense and threatening. Indeed, our entire relationship seems to be plunging headlong into chaos.

We may be severely tempted to abandon the whole enterprise at this point. Many people do. But it is only during this tumultuous period of transition that the real breakthrough can occur. If we stick to our good, intentional attitudes and behavior during this terrible trial-by-fire, we can triumph. From the ashes of our old, fragmented self, our old, self-absorbed life, and our old, combative relationships will arise the phoenix of paradise: a real love that transforms our entire world.

🕭 *Today, think back over past crises in your life. Identify at least three conscious attitudes or behaviors that helped get you through these crises in a positive manner.*

I breathe in the courage that lives within me, recognizing that the phoenix must burn before it can rise in glory once again.

*When you love someone all your saved-up wishes
start coming out.*

—ELIZABETH BOWEN

One of the joys of being single is developing a wish list for a committed relationship in the future. Like any shopping spree, we need to know who we are and what we are looking for in order to make a good purchase for ourselves. Without first thinking about what we need, or what we'd like to buy, we can find ourselves making purchases that do not work once we get them home.

What dreams would you like to realize in the course of such a relationship, dreams that your mate may want to share?

Sailing together all through the Caribbean?
Joining forces to run an after-school center for teenagers?
Having a small apartment in the city and a large house in the country?
Cohosting lavish parties to entertain your friends?
Collaborating on a book about health issues?
Conversing with each other in French?

Now is the time to ply your mind, plumb your heart, and draw up a list of ambitious and exciting possibilities. You may never be able to make all your wishes come true, but wishing in itself can be inspirational. Besides, it's always good to be prepared. How well a relationship succeeds in fulfilling your dreams depends to a large measure on the dreams that you bring to it.

❧ *Today, begin a "wish list" for your future life with a committed partner. Identify at least three dreams you have of what that life could include.*

Entering the silence today, I access the dreamer within. As my imagination flows, I become aware of the life I want to live with the love of my life. I hold this thought: "My dream can become my life."

Happiness must be cultivated. It is like character.
It is not a thing to be safely let alone for a moment,
or it will run to weeds.
— ELIZABETH STUART PHELPS

Through our relationship with an Imago match—and only through that kind of relationship—we can find those vital parts of ourselves that we lost in the process of growing up. Specifically, our Imago match inspires us to rediscover the ways that we once gave ourselves pleasure but relinquished because our parents, our peers, or society in general frowned upon them. At one time we may have found delight in rubbing our bodies or in raucous, rip-roaring laughter. Maybe we loved playing in the mud or harbored a secret desire to fly a plane. Our parents may have scoffed at our compulsion to sketch or harped on our sitting outside, watching clouds, or just doing nothing at all.

We see these lost possibilities when we look at our Imago match. It's the "you're everything I always wanted" piece of the Imago puzzle. The challenge is for us to merge with our Imago match in a fully committed relationship so that *we* can become everything we've always wanted.

❧ *Today, take another look at some of the most likely characteristics of your Imago match. Review the list of your lost self traits that you made on Days 215–220.*

Renewing my spiritual courage, I awaken lost parts of myself so that I can once again experience the wonder and limitless possibilities of my dreams.

> *What we need is a cup of understanding, a barrel of love, and an ocean of patience.*
>
> —ST. FRANCIS DE SALES

Any project worth pursuing—especially one involving self-realization—requires a great deal of concentration. With this concentration comes greater insight, faster development, and stronger motivation. The more we value and systematically practice techniques that help us to focus and stabilize our attention—from intentional dialogue skills and good study habits to prayer, meditation, and visualization—the faster we will see results. These ways of consciously applying more of our general energy to the specific task at hand enable us to appreciate just how deep our human resources go. We don't have to be content with a superficial, half-conscious, day-to-day life that is mostly dependent on what happens to us. Instead, we can strive to awaken our inner power and become more and more capable of independently making things happen. Our good efforts applied toward increasing our day-to-day attentiveness, in whatever forms we choose, are returned in a universal way; for in changing the ways that we live, we change the world in which we live.

🏵 *Today, make a new experiment in learning to focus your attention. For example, try praying a special prayer or visualizing a cherished goal or looking at, or listening to, someone or something special with extra attentiveness.*

In this sacred space, I recognize the strength and power I have to transform my life so that I may create a conscious whole that enables me to experience my full aliveness.

To understand is to forgive, even oneself.
—ALEXANDER CHASE

What does it mean that we must first *own* our lost and denied selves if we are ever going to change for the better? The modern psychological term *ownership* is just a new word for *confession*. It is part of the healing—or salvation—process. Without owning, or confessing, the truth about ourselves, there can be no change. Just as it is axiomatic in prison-reform theory that the prisoner must have remorse if he or she is to be rehabilitated, so it is with us. Both to ourselves and to others, we need to avow both the positive and negative aspects of our identity.

The healthiest, most helpful type of confession is free from guilt or judgment, two of the old brain's greatest allies. Instead, we must simply and purely acknowledge the truth. In order for us to be healed as individuals, we must bring our wounded, negative, and distorted parts into our consciousness without censorship. We simply have to have faith that everything will work out okay after this happens, that we will still have our self-respect and the acceptance of our friends and family. In actuality, confession of this type is essential if we are ever to develop true love for ourselves and another person.

⇛ *Today, confess to yourself at least two things about yourself that you have been afraid to admit. Choose one of these things and consider confessing it to someone who is close to you—for example, a lover, friend, or family member.*

In this sacred time alone, I move into my internal place of courage and I begin to look at those less than perfect areas of myself. I hold this truth: "Guilt only serves to strengthen the prison bars."

Due to the forces of socialization, we may lose our innate capacity to feel and express our emotions, and to compensate, we might develop a highly active physical life. Or we may become so "uptight" about our bodies that we're very "sloppy" emotionally. When Woody Allen said, "I am at two with nature," he was talking about the urbanized, intellectual filter through which his feelings and senses could not penetrate.

Socialization has, to some degree, wounded us in all four dimensions of our core energy: thinking, feeling, acting, and sensing. Some get off pretty lightly, while others are sorely constrained in one or two areas. A few have suffered severely in every area. Through our relationships, we seek to repair this damage—first unconsciously, through our irresistible, Imago-led drive to interact with a partner who exhibits our opposite traits, and then consciously, using the necessary tools to apply our relationship skills and reclaim our wholeness.

❧ Referring again to your assessment of how the socialization process thwarted your natural instincts (Days 187–193), think of one thing you can do this week to help free that part of you that's the most blocked. If that part is "thinking," for example, you could try reading an intellectually challenging book. If it's "feeling," you may want to do some sort of charitable work. To indulge your sensual self, you may enjoy taking a bath in aromatic oils. To develop your action-oriented self, you may plan to take a longer-than-normal bike trip.

I open my spirit to a time of renewal today, visualizing the strands of my energies intertwining into a pulsating whole.

The greater the pleasure that man and woman give to each other—in bed and in every other dimension of their relationship—the more God is present with them.

—ANDREW GREELEY

However "safe sex" may be defined in terms of public health, "safe sex" from an emotional and spiritual perspective is sex that allows us to feel safe in the other person's company. This means not only feeling safe from having our bodies harmed or our feelings hurt, but also feeling safe to express our needs and desires and to consider the needs and desires of the other person.

Safe sex is truly consensual. It involves *talking* as well as *having sex*. Intentional dialogue skills can be a big help in overcoming shyness or awkwardness and allowing freedom of expression in sensitive discussions about sex-related matters. Safe sex also includes each partner working toward a *mutually* pleasurable experience, instead of just a *personally* satisfying one.

When sex is safe in all these ways, it can be transformative, reaching far beyond the mere meeting of two bodies and the releasing of two people's sexual tensions. This kind of sex frees two spirits to become one and to feel the creative energy of the universe.

❧ *Today, make a commitment to discuss sex-related matters more openly and honestly, using intentional dialogue skills, the very next time you and another person become involved in a sexual situation.*

In this time of quiet stillness, I reach into my core to shed light on the shadowed area of my sexuality. I ponder this wisdom: "Sexuality that is safe both emotionally and physically will reconnect me to the joyful tapestry of being."

It is a bad plan that admits of no modification.
—PUBLILIUS SYRUS

How we behave in the world at large and within each relationship we form is largely determined by those beliefs that have become our general truths: "Friends should never do business together." "I'm not special." "One person has to be the leader in a marriage." Whether our beliefs are true or not, we take pride in living by them. They give us a black-and-white plan for tracking our way through an uncertain world.

The problem is that some of our general beliefs can be so rigid, so inaccurate, or so inappropriate to the actual situation at hand that they hinder us rather than help us. We need to reexamine our beliefs and assess their merits and demerits more carefully. Do they really reflect *all* of our experience, instead of just one or two specific incidents? Do they even come from our experience at all, or were they foisted on us by someone else? How might they be keeping us from living a fuller, more satisfying life?

Over the next four days, you'll review some of the belief systems that motivate your behavior and your relationships. Remember that accepting your beliefs at face value can blind you to seeing things as they really are.

🍃 *Title a page in your notebook "My Beliefs." Write down at least two beliefs that you have about the world at large (for example, "Surviving in this world is very tough" or "The world is a vast playground of opportunities") and at least two beliefs you have about people in general (for example, "People are basically good at heart" or "You can never trust anyone completely").*

Seeking a broader perspective today, I acknowledge that my beliefs can sometimes be a foundational tool, but can also be a shackle. I pledge to find the beliefs inside that will release me from my shackles.

The greater part of our happiness or misery depends on our dispositions and not our circumstances.
—MARTHA WASHINGTON

In some ways, our belief systems perform a valuable service, because they temper our "old-brain," instinctual nature. By conceptualizing the teachings we get from people we respect into a code to live by, we can often function more rationally than we otherwise might. When a personal crisis looms and we're about to lose control, we can say to ourselves, for example, "*This* is the way I should behave when . . ." or "If I do *this*, then *that* will happen." Our pattern-forming "new brain" enables us to bypass our primitive instincts to fight or flee; instead, we come up with a more logical response.

Unfortunately, our belief systems can become as unyielding and automatic as our basic instincts are. Our belief about how we should behave on a certain type of occasion becomes a belief that affects our conduct in all sorts of other occasions. And our belief about our capability in one area evolves into a belief about our overall competence as a human being.

❧ *On yesterday's page entitled "My Belief Systems," write down at least three beliefs that you have about* yourself. *You can try filling in the blanks in the following statements:*
* *When I'm attracted to someone, _____ is how I should behave.*
* *If I go to a party where I don't know anyone, then _____ will happen.*
* *I'm not the kind of person that can _____ when something bothers me.*

In quiet prayer, I offer thanks for the beliefs that have provided safety in the past. In newfound freedom, I let go of those beliefs that no longer ring true for my future.

Only that which is deeply felt can change us.
Rational arguments alone cannot penetrate the
layers of fear and conditioning that comprise our
crippling belief system.
— MARILYN FERGUSON

Because we formulate so many of our beliefs without questioning their source or value, and because they so powerfully influence our behavior without our awareness, we must work hard to become more conscious of them and to insist that they reflect reality. Otherwise, they will bully us into living stunted, mechanical lives.

Our belief systems involving our own gender and the opposite gender can be especially strong and insidious. From early childhood, we are trained to have firm opinions and attitudes about the differences between men and women: what each gender is like, what each gender can do, what type of life each gender should lead, and what types of actions or reactions each gender will exhibit in a given situation. Modern research and experience have thrown many of these assumptions into question, allowing us to reevaluate old stereotypes, discover the many varieties of reality, and realize our full potential.

&. *On the page titled "My Belief Systems," which you began two days ago, list at least two beliefs that you have about your own gender and at least two beliefs that you have about the opposite gender. For example, you might try completing these statements for each gender: "Emotionally, men/women are . . ." or "What a man/woman wants out of life is . . ."*

In reverential stillness, I deepen my breathing and visualize new possibilities with every indrawn breath.

*I truly feel that there are as many ways of loving as
there are people in the world and as there are days
in the lives of those people.*
— MARY S. CALDERONE

As accurate or as helpful as our beliefs can sometimes appear to us,
they are, by definition, entrenched in our minds. If, from our
experience and what society tells us, we come to have fixed beliefs
that all a man cares about is sex, that it is normal for family members
to shout at one another, or that our best response to criticism is to
keep quiet, we will find it extremely hard to think otherwise on a
case-by-case basis. Each situation in life—especially each human
relationship—has unique components and holds unique possibilities
that shift from moment to moment, day to day, and year to year. To
be locked into our belief systems is to misinterpret, misuse, or miss
altogether those moments, days, and years.

As single people, part of our preparation for the journey of
relationship is to uncover the world of beliefs we carry around in our
head. We need to begin taking on the responsibility for changing our
world. Full change will come with an altogether new experience of
living that replaces the old experience and inspires more temperate
and constructive opinions. This altogether new experience is what a
conscious and committed love relationship provides.

🐚 *On the page titled "My Belief Systems," list at least three
beliefs that you have about love relationships, for example: "Relationships tend to be passionate in the beginning, but they inevitably get boring after six months" or "The other person should
always be there for you when you need him/her."*

**In meditation today, I rejoice in having loosened the shackles of my
beliefs, recognizing that each clink of metal can be heard as a
resounding cry of freedom.**

Did you ever look for romance and, instead, find a good friend? The next time you're attracted to someone for his or her companionable qualities but don't feel any heavy Imago energy, why not practice utilitarian dating? Just because we sense that a person is not the love of our life doesn't mean we have to shy clear. On the contrary, this individual may be the perfect person to practice healing for the "real thing."

When we first start practicing utilitarian dating, it can seem like a haphazard, one-sided enterprise. We take care to mirror what our date says and to illicit more information, delaying our own contribution until later. We boldly share an aspect of ourselves that we're used to hiding because we're too shy. And instead of using "you" language to complain about the other person, we use "I" language to make a behavior-change request. Soon we find that our efforts are paying off. The other person is responding in kind, as people in relationships tend to do. We become confident enough to let this person in on what we're doing and offer to take turns with them in trying out new behaviors. Eventually, we have a playmate for change—an egalitarian and utilitarian partnership!

❧ *Today, plan a utilitarian date for sometime in the next two weeks.*

In this time of meditation, I open up to the many ways I can work on healing myself, holding this truth: "Every relationship is an opportunity to strengthen my awareness."

*Honest criticism is hard to take, particularly from
a relative, a friend, an acquaintance, or a stranger.*
— FRANKLIN P. JONES

As problematic as criticism can be, there is much that we can learn. Behind every criticism we launch against our partner and every one that we receive, there's a projection of our denied self—a self that we otherwise don't see. Just how accurately either form of criticism reflects our denied self can be gauged by how we feel at the time.

For instance, if we're especially exasperated at something our partner has done and find it almost impossible to speak about it without flying off the handle, it's a clue that we're unusually sensitive about that issue. Our volatile reaction indicates that our denied self was fleetingly palpable, and we didn't like the feeling. In a similar fashion, if we're extremely rattled by our partner's criticism of us, it's no doubt because it contains a kernel of truth that we've trained ourselves never to face. If we're smart, we'll not only pay attention to these denied-self indicators, we'll act on them. By responding to criticism with a positive behavior change we are working toward our own self-development. Changing our own behavior in the same positive direction that we are asking others to change *their* behavior will help us progress toward wholeness. In this way, we can diffuse the missiles of criticism before they explode into full-blown power struggles.

❧ *Identify at least two criticisms that you expressed toward past romantic partners. How accurately do the criticisms reflect your own denied self? Then, identify at least two criticisms that past romantic partners made about you and ask the same question.*

As I breathe into this silent time of prayer, I honor the reality that behind each criticism is an important kernel of truth that will further my path toward wholeness.

When we pick up a conch shell and put it to our ear, we hear the ocean from which it came, as if the ocean's vastness were somehow magically contained deep within the shell's coil. In a similar fashion, each human life sounds a common chord from its very depths—a testament that it is but one part of the boundless, living universe.

We were most aware of this heritage when we were infants and could barely sense the distinction between ourselves and others. At that time, we felt vitally linked to all of creation—beginning with our mothers and extending to everyone we encountered. As adults, we most fully recapture this awesome and empowering sense of connection when we merge with another human being in a committed love relationship.

❧ Today, pause every now and then to look more benevolently at the people around you. Remind yourself of all the things that you share with these people as a human being—not just the everyday things, such as a job, a car, or an interest in sports; but also the everlasting qualities, such as the desire for safety and happiness and the need for love.

Seeking a broader perspective today, I open up to this time of meditation and visualize the awesome yet invisible network that lovingly binds me to all of humanity and life.

*The questions which one asks oneself begin, at last,
to illuminate the world, and become one's key to the
experience of others.*
                                            — JAMES BALDWIN

Our childhood offers deeper insight into our most persistent relationship difficulties as adults. We need to peer down the corridors of
memory to unlock more information from long-closed rooms. As
children, our "old brain" developed defense mechanisms for anything
that seemingly threatened our survival. Those mechanisms stayed
intact as we grew older and developed more understanding and
control over our lives. The "old brain" remained in operation, not
realizing that it no longer needed to trigger those age-old responses
to protect us. If we hope to be truly free to live in the present, we
must carefully disengage the "old-brain" mechanisms that were put
in place to keep us safe.

Now if we cling to our partners, if we recoil from affection, we can
be sure that our problematic behavior can be traced back to our
childhood defense mechanisms. As long as we remain unaware of our
defense mechanisms and their causes, our major frustrations in
relationships will continue. We need to become aware of our intricate
defense mechanisms and learn how to rewire that alarm system to
benefit us as we are today. Only when we can identify how we were
wounded in the past, and see the effects of that wound in the present,
can we start changing for the future.

᠔ *Review the lists of childhood wounds and character defenses
you made on Days 171–178. Have you become more aware of
any of these wounds or defenses since you made these lists? How
so? Write your responses in your notebook.*

**Moving to a place of inner calm today, I take a moment to thank my
"old brain" for keeping me so safe when I was small. Breathing
deeply I recognize that, as an adult, I no longer need the alarms of
my childhood.**

Our Imago match can eventually heal us, partly because they possess those traits we need to cultivate. After "falling in love," however, there's a period of intense struggle, turmoil, and doubt. This happens precisely because in recapturing our missing traits through our partner, we are awakening a sleeping beast within ourselves, the part of ourselves that we still believe is dangerous to possess: our repressed sexuality, our neglected intellect, our lost sense of daring.

As children, we took many pains to stifle this beast of troublesome qualities. When, as adults, we connect with a partner who also has these same qualities, the beast starts waking up. Our "old brain" tells us that we're in danger—that our partner is, in fact, pushing us beyond the brink of safety. And so we lash out at our partner in order not to have to wrestle with our newly awakened beast. Consciously or unconsciously, we avoid commitment because it would mean having to come to terms with the beast.

* *Today, refamiliarize yourself with the sleeping beast inside you. Review the lists you made of the traits and qualities you lost through socialization (Days 187–193). These are some of the Imago-related traits that you're disposed to look for in a romantic partner.*

Today, I visualize the beast within me. Rather than being afraid, I recognize that the loud roar comes from a feeling of hurt at being neglected.

I can't mate in captivity.

> —GLORIA STEINEM, WHEN ASKED WHY
> SHE HASN'T MARRIED

Gender-related stereotypes and roles can wreak havoc on our sex life. The way women are socialized tends to cut them off from enjoying the *physical* experience of sex, while the way men are socialized tends to cut them off from enjoying the *emotional* experience of sex. We've all been raised hearing the same subtle and not-so-subtle messages:

- Women *give* their favors; men *take* their pleasure.
- Men prefer sex to love; women prefer love to sex.
- Men use women to get sex; women use sex to get men.
- Men who engage in a lot of sex are studs; women who engage in a lot of sex are whores or nymphomaniacs.
- Men who submit to women are wimps; women who dominate men are bitches.

In matters of sex, people of both genders find themselves to be captives. We need to override these social messages with a personal one: "I have the right to express and enjoy my sexuality in any way I choose, as long as I don't hurt anybody, and my partner has the same right." This leaves matters of sex up to you and your sexual partner to negotiate fairly.

❧ *Today, identify at least two situations when you felt sexually pressured by, or frustrated with, a romantic partner. For each situation, ask yourself how gender-related stereotypes may have contributed to the problem. Be sure to bear in mind not just the other person's responsibility for the problem, but also your own.*

Easing into a time of meditation, I hold this truth: "As long as I don't hurt anybody, I have the right to express and enjoy my sexuality as I choose."

Shedding light on the parts of ourselves that we relegate to the dark is scary. Our "old brain" feels it's dangerous to be ourselves. And the socialization process built a prison for our split off parts. In waking up, we put ourselves in touch with those lost parts behind the prison walls.

It's a painful recontact, and with pain inevitably comes fear. We ask ourselves what will happen if we try to liberate those imprisoned desires and needs. We've come to believe that we must keep these aspects of ourselves walled up if we're going to get along in life. We've learned to live with our losses. Why should we invite trouble now? And, we also fear that, once out of prison, these desires will take over our lives and thrust our carefully created order into chaos. The answer to these fears lies in our innermost heart: we know that we will never be free as individuals unless we first release our lost self from its self-created prison.

&bramble; *Today, review the aspects of your lost self that you identified on Days 215–220. Choose one of these aspects and identify at least two specific ways that you could allow this aspect more freedom in your life during the coming week.*

Drawing hope as I sit in stillness, I relax into the reality that wholeness can be possible only when I free those parts of myself that have been wrongly imprisoned.

Seek not outside yourself, heaven is within.

—MARY LOU COOK

As we develop the practice of regularly withdrawing into our own, inner world—whether it's through prayer, meditation, contemplation, or quiet reflection—we come to realize that we have infinitely deep resources of strength, peace, and hope. It is our most precious and sacred heritage as children of the universe. We were not created to fret over day-to-day events but to transcend them, thereby realizing oneness with the eternal universe. We sense this higher purpose whenever we let go of our transitory cares and realize how rich and wondrous it is simply to be alive.

Returning from this inner world, where we reexperience our connectedness with all creation, back into the chaotic, disorganized outer world of our jobs, homes, and relationships, we are delighted to feel ourselves refreshed and revitalized. For, once we are connected with the joyful tapestry of being, the normal everyday occurrences that would frustrate us and anger us no longer hold the same power. It is not that these everyday occurrences have diminished— but we ourselves have changed. We are calmer, more collected, and therefore all the more peaceful.

❧ *Today, spend a little more time enjoying your inner world. Offer a special prayer to express your thankfulness for life, allow your mind to dwell peacefully for a few moments on one particularly beautiful aspect of your world or devote extra attention to performing the meditation below.*

Today, I enter the stillness and descend more deeply into my core and, resting there, experience the calm that is my essence. From this place I detach myself from the shimmering world of hectic activity and small details.

We can fool ourselves when we're alone, or when we're with people we know how to control, but it's much more difficult to do in our day-to-day lives with an intimate partner. Our Imago match, the one to whom we're most attracted as a potential life-mate, is someone in whom we can't help but see our own denied self. An Imago match possesses the negative qualities or behaviors that *we* possess but do not acknowledge. If we get particularly infuriated by this person's pettiness, vanity, or temper, it may very well be because we, ourselves, have these same traits but won't admit it.

The fact is, we aren't even conscious of having these negative traits until our inevitable struggles with our Imago match bring them to our attention. And this is the wondrous magic of an Imago relationship. By compelling us to take a good look at our denied self and to work out the interpersonal problems that result, our Imago match helps us to heal that self. In short, a miraculous transformation occurs: through becoming one with our Imago, we become whole and healthy as individuals.

❧ *To become more familiar with the characteristics of your Imago, review the list of your denied self traits that you made on Days 230–232.*

As I retreat today, in my twenty minutes of stillness, I open my heart to the realization that what often initially feels bad leads to a richer, fuller awareness.

You want to be loved because you do not love; but
the moment you love, it is finished, you are no longer
inquiring whether or not somebody loves you.

—J. KRISHNAMURTI

Many of us have a hard time with the concept of unconditional love—or, more accurately, unconditional giving. Too often we tend to think in terms of a balance sheet, of *earning* someone's love or having him or her *deserve* ours. It's an economic model, not an emotional one. Unconditional love depends upon *not* keeping accounts. At first hearing, unconditional love sounds like a willingness to love our partners no matter what they do, even if they neglect or abuse us. "I can't agree to that," we react. But that's not really what it means.

Loving our partner unconditionally simply involves giving them what they need without asking for anything *in return*—that is, without rendering a bill for our service. Instead of saying something contractual like, "I'll be nicer to your friends if you'll be nicer to mine," we learn to say something compassionate like, "I'll be nicer to your friends because you need me to get along with them." Rather than strike a cold-hearted deal like, "I'll be quieter when you're studying this afternoon if you'll take me to the movies tonight," we learn to make a warm-hearted offering like, "I'll be quieter when you're studying so that you can concentrate better." In the stock market of life, this kind of investment earns the most interest of all!

&. *Today, think of at least two ways that you can express unconditional love to someone who is close to you (a family member, friend, or lover) during the coming week.*

In my time of meditation today, I imagine I am in a room with a screen depicting images of selfless, unconditional love. Slowly, I experience an insight: "Love does not need an adjective. There is no other kind."

Ultimately, we want people to like us. Only when we feel that we are unlikable or if we have been hurt too often, do we take on a grumbly personality that adopts the adage of hurt or be hurt. Like a mild-mannered sheep shedding a wolf-skin disguise, we can learn how to discard outdated defenses, negative or *acquired* behaviors, so that everyone can see the goodness within us.

In this unit, you'll be identifying negative behaviors that you'd like to start changing, either because you yourself are fed up with them or because they seem to cause trouble with the people you care about. Some of these traits you've already examined in this book: the disliked aspects of yourself that you tend to project onto other people, or the unwanted characteristics that are part of your denied self. Now you'll learn a specific way to change your negative behaviors into positive ones.

❧ *Today, take a few moments to think about one or two situations in past relationships when you behaved badly and wished right away that you could have handled the situation differently. Try especially to recall an incident when you knew that your bad behavior didn't reflect the real you.*

I draw upon my spiritual strength to find the courage to look at my dark side, knowing that it is a source of transformation. I hold this thought as a prayer: "To be whole, I must accept all of me."

*The remarkable thing is that we really love our
neighbor as ourselves: we do unto others as we do
unto ourselves. We hate others when we hate
ourselves. We are tolerant toward others when we
tolerate ourselves.*

—ERIC HOFFER

Consciousness can be painful. Subconsciously, we are driven to find
fault in others, rather than identify it in ourselves; and the negative
traits that are most visible to us in others tend to be the ones that
we don't want to look at in our own behavior. As we learned in an
earlier unit, this pattern of assigning an undesirable or unattractive
quality in ourselves to someone else is called *projection*.

Among all our negative behaviors, projections can be particularly
offensive to other people. On the one hand, we are accusing them of
having a trait that they may not have at all—or, if they do, it's not to
a degree warranting such an emotionally charged attack. On the
other hand, we're infuriating them with our failure to acknowledge
the same trait in ourselves; to them, we're either being hypocritical
or willfully ignorant. In seeking to change our negative behaviors, it's
often best to begin with our negative projections.

ᎧᎧ *Reexamine the projections you identified on Day 127. Try to
think of any other negative traits in yourself that you have a
tendency to project onto others. Keep in mind that the negative
traits you project most are those that have the most energy when
you perceive (or think you perceive) them in others. Then, choose
one of these negative traits that you feel you are ready to
start changing.*

**As I relax today for my twenty minutes of silence, I draw upon the
courage to allow my criticisms of others to be a mirror for myself,
knowing that to see these "faults" in myself is my hope and my salvation.**

Oh wad some power the giftie gie us
To see ourseles as others see us
It wad frae monie a blunder free us.

— ROBERT BURNS

As we've learned earlier in this book, the denied self consists of those negative aspects of ourselves that we deny having—both to ourselves and to others—but that others can see quite readily. Often, people are too polite or too inhibited to bring these traits to our attention. Other times, when people *do* point them out, we simply discredit or ignore what they say.

In some cases, we may dread to admit certain traits because they're ones that we particularly disliked in our parents: a tendency to nag, to be stingy, to hover over people when they're trying to work, or to insist on always being right. In other cases, our self-esteem is simply too invested in *not* having those traits for us to face up to them. We may in fact be cowardly, but we like to think of ourselves as brave. Our profession demands compassion, so we're deaf to our frequently cruel remarks. We're intelligent, college-educated people with open-minded sympathies, so how on earth could we be prejudiced? The process of changing these denied, negative behaviors is the art of truly becoming the good person we already think we are. And, the reality is that it takes much more energy to keep denying those traits we dislike, than owning them once and for all and moving on.

🍃 *Reexamine the "My Denied Self" list of traits you made on Days 230–232. Try to think of any other traits that belong on this list. Then, choose one of them to start changing.*

In my time of quiet, I take the risk today of seeing myself as others see me, knowing that whatever I see through the eyes of others is a part of my total self.

When the evil Mr. Hyde wanted to change into his good alter ego, Dr. Jekyll, all he had to do was drink a special potion. Regrettably, we can't do the same thing to transform our own negative behaviors into positive ones. Virtue doesn't come in a bottle. We have to work toward achieving it, small step by small step, over an extended period of time.

Nevertheless, there *is* something very important we can do to get off to a good start that only takes a few moments. For every negative trait that we possess, we can identify a counteracting positive trait: one that we can aim toward as a goal for our change. The counteracting positive trait that's most appropriate for the situation (or for us as individuals) might be an exact opposite; for example, if we see that we are, in fact, stingy, we could identify "generosity" as our goal; if we're inclined to be impatient, we might choose "patience." Or we might decide on another kind of positive trait, not necessarily an opposite trait, but one that has the effect of ameliorating the negative trait; for example, to counteract "stinginess," we might choose "compassion"; to counteract "impatience," we might choose "tolerance," "agreeableness," or "calmness."

֍ *Title a notebook page "Changing My Negative Behaviors" and write the two negative traits or behaviors that you singled out during the first two days of this unit. Then, identify a counteracting positive trait or behavior for each negative one, using positive language. For example, a counteracting positive trait for "aloofness" might be "warmth."*

Whatever I do that is experienced as negative by others is an attempt to keep myself safe. In my time of meditation today, I open myself to more constructive ways to keep both myself and others safe.

My religion is very simple—my religion is kindness.

—DALAI LAMA

Working toward a positive goal is saying "yes" to ourselves instead
of "no." But how do we go about achieving vague goals like "generosity" or "warmth"? We can break them down into more specific
activities, so that we can visualize them, plan how to do them, and
measure our progress. For example, a person who has "generosity"
as a goal might develop the following list of positive activities:

- I will set aside $25.00 a month to donate to charity.
- I will give Adam my signed football he's so fond of.
- I will be more tolerant of Amy's extravagances.

Whereas a person having "warmth" as a goal might choose:

- I will say hello to people at the coffee shop.
- I will eat lunch in the faculty cafeteria twice a week.
- I will call my sister Louise this week and tell her how much she
  means to me.

However, achieving these goals lies not only within the specific
activities. If we give our football away because we want to be
generous, but ultimately regret the act, then we have not achieved
generosity. The activities we choose in order to cultivate positive
qualities must be done with an open hand and heart.

❧ *On the page in your notebook titled "Changing My Negative
Behaviors," list at least two specific positive activities you can do
toward achieving each of the two positive traits or behaviors that
you identified yesterday. Make sure each activity has some sort
of time frame attached to it.*

**In prayer today, I confess the fears behind my negative traits.
Accessing my deepest self, I turn away from the hurtful ways I have
protected myself and toward positive acts that communicate my
true self.**

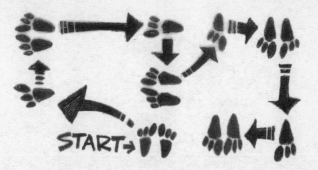

START→

It is normal to feel afraid, foolish, or clumsy when we first begin to practice new behaviors. As we practice, we'll be naturally motivated to continue and the more natural it will seem.

Once we have mastered a few activities that lead to our goal, we should develop other activities right away. Eventually, we'll discover that we're naturally inclined to live in accordance with our target goal. We no longer have to tell ourselves to stay on target, we will simply *be* on target: a person who authentically acts and responds positively rather than negatively.

Also, the more we can involve others, especially intimate others, in our behavior change, the faster and deeper the change will be. By "confessing" our negative traits we help ensure that we will no longer deny these traits or project them onto others, plus we may get some valuable advice. By making such people the beneficiaries of specific activities relating to our positive goal trait, we help guarantee that we'll get some especially gratifying feedback.

❧ *Today, sit back and visualize an imaginary person acting out one of your positive goal traits. When you have an image that's clear and inspirational to you, substitute yourself for that person. Then, spend a few moments watching yourself exhibiting that positive trait.*

I draw upon the power of my imagination and re-create myself in my original image, prior to developing the defenses that now injure my relationships. I meditate on this truth: "Fueled by my spiritual strength, I can make all things new."

We've all observed how some people seem determined to be gloomy no matter how much the sun may be shining. Their house may be lovely, but they complain that it isn't big enough. They admit that they have a good job, but insist that it could be better. Other people, however, seem capable of deriving happiness from the smallest of life's wonders. We each have the power to be one type of person or the other. We can choose to make ourselves miserable or content, regardless of the outside circumstances. When we're struggling with our own specific health, work, home-life, or relationship crises, or when we're faced with some of the more general problems that every single person occasionally faces—loneliness, rejection, self-doubt, and disappointment—we need to remember this inner power and choose wisely how, and who, we want to be.

❧ *Title a page in your notebook "Negative to Positive." On the left-hand side list four complaints that you have about your life. On the right-hand side, list a contrasting positive perspective. For example, if you complain about being bored by all the paperwork in your job, you might counter that complaint by stating how much you value your job security or certain coworkers.*

I am learning that reality is larger than my perceptions, and that I usually globalize my experience. Today, in my time of quiet, I surrender this limited view and allow myself to see from a larger perspective.

*Miracles occur naturally as expressions of love. The
real miracle is the love that inspires them.*
                              — *A COURSE IN MIRACLES*

Like the romantic phase of a relationship, the power-struggle phase
is supposed to end. Those who hang in through the power struggle
will emerge and celebrate with real love's trophy: a passionate partnership.

Passion, that chemistry that makes romance so intoxicating, is the
most striking feature of real love. The Greeks call that passion *eros:*
the fundamental life force, a pulsating energy that, under conditions
of safety, undisturbed by fear, is experienced as a feeling of full
aliveness. When released from the prison built from rigid character
defenses, eros courses through the channels of the wounded self—
healing the hurt places, restoring the body to its full capacity for
sensate experience, softening tightened muscles, enriching starved
feelings, and spurring creativity of thought and action.

The resulting experience is not one of sustained intoxication,
although there are many moments of ecstatic highs, but rather an
ongoing sense of total well-being, a life lived in relaxed joyfulness.
It's a gift of real love, the gift of a world that is altogether a more
physically enjoyable, emotionally satisfying, and spiritually meaningful place.

ᘒ *Today, do something to restore your sense of aliveness. Exercise your body with long lingering stretches, indulge your sensual
craving for chocolate, delight your soul with some favorite poetry.*

In this time of stillness, I imagine myself full of life energy and
radiating with inner peace. I recognize that this image can be my reality.

Our discomfort grows as the stakes get higher. When the relationship starts to intensify, so does each partner's anxiety. A commitment sends the old, "fight-or-flee" brain into panic because it activates the blocked parts of ourselves.

Fear of facing the lost self explains why many couples break up. The terror of giving up the safety of the acceptable, if limited, presentational self explains why many couples have their first serious fight within forty eight hours after their engagement. No longer can we drift along simply complementing each other—serving as each other's lost self. Instead, we get a peek at the work we must do to become whole and to help our partner become whole. It's hard work, to be sure; and a breakup can seem easy by comparison, but the work is well worth it.

  Today, think of a time when you broke up with someone after a relatively lengthy relationship. Ask yourself these questions:
- *What was our last or largest argument about?*
- *Was I suddenly seeing things in my partner I hadn't noticed before?*
- *Was I finding fault with qualities I'd once found attractive in my partner?*
- *Why did it seem harder to stay with this person than to break up?*

During this time of quiet aloneness, I allow the romantic notions of love to fade. As my mind clears, I welcome in the deeply gratifying option of cultivating real love in my life.

*My advice to the women's clubs of America is to
raise more hell and fewer dahlias.*

—WILLIAM ALLEN WHITE

Biases relating to gender exist in all aspects of socialization, but one
of the strongest and most unfair biases involves our early training in
coping with anger. Men are allowed much more latitude to express
their anger. Women under the same conditions are supposed to be
much more demure and compliant, lest they be condemned as
"shrews." Instead of being encouraged to use their anger to show
dominance or mastery, women are trained to hide their anger or
subdue it until it is nothing more than a "complaint."

   Both forms of anger-related socialization—masculine and feminine—do the individual a profound disservice when it comes to
establishing intimate relationships. A man can strike out in anger
before he can process that anger internally; and he can be so turned
off merely by a woman's expression of anger that he's incapable of
sympathizing with her. Alternatively, a woman can suppress anger to
the point of becoming a sour, depressed person. Meanwhile, she's
so overwhelmed by a man's display of anger that she can't help being
afraid and resentful.

❧ *Today, think of your own socialization regarding gender-
appropriate displays of anger: How were you (as a man or a
woman) taught to express anger? How were you taught to
regard—or react to—displays of anger by the opposite gender?*

**In my period of quiet today, I move into a space within that lies
beyond the "rules" of socialization. Tapping into my connection with
the transcendent, I may experience my full richness as a person.**

The effects of change are cumulative. The more we achieve, the faster the process goes, and the more we are motivated to proceed to the next step. At a certain point we will crest the initial steep incline, and then change will proceed at a swifter, more effortless pace. Thanks to their more objective point of view, other people in our life will notice our progress even before we do. In fact, we may first appreciate the extent of our transformation by observing their more positive attitudes and actions toward us. When we realize that our efforts are paying off and that we have changed, we are going to feel very good about ourselves indeed. The energy that had been bound up in our character defenses and used to protect ourselves from hurt will be freed—extra energy for feeling alive—and we will naturally find ourselves moving toward a healthy and healing partner.

❧ *Today, reward yourself for all your efforts at change by doing something that will make you feel good.*

Moving into my center during quiet reflection, I allow myself to simply relax and acknowledge the joy that can be found in this process toward wholeness.

*The pleasure of love is in loving, and we are made
happier by the passion that we experience than by
that which we inspire.*
— DUC DE LA ROCHEFOUCAULD

In order to set in motion a two-way healing between our partner and
ourselves, we must give our love to our partner with no strings
attached. The unconscious mind is not interested in bartering. In the
final analysis, our unconditional love for the other turns out to be the
key to our personal welfare. The ancient Greeks coined the term
agape to describe this kind of love. At that time, it referred specifically
to the best strategy for incorporating conquered tribes into the
commonweal: instead of subjugating these tribes through violence,
the Greeks found it more effective to shift their perspective entirely
and treat them as kinspeople.

As applied to our present-day relationships, agape love involves
ceasing to view the other person as if he or she were an alien being
or a potential threat. Instead, agape views the others as "one of us,"
someone we love as dearly as ourselves. In practicing agape, or
unconditional love, we stretch beyond self to meet the other person's
needs. We do not do this because we want a particular outcome, but
simply because such action *should* be done for no other reason than
to offer love to our partner. Unconditional love is the best and most
productive way to behave.

❧ *Today, do something especially nice for someone you care
about without asking — or expecting — a return.*

I strengthen my inner spirit with this thought: I must view myself
with agape love, just as I must bring my unconditional self to those I
really trust and love.

Hoarding up all of our love until that one special person comes along just doesn't make sense. Life thrives on love. Not only do we need to receive love, but we need to *express* love; and, like a muscle, the more ways we exercise the part of ourselves that loves, the more loving—and lovable—we become. Our sense of safety and belonging in this world increases, and so does our capacity to appreciate the possibilities for beauty and self-fulfillment that lie all around us.

The world today is beset by anxieties. With each passing day, our planet is being exploited more ruthlessly, our cities are turning ever more dangerous, and our far-flung communities are increasingly in danger of losing their heart. If we tap the deep capacity for loving action that exists within us, we, as individuals, *can* make a difference. If we make a loving effort to be less self-absorbed and to reach out to others, we can make an invaluable contribution to the world, as well as to ourselves and our future partner.

❧ *Today, think of one way that you can spread your love out into the world around you. Maybe you can help out a friend in need, join a community group that does charitable work, or make the road that you live on nicer for everyone by cleaning up the litter. In the future, be on the lookout for other opportunities to expand your ability to love.*

Taking twenty minutes of contemplative silence, I visualize my heart opening like the petals of a flower to receive the warming rays of the sun. From this grounded place in my center, I recognize that this is a way to give and receive love.

*We want people to feel with us more than to act
for us.*

—GEORGE ELIOT

Empathy is an indispensable element in any successful relationship
and a key part of intentional dialogue. Unfortunately, we've each had
to develop a certain amount of self-centeredness just to survive our
childhoods and carve an independent life for ourselves. Now, as
adults seeking to connect more meaningfully with others, empathy is
a sensitivity that needs to be cultivated.

In our attempts to be empathic during conversations with other
people, it helps to think of empathy as having two different levels.
First-level empathy communicates that we hear and understand
another's feelings, that we can *imagine* the feelings that he or she
must have. For example, "I can understand why you're upset; I can
imagine that my not calling you made you feel abandoned and angry."
Second-level empathy communicates not only that we hear the
other's feelings, but that we are experiencing his or her feelings
ourselves. For example, "I can feel the pain and hurt you must have
felt when I didn't call."

Second-level empathy requires an extra degree of self-transcen-
dence, a relaxing of our defenses, which makes it more difficult to
achieve than first-level empathy. Our perseverance in trying to reach
the second level however will be an experience of self-expansion. It's
a deeply healing process for a relationship, and it opens us up to a
much wider range of living.

&• *Today, in intentional dialogues with other people, practice
experimenting with first-level empathy and, if you feel capable,
second-level empathy.*

**I access the inner courage necessary to stay true to myself while
being available to participate in the feelings of those I care about.**

A fantasy can be equivalent to a paradise and if the fantasy passes, better yet, because eternal paradise would be very boring.

—JUAN RAMÓN JIMÉNEZ

It can be one of the most discouraging experiences in single life. We meet, date, or, perhaps, even live with a person who is remarkable for having many of the qualities we most often fantasize about: a great sense of humor, a keen mind, an uncanny ability to charm our most cantankerous friends. In fact, this person comes achingly close to our image of the perfect mate, closer than anyone else we've ever known. And yet, when all is said and done, this person doesn't really turn us on.

This is due to the reality that our fantasy of the perfect mate seldom represents the type of person we really need and, therefore, the type of person we're unconsciously programmed to want. He or she does not have that particular combination of positive *and* negative attributes to qualify as our Imago match. Without the grist of negative traits for our mill, we stagnate and cease to grow. We need someone who can help us not only to recover what's missing in our lives, but also to reengage in core struggles and problems so that we can finally resolve them once and for all. We stay involved with a fantasy partner as long as we can, but inevitably we get bored and have to move on to the real business of love: a connection with our Imago match.

❧ *Today, try to recall and jot down a few sentences about a time when you seemingly found the perfect lover or when you had a choice between two or three love interests. Did you wind up choosing what you at first thought was the least ideal candidate?*

In the serenity of this time alone, I make the commitment to shed my fantasies of perfect love. By doing so, I usher in the possibility of real love.

.. I guess what I'm seeing is what happens when power is threatened. I guess I'm seeing what happens to people who challenge the insurance industry. But it is so antithetical to the America that I walk around in that I'm not sure how to relate it to anything...

It's a popular misconception that listening is just a passive, inferior activity: less communicative, less satisfying, and less important than talking. Furthermore, it's easier to fake than talking, at least on a superficial level. If the person we are listening to is not keyed into how receptive we are or aren't being, then it is easy to check out and daydream. Therefore listening doesn't call forth our creative energies as automatically and emphatically as talking does.

How tragic it is that listening is so often devalued, and that we're so lax about developing our listening skills! In fact, listening is an extremely powerful tool in building a better relationship with someone. It not only gives them support and encouragement to draw closer to us, but also gives us valuable insights into the wondrous world that the other person inhabits. Think about how important it is to you that your stories and feelings are received with the proper emotion and enthusiasm. And also think about how upset you become when you receive hard evidence that someone doesn't remember an important conversation or insight you shared with them. We must learn to listen not just with our ears, but with our eyes, our hearts, and our minds. We must be attuned to the other person's body language as well as his or her verbal language. We must keep ourselves keenly receptive to the message behind the words, the meaning behind the acts, and to the feelings behind the thoughts.

❧ *Today be especially conscientious about becoming a better listener through practicing intentional dialogue skills.*

Today, in my twenty minutes of meditation, I hold still and allow myself to practice listening—to my beating heart, my breath, the wind. I make this decision: "I am open to greater messages that come to me."

Self-love, my liege, is not so vile a sin
As self-neglecting.
                                        —WILLIAM SHAKESPEARE

We defend ourselves from love because we are afraid of reactivating the clear, punitive voices of the past, which told us to reject parts of ourselves. Already we hate those aspects of ourselves that our parents rejected when we were growing up: our quick temper, our unrestrained sensuality, our rebellious spirit. Allowing ourselves to love our Imago match inevitably forces us to reconnect with those despised traits, and this exposes us, once again, to the death threat we perceived in our parents' rejection. Our hatred for ourselves prompts our fear that others will hate us too. And yet, to keep our romantic partner's love, we feel we have to keep our self-hatred intact, just as we kept it intact to ensure our parents' love when we were children. It's a self-destructive paradox.

In order to break through this paradox, we need to start loving ourselves more and hating ourselves less. This means developing a new form of behavior with others, especially our romantic partners: *learning to love the hated parts of ourselves that we project onto them.*

🕿 *Today, refamiliarize yourself with the projections you tend to make on people of your own "despised" qualities. Review the projections you identified on Day 127.*

As I make time for twenty minutes of solitude today, I recognize that my future partner will be a mirror, offering me the chance to embrace those aspects of myself I have kept in shadow.

We possess, to some degree, traits that we especially admire in others. Such traits are parts of our disowned self. We reject them either because we're taught to do so by our childhood caretakers or we discovered that they were not acceptable in a social context. A young boy's sensitivity to the pain of others may be discouraged as he's trained by his father, his peers, and his coaches to play sports more aggressively. An adolescent girl winds up dismissing her talent for singing because singing in general isn't particularly valued by her family and friends or because she's led to believe that other people sing so much better. As a matter of fact, children who are strongly discouraged, intimidated, or denied in *any* area of life may develop such a sense of overall inferiority or hopelessness that they downplay many of their virtues.

Disowning parts of ourselves, and then projecting those parts onto others, is ultimately an act of self-betrayal. We idealize movie stars and others in our lives, not realizing that they have qualities that we have repressed in ourselves. But we can't become whole until we own all of our qualities.

❧ *Today, think of at least three famous living people whom you especially admire. What qualities do you like in these people? In what ways might you possess those very same qualities or see them as potentials you might develop in yourself—ones that you're inclined to disown?*

Today, in silence, I surrender my self-betrayal. I watch images on a screen in my mind where I see myself becoming what I admire in others.

*The test for whether or not you can hold a job should
not be the arrangement of your chromosomes.*

—BELLA ABZUG

Our Imago can help put us in touch with our missing contrasexual
traits. Through our Imago, we can connect with qualities and behaviors that we were drawn to as children but were discouraged from
developing because they didn't fit our gender stereotype.

To appreciate this aspect of our Imago, we need to think about all
the ways in which we were forced to conform based on the gender-
related distinction our parents and other powerful people in our lives
taught us to believe. Do any of these clichés seem especially familiar
to you?

- Men are self-reliant; women are dependent on men.
- Women are good at nurturing; men aren't.
- Women like to enhance their appearance; men don't.
- Men enjoy competing with their friends; women don't.
- Women love to make a home for themselves; men don't.

Our attraction to our Imago match compels us to reexamine such
clichés. As we reexamine them, we move away from the dualistic
tendencies that we were taught in childhood. We learn to free
ourselves from narrow definitions of gender identity so that we can
grow as human beings, tapping all our personal sources of aliveness.

&* *Today, think back to a past intense relationship that you had
with a member of the opposite gender. Ask yourself, what specific
traits in this person—traits that are commonly associated with his
or her gender—did I particularly like? How might I go about
incorporating similar traits in my own life? Write your thoughts
down.*

As I move into quiet contemplation today, I relax into the possibilities
that exist beyond stereotypes. I jump over these often destructive
boundaries, allowing myself to freely experience my complexity.

From giggles to guffaws, rib-ticklers to belly-busters, laughing is a fine art and a natural gift. But it can still use cultivating. As young children, we had an amazing repertoire of laughs at our disposal. Our individual ha-ha capabilities were excercised daily, if not hourly!

As we matured, the forces of socialization went about stripping us of our laughing skills, until most of us were left with watered-down belly laughs or self-consciously suppressed giggles. Indeed, we all tend to have one certain way of laughing that we rely upon for most laugh-worthy occasions: our signature laugh for showing that we are happy or having fun. Why not work on enlarging our laughter repertoire to somewhere near its former, and enormously gratifying, size?

𝄪 *Sometime this week do one or more of the following:*
- *Watch a funny movie or comedy act.*
- *Learn several jokes or funny stories and tell them whenever you have an opportunity.*
- *Listen to a canned-laughter tape and join in!*

It is with a feeling of joy today that I move into my twenty minutes of time alone, and rather than seeing this as a time of quiet, I call to mind something that I recently found to be hilarious—allowing myself to laugh out loud.

So much that was beautiful and so much that was
hard to bear. Yet whenever I showed myself ready to
bear it, the hard was directly transformed into
the beautiful.

—ETTY HILLESUM

Feeling fully alive is not possible if we have not properly grieved the people and things we've lost. These losses can take many different forms, including: a friend who moved away, a pet that died, a jilted romance, learning that our parents were divorcing, getting fired from a job, a missed opportunity to travel, a treasured possession stolen from our home, a career choice given up to raise children.

As long as we repress, consciously or subconsciously, the expression of our sadness, the loss will continue to weigh upon our minds, hearts, and souls. It will diminish our capacity for joy and inhibit our ability to be open and responsive to the sources of aliveness all around us. Sadness is an important part of our aliveness process. Grief can be a powerful way to honor the memory of someone we cared about who died. And as we let the healing tears flow, we make room for new heart connections to grow. So it is important for us to learn how to honor and express our sadness. In doing this, we will transform our sadness from something distressing and ugly in our lives to something that's beautiful and sacred.

❧ *Go back through your childhood, adolescence, and adult life and think of at least five losses you have sustained. Which ones still cause moments of painful sadness from time to time?*

Feeling the heaviness of uncried tears, I go within to my strength and allow tears that have kept me attached to people long gone to flow. In so doing, I release all attachments to a past that has ended. I trust this thought: "Whatever I hold from the past prevents me from experiencing the full flow of the present."

How dry eyes can get when they are not allowed
to cry!

                                                          —MARIA AUGUSTA TRAPP

Without sadness, there could be no joy. They are two sides of the
same emotion. The heights we can achieve in our joy, are mirrored
by the depths with which we express and feel our sadness and pain.
Therefore, if we don't allow ourselves to express sadness, we place
limits on our capacity to express joyfulness. When we choke back
our tears, we become emotionally dry. But when we allow our tears
to flow, we oil our ability to feel profoundly on all levels and in turn
experience life in a fluid and alive way.

‌ *Today, try the following exercise for expressing your sadness.*
Choose one of the losses that you identified yesterday that still
cause you pain from time to time. Then, take two chairs. Place
one in front of you and sit in the other. Place the "loss," either an
actual picture or symbolic image, in the chair facing you.

Begin speaking out loud to the loss, addressing this loss as
"you." Put into words all your feelings, how your life has been
positively affected and how much you hurt from this loss. Express
any love or anger you may still be harboring or that you've
developed since that time. If you feel like crying, let the tears well
up. Give yourself the same freedom to moan or pound your fists
or double over.

When you've finished grieving, imagine that you are at a burial
site and you are now going to say a final "good-bye." Imagine the
loss being lowered into the ground and covered with dirt. Visual-
ize the flowers that are placed on the final mound. Then leave the
scene in your imagination.

Death comes in many forms, all of which are transitions to another
reality. Today, in deep contemplation, I accept the deaths of the past
and open myself to a yet undiscovered and unimaginable future.

I saw sorrow turning into clarity.

—YOKO ONO

All past losses follow us into any relationship. And whenever we experience new loss, it dips into the reservoirs of the loss. The more we can solemnize those losses and learn to grieve for them in an appropriate and satisfying way, the less unconscious and unprocessed emotion will erupt as we search for, and enter into, a new relationship.

We may never be able to overcome a loss in the sense that we forget it entirely or cease to think of it without sadness. In many cases, it would be unnatural or unrealistic to expect our sorrow to disappear entirely. For example, we will always miss our departed loved ones and, on occasion, feel some degree of pain that they are gone. Our goal is not to eliminate sadness but to learn to give full and proper expression to it, so that it can be a source of spiritual consolation in our life, rather than a source of agony. Even if we've already buried our loss, literally or imaginatively, sorrow will come back from time to time. When it does, we can revisit the burial site and speak again about our feelings until the memory is no longer charged with such deep sorrow.

ع *Today, focus on a specific loss of someone or something that was dear to you—a loss that you'd like to commemorate in some way, such as the loss of a parent, a beloved pet, an idyllic summer cabin where your family vacationed, or a cherished dream. Then, think of a consoling and inspiring way that you could commemorate that loss sometime this week: a special hour spent looking at photographs, writing a journal entry, revisiting a "sacred" place, or performing some activity that relates to your loss or sadness.*

In the quiet of meditation today, I celebrate the past that was, and feeling my fullness, I claim the joy that will give birth to tomorrow.

*When marrying, one should ask oneself this
question: Do you believe that you will be able to
converse well with this woman into your old age?*

—FRIEDRICH NIETZSCHE

Partners in a conscious relationship accept each other's absolute separateness as individuals, each other's unique way of perceiving reality, and the sacredness of each other's inner world. Becoming part of a committed couple does not mean becoming invisible as a person. It means the opposite: having one's identity confirmed and strengthened by a partnership based on respect, mutuality, and unconditional love.

Conscious partners are people who work together in harmony, functioning as equals. To sustain this kind of cooperative love, they rely on their intentional dialogue skills. They take turns mirroring each other's worlds, validating each other's experience, and empathizing with each other's feelings. Only this type of open and caring dialogue carries them through the worst crises and allows them to savor the best of times.

&. *Today, concentrate more on using intentional dialogue skills in your conversations with at least three people.*

Today, in my time of quiet contemplation, I ponder the paradox of the absolute separateness and uniqueness of each human being and my assumption that others know what I need and want. I make a decision to live in relationship, rather than fusion, and choose to learn and use dialogue.

Confronting the negative or problematic parts of ourselves—such as our childhood wounds, our lost self, our denied self, or our contrasexual self—goes against the grain, but it also goes against the socialization that produced these problems. We've been conditioned by society in general, and modern psychology in particular, to look always on the bright side of things, to have what is technically known as "unconditional positive regard."

All too many people, however, disparage themselves unmercifully. Perhaps because of this self-punishing extreme, it is common today to address personal healing only from the upbeat side, inundating ourselves with affirmations and self-love, while simultaneously pushing aside the hard-to-face negatives. This "all good and nothing but the good" approach is potentially dangerous, for the denial of our shadow side encourages further internal splits in the psyche. The surface may look happy and bubbly, but in the depths below, the negative parts of ourselves are seething and boiling.

We cannot truly heal ourselves consciously until we clear away the shaky foundation of self-hatred. Covering up this foundation with a brittle veneer of ersatz self-esteem only increases our underlying anxiety. We have to see the negative *and* the positive—equally well and at the same time—in order to work toward wholeness.

❧ *Today, think of at least three negative aspects of yourself that you have identified through working with this book. Then, for each negative aspect, identify a positive aspect of yourself that might help you to deal with it.*

During my quiet time alone, I visualize myself embracing with love and acceptance those parts of myself that I have abandoned and denied.

Do you ever look up at clouds in the sky and try to identify various images in their fleecy twists and turns, bulges and tucks, lights and shadows? Do you ever linger to watch in delight as one cloudy image slowly evolves into another and another and another—as if you were witnessing Nature's very own stream of consciousness? Children are instinctively drawn to cloud watching, and for good reason. It not only stimulates their highly active imaginations, it also reconnects them with the living universe to which, as infants, they so recently felt more bound. Within each of us, this child still exists. Even though we are now adults, we can derive the same spiritual exercise and pleasure by looking up toward the clouds in the sky and freeing our minds to dream. In doing so, we transcend our earthbound concerns and experience once again the fluid, vital force that moves throughout creation and that fuels our innermost lives.

❧ *Today—or the very next day that the sky is filled with inspirational clouds—spend several minutes gazing at the clouds and imagining shapes in them.*

Today as I relax into the safe place, I free my mind from all fixed images and allow my imagination to soar. I savor this truth: "I am as free as I can imagine."

Perhaps it was right to dissemble your love,
But—why did you kick me down stairs?

— JOHN PHILIP KEMBLE

We can be so afraid of love, or so out of touch with how to express our love, that we unconsciously go about sabotaging it. When it crops up in our life, our immediate reflex is to mow it down, as if it were an offending weed.

How do we do it? We may tease our dates unmercifully, ignoring their pleas for us to stop, until finally they run away for their own safety. We may test their commitment to us by behaving in unreasonable ways: such as constantly being late, expecting them to be more intimate than the early stage of the relationship warrants, or by letting our emotions blow hot and cold. Or we may play the "gotcha!" game with them, penalizing them for not anticipating our desires, competing with them to gain more attention at parties, or trying to second-guess their every move and motive.

How do we stop doing it? First, by being truthful with ourselves and becoming more conscious of the specific, negative behaviors that we're inclined to inflict on the people we care about. Second, by replacing those behaviors with the relationship skills and communication tools that we're learning in this book. In this way, we can be sure to cultivate those plants that will blossom into the flower of lasting love, while weeding out those that choke our vibrating life force.

&❧ *Today, identify two of your own negative "love" behaviors that alienate others—thoughtlessness, impulsiveness, or other inexplicable things that you're inclined to do. Ask yourself, how could I keep myself from doing this? What relationship skill could I utilize instead?*

In quiet time today, I make the commitment to identify those ways in which I may be unconsciously preventing love from flowering.

If we're ever going to grow as individuals and as lovers, we need to challenge ourselves. We need to aim high, perhaps higher than we think we can manage, rather than sticking with what we *know* we can get away with.

What does this mean on a day-to-day level? At work, we should try to do the best job we can, rather than merely an acceptable job. When we get home, we should resist the temptation to collapse on the couch with the remote control and a bag of corn chips, and use our time more creatively. We should make an effort to talk to people who interest us, rather than shying away as we usually do. Instead of telling ourselves that the extremely attractive person we just met is way out of our dating league, we should ask for a date.

Life and love call for the best we have to give, no matter how scary that may seem. If we play it safe and offer very little, then very little is what we'll get in return.

❧ *Today, think of one way that you can challenge yourself: at work, at home, or with other people. Then, take the challenge!*

As I move into quiet time today, I allow myself to tap into the wellspring of excitement that is teeming at my core. I recognize that fear is the volume control, keeping me from hearing the many wonderful sounds of being fully alive.

One's own self is well hidden from one's own self: of all mines of treasure, one's own is the last to be dug up.

—FRIEDRICH NIETZSCHE

We're often attracted to people who possess qualities we unconsciously admire but didn't develop in ourselves because they were dismissed or disdained by our childhood caretakers. When we first start getting close to such people, we feel better about ourselves, more complete through the association. We never cry at the movies, perhaps, but we enjoy going to the movies with our best friend who sobs through the sentimental scenes. Or we're the type of person who is always seeking compromises, temporizing judgments, and trying to understand both sides of an issue, but we feel oddly liberated in the presence of a cousin who has strong opinions and takes firm stands.

What this strange attraction is telling us is that we have a desire and a need to change—to stretch ourselves to accommodate lost or disowned aspects of our identity. It isn't easy. In fact, the very same traits that we admire in others can, in time, become major causes of our dissatisfaction with them, because we cannot accept in others for very long what is forbidden in ourselves. Nevertheless, we must acknowledge that these traits are calling us to go where we've never been before.

❧ *Today, identify at least two examples of people to whom you are/were attracted to because they possess/ed a specific trait that was discouraged by your childhood caretakers. For each example, ask yourself: "In what ways does/did my association with this person help me develop that trait? In what respects do I still need to develop that trait?"*

I never cease to wonder at how many ways I am called to my wholeness. As I relax into my quiet place today, I listen to the voice of admiration, knowing: "I am potentially what I affirm in others."

*The interval between the decay of the old and the
formation and the establishment of the new,
constitutes a period of transition, which must always
necessarily be one of uncertainty, confusion, error.*
                                        —JOHN C. CALHOUN

Deep down, human beings are drawn to habitual activities that
provide the illusion of security. This poses a major stumbling block
when we try to learn new skills and behaviors so that we can lead a
more dynamic and fulfilling life. However dull, difficult, or unre-
warding our present life may be, we're familiar with it, and that fact
alone can make us reluctant to do anything that might disturb it.

Even if we feel that change will do us good and know precisely
what's necessary to effect that change, we have to psych ourselves
up to take each scary plunge. We'll inevitably make mistakes, and
these mistakes often reinforce our belief that change is scary—but
they are necessary stumbling blocks on the way to wholeness. In the
end, we'll have a vastly improved life—and we'll marvel that we ever
hesitated to bring it into being.

❧ *Today, create some self-motivation! On a page in your notebook entitled "Good Reasons to Change," list at least five things
about your present single life that you don't like, leave one or two
lines blank after each entry. Then, in the space you left, write
down what you would like, as a positive alternative, in your
partnership future. For example, you might write, "I'm often
depressed during evenings at home." A positive alternative might
be: "I would like someone with whom I could do fun things
during evenings at home."*

In the safety of this time alone, I use the strength at my core to help
me access the fear I have about change. I hold this truth: "Change is
a necessary stage of evolution that can usher in gratifying results."

Do you like being thanked or admired in front of others who are special to you? Chances are good that you do and that you wish it would happen more often. Consider, therefore, how much other people may enjoy it if you are thoughtful enough to praise them when the two of you are with friends or family members.

When we call public attention to something nice that the other person has done for us or to an especially positive quality that he or she possesses or to the overall importance that he or she has in our life, our kind action is doubly meaningful. Not only does it demonstrate to the object of our praise just how sincerely we value them, but it also helps to spread joy and positive regard among the entire circle of people around us. We should certainly be careful not to embarrass the other person by being too effusive ("You're just the sweetest person on earth!"), too intimate ("I want everyone to know how hot you were last night!"), or too manipulative ("Let's all give three cheers for the hero!"). But we should be even more careful not to let golden opportunities for public praise pass us by.

❦ *Today, think of at least two opportunities you might have in the near future to acknowledge publicly your gratitude or admiration for someone who is close to you.*

Today, I hold this spiritual thought: "What I give out eventually comes back to me. In this quiet time, I decide what I want to come to me."

Within the past thirty years we have born witness to a sexual revolution. Talk about sex has come out of the closet and onto the airwaves. Birth control and sex education are widely accepted and readily available. And premarital sex is the norm, rather than the exception, for both genders.

We need to create our own, internal sexual revolution, one that is not only personally liberating, but ethical as well. To enact this liberation, we need to create a new sexual identity for ourselves. We must consciously refuse to follow gender-related sex stereotypes and roles that stand in the way of our truest sexual enjoyment and fulfillment. We must try to give expression to those sexual aspects of ourselves that we've been socialized to repress. We must be willing to experiment and play with sex, but we must also be willing to work and challenge ourselves. Above all, we must value ourselves, others, and sex enough to strive toward building the best possible kind of relationship—one that allows us to grow in physical *and* emotional intimacy with an equally free and responsible partner. That is real sex education.

🍂 *Today, review the sexual relationship vision that you created on Days 269–274. Start your own sexual revolution by recommitting yourself to this vision.*

In wordless prayer, I move into the sensuality radiating at my core. Here, I commit myself to creating an internal revolution of awareness and trust with which to express my sexuality.

*It is easier to live through someone else than to
become complete yourself.*

— BETTY FRIEDAN

We can't know true happiness in a relationship—or, for that matter, true happiness as individuals—until we recover and rehabilitate our lost self. Only then will we be fully integrated and capable of experiencing personal fulfillment.

It's tempting to try to dodge the difficult work of self-integration by living through our romantic partners. We talk about *possessing* them or *being possessed* by them because we like to feel that they actually *are* part of us. If we're shy around new people and our partner isn't, we can depend upon our partner to bring new people into our world. If we find it very hard to express negative feelings such as sadness or fear, we can let our partner be sad or fearful for us. If we find it difficult to make decisions, we can foist that task onto our partner. Unfortunately, this strategy just doesn't work in the long run. We need to stop searching outside ourselves for what we need in terms of self-development. For if we continue with this pattern, we will shadow our opportunity for real love with codependency.

We must respect the truth told by every inspirational story from King Arthur's search for the holy grail to *The Velveteen Rabbit:* The secret to personal wholeness lies within us. We are the ones who must bring it to consciousness.

🍂 *Identify some of the favorite stories, myths, or legends you had as a child. What did they teach you about becoming a wiser, happier, more fulfilled human being?*

Today, I commit to developing those aspects of myself that I have usually foisted onto others in my life, and I offer this prayer: "That which is worth cultivating, I must cultivate within myself."

Play is the exultation of the possible.

—MARTIN BUBER

Through play, kids can experiment with ideas, explore emotions, and master skills in a safely controlled environment. It's their job to play if they're going to live a satisfying life, and they take to that job with gusto!

As adults, we would do well to indulge in play with a like spirit from time to time. It can do wonders to rekindle our sense of aliveness and to put us back in touch with parts of ourself that we've lost, disowned, or covered over. But how do we get over our inhibitions?

One way is to approach the challenge in an adultlike manner. We can draw up a plan of possibilities and then work to make some of those possibilities happen! Another way is to visit an amusement park or carve out an afternoon and go to the nearest Toys "R" Us. If you feel embarrassed about being in a toy store, pretend that you are there shopping for a niece or nephew—no one has to know you're actually shopping for your own child within!

🙋 *Today, title a page in your notebook "Play Plan" and divide it into thirds horizontally. Subtitle the first third "games and activities," and list the ones that most appeal to your sense of play (sports, card games, board games, party games, sketching, dancing, singing, etc.). Subtitle the middle third "places," and list specific places that might provide interesting play sites. Subtitle the last third "people," and list specific people in your life who might be interested in becoming playmates. Then, play around with your three lists and start making some connections!*

It was long ago that I "put away childish things," thinking that was part of growing up. As I enter the quiet place within today, I reconsider that decision and ponder this thought: "The ability to play without conflict is an indication of becoming an adult."

It takes a great deal of sheer effort to reach the paradise of real love, but once there, a miraculous change occurs. Spontaneous behaviors replace intentional efforts. It is not necessary to remind ourselves of our partner's needs, because we are motivated out of sheer joy and understanding to express our care automatically, in specific actions.

And the most remarkable thing of all is that our core relationship difficulties seem to simply dissolve. The grueling struggle for wholeness is now in the past; working together becomes a joy. Our partner's needs dissipate along with our own, and we find ourselves in a partnership that feels heavenly. Laughter is abundant, the humdrum dailiness of life takes on deeper meaning, pillow talk is tender and intimate, orgasms easy and plentiful. There's no more walking on eggshells, because we're home where we belong. Expectations of pleasure give way to *experiencing* pleasure. Instead of desiring our partner to meet our needs, we *value* our partner's sheer presence in our lives. The future has arrived to replace the past. Paradise has been regained.

❧ *Today, restore your energies for the hard work of change. Do something relaxing, playful, or celebratory. Treat yourself to lunch at a favorite restaurant, invite a good friend over for a game of cards, go to a funny movie.*

As I sink into the sacred depths of my being, I celebrate the joy in knowing that a conscious partnership with real love can hold more for me than the sum of all fairy tales combined.

The person who makes a success of living is the one who sees his goal steadily and aims for it unswervingly. That is dedication.
—CECIL B. DEMILLE

Knowing the details of our Imago portrait shows us more clearly what our self-completion issues are. It indicates where change and modification are necessary and pinpoints how that can be accomplished. If we are able to reclaim some of our split-off parts while we are still single, we will not need to seek those parts quite so desperately in another person. If we can begin to get some of the nurturing and validation we need to heal our childhood wounds while we are still single (for example, by conducting more conscious relationships with our friends and relatives), we will diminish the intensity of our negative Imago traits. There will be less emptiness to fill up, fewer needs to torment us and our future partner, and a reduced tendency to fight, flee, panic, or play dead when problems arise. When we do find ourselves in relationship, we will have fewer power struggles and we will have curbed some of the tendencies that we might have unconsciously used to sabotage the relationship. The Imago will literally mutate and will become a picture of someone who, like us, is a bit more emotionally developed and well-rounded. We will fall in love with a healthier person. And a healthier person will fall in love with us.

❧ *Today, review your Imago portrait. Identify at least two positive traits in this portrait that you can begin to cultivate in yourself during the next week, so that you won't so desperately need to find them in another person.*

Unlike a river whose flow is determined by its geography, I can choose my course. In my moments of quiet today, I visualize myself overcoming all resistances and reaching my full potential.

If we're intent upon establishing an intimate and lasting relationship with another person, we need to start practicing the art of *thoughtfulness* right now with the important people in our lives. Among other things, this means keeping mentally alert for clues about what interests and concerns them and then going one step further to make mental notes about our discoveries. For example, if a favorite uncle happens to mention that he likes jazz music, we should take care to stash this detail in our "potential birthday gift" file. If a close friend talks about her hatred for onions, we should work this revelation into our long-term memory, so that we don't wind up serving her onion stew for dinner. If a date confides in us a preference for quiet evenings of togetherness at home, we should take heed, or we may seriously upset this person with our surprise night out at a jam-packed disco.

Cultivating thoughtfulness is a wonderful way to express appreciation to those we value in our lives. And we will be paid back in kind for the thoughtfulness we show to others.

🍃 *Over the next three days, pay especially close attention to what a person close to you says or does, in case he or she reveals something that it would be thoughtful of you to remember. As others offer insights, take the time to write them down so you can review and act on them later.*

In my safe place today, I choose to release my self-absorption and tune my ears and heart to the needs and yearnings of others, seeing them as a sacred trust and as an opportunity to practice loving.

Plans get you into things but you got to work your way out.

—WILL ROGERS

Careful planning is an indispensable part of getting things done well, but let's not forget that the actual *doing* of those things is a far more important part. Over the past year, we've figured out all sorts of occasions for experiencing more aliveness, using intentional dialogue, expressing our anger, making behavior-change requests, finding our lost self, owning up to our denied self, and changing our negative behaviors. But how many occasions have passed us by without our having put into action all that we've figured out?

We shouldn't dwell on lost opportunities or wallow in self-blame. But we should look back with a clear, calm mind and assess just how often we practice what we know to be right. Only in this way can we cultivate the awareness necessary to enable us to use these tools.

❧ *Today, look closely at the past month, and, for each of the skills listed below, rate how often you've applied the skill on the following scale: 1 = never; 2 = once or twice; 3 = several times; 4 = many times. If you can only rate a particular skill "1" or "2," give yourself a practice "boost" by reviewing the unit in this book that discusses it.*

- *Experiencing more aliveness: Days 28–31.*
- *Using intentional dialogue: Days 35–38, 57–59, and 82–85.*
- *Making behavior-change requests: Days 146–151.*
- *Finding my lost self: Days 215–220.*
- *Owning up to my denied self: Days 230–232.*
- *Changing my negative behaviors: Days 300–305.*

In this time of reverential stillness, I recognize that there are many opportunities to use the tools I am cultivating. I ponder this truth: "An often used tool becomes an ally on my journey toward wholeness."

Changing long-established patterns can be difficult and frustrating, and the results of all this effort and discomfort are not immediately apparent. It isn't like buying a new suit or learning some sure-fire jokes or radically changing our hairstyle. In fact, it is hard to monitor change in oneself because the slow process of becoming whole happens in such subtle, day-by-day increments.

We are so used to seeing ourselves in a certain way that we often overlook the initial effects of the work that we are doing. From our point of view, it often seems as though the outside world has changed, rather than ourselves. We are mystified by our boss's apparent change of heart toward us and speculate that her home life is happier or she got a raise, when, in fact, it may be our more positive attitude toward the job or our newly acquired skills in being relaxed with who we are. We are delighted at the lucky turn in our dating fortunes—our dates are more interesting, they like us better, and we like them better—when in fact, it's not luck, but the fruits of our hard labors to change ourselves and develop greater sensitivity to, and appreciation of, other people—and ourselves!

  Today, take a break from worrying about whether—and how—you've improved over the past year. Instead, celebrate the present! Think about all the things that you enjoy in your life right now.

During this time of solitude, I allow myself to acknowledge the slow yet profound changes that are taking place inside of me.

> *How could a man live at all if he did not grant*
> *absolution every night to himself and all his fellows?*
> — JOHANN WOLFGANG VON GOETHE

In moments of sorrow, sleeplessness, or soulful reflection, have you ever tortured yourself by dwelling on the many ways that you've hurt other people, intentionally or not? It happens occasionally to all of us. Maybe we still feel sorry about gossiping behind a friend's back, conspiring to get ahead of a colleague at work, hurting a family member's feelings during an angry tirade, or breaking vows of loyalty or love to a former romantic partner.

Whatever we may have done to the other person, we are now hurting ourselves as well, dwelling on our regret and, in the process, perpetuating our sense of self-failure and self-unworthiness. If we haven't already made amends to the other person through confession and apology, it might help us to overcome our obssesive regret if we did so. But whether we have or haven't, can or cannot, we must go ahead and forgive *ourselves* for these acts, promising ourselves that we will make a conscious effort to do better in the future. For in the process of forgiveness, we allow ourselves to experience our humanity, and as we become more adept at forgiving ourselves, it becomes easier for us to forgive others.

🍃 *Today, recall at least three ways that you have hurt others in the past—episodes that still bother you today. Then, forgive yourself for each episode and promise to do better in the future. Also, if you haven't apologized to these people already, and if you don't feel too uncomfortable about the prospect, consider doing so now.*

In my place of safety and quiet today, I surrender my regrets through self-forgiveness, giving up the magical fantasy that my suffering will undo my wrongs.

Two people working to build a conscious relationship accept all of each other's feelings, especially anger. They realize that anger is an expression of pain, and this pain usually has its roots in childhood. They try never to burst out spontaneously with anger or frustration in front of each other, for they know that "dumping" negative feelings is destructive. They don't waste time thinking up devious ways to hurt the other person. Instead, they develop constructive and imaginative ways to process their anger and other negative emotions, and they help their partner to do the same.

When we learn to express our anger in appropriate ways, the energy behind that anger can be channeled into passion and bonding. Otherwise, whether our anger is justified or not, we wind up hurting our partner, ourselves, and our relationship.

🌢 *Today, refamiliarize yourself with the techniques you learned for expressing anger more effectively (Days 136–139).*

Today, I enter my safe place, and breathing deeply and relaxing more deeply still, I allow myself to feel the intensity of my rage, recognizing it as my life force protecting itself from death. With deep wonder, I ponder the truth that this energy can create passion or destroy relationships. I choose to transform all my anger into passion.

Love has to be learned, but we can't learn it from books, not even this one. It's something we must teach ourselves, because we have to transcend the specific instinctual impulses, negative behaviors, and emotional conflicts that stand in the way of our personal quest for love.

Learning to love takes courage, imagination, and, more than anything else, practice—right now, with anyone we're close to, such as our family members, good friends, and steady romantic interests, and, eventually, with the one special person with whom we establish a committed relationship. Practicing love means making active efforts to express love, to put love into motion. It doesn't mean sitting back and waiting for love to happen on its own, nor does it mean making mechanical stabs at being "nice" so that one receives love in return. Instead, it's a matter of seeking better communion with other people and caring about their welfare so that we can transcend the self-absorption and separateness of our own lives and renew our connection to the universe.

🍠 *Today, recall at least three specific moments when you have successfully shown love to other people and made their welfare as important as your own: family members, good friends, lovers. Try to remember exactly what happened and how you felt. Bask in these good memories.*

In quiet today, I open my heart to the courage to love, knowing this: "Only by loving can I become whole."

*Love is a choice — not simply, or necessarily, a
rational choice, but rather a willingness to be present
to others without pretense or guile.*

—CARTER HEYWARD

So what is this thing called love? Here's a "Vision of Love" that can
serve as a definition.

First, love is an *attitude* that gives value to the other person
independent of any value they have for us personally. This means
that the other person does not exist just for our benefit and their
value is not determined by an accounting of what they do or do not
do. They are given existence by the universe, and their presence in
our life is a gift, freely bestowed by their choice.

Second, love is a *behavior* that expresses that attitude at all times
during the relationship, not just when the other person meets our
needs. And it endures even when the other person is a source of
frustration. In fact, it can grow in times of conflict and tension over
our differences, not just in good times and delightful feelings.

Third, love is a *commitment* to the total welfare of the other
person, including their emotional healing, psychological growth, and
spiritual evolution, and this gift is bestowed without conditions. This
means that the other person is always safe in our presence and their
existence is at the center of our consciousness.

≥• *Right now, repeat this "Vision of Love" out loud, so that you
can literally hear the words in your head.*

**In deep silence today, I ponder this truth: "Love is something you *do*
no matter how you *feel*."**

Love doesn't just sit there, like a stone, it has to be made, like bread; re-made all the time, made new.

—URSULA K. LE GUIN

It's not enough to know what love *is*. We also have to know what love is *not*. It is not just a feeling, which means we have to detach it from the many emotions that are associated with romance, sexual ecstasy, self-gratification, and obsession. Love is also not a static state of being. It is an organic process that must be continuously nourished, intentionally kept alive, if it is to thrive into its fullness. Real love comes after our emotions have had their play—and real love is a foundation that makes it safe for us to feel the variety of our emotions. In a conscious relationship, feelings of appreciation and joy accompany love, but they are not its substance.

Part of tending love in our lives, and thereby giving it substance, involves training our minds to know what love really is, and to look for nothing less. By actively visualizing moments of love that we've experienced, and by repeatedly verbalizing a specific "Vision of Love," we can help love come to pass.

୬ *Today, make a commitment to practice visualizing moments of love (as you did the first day of this unit) and verbalizing the "Vision of Love" (as you did yesterday) once a day for three days, beginning with today. Set a few minutes aside at a regular time each day to do this. In the future, you may want to perform this activity on a weekly or monthly basis, or whenever you feel the need to get your bearings again.*

Today, as I enter the silence, I visualize love as a plant, growing in the sunshine of my care. As I water it with my attention, I can see it growing and its blossoms open. I become aware that this plant is in my heart.

Once more upon the waters, yet once more!

—LORD BYRON

Many of us get discouraged with dating because often we find ourselves bored on dates. Fairy tales offer exciting stories of instantaneous love, being swept off of our feet, and riding away into the sunset. We wait to be transported into this dreamworld and become disappointed when our date remains a frog.

The reality is that fairy tales lack substance. Though it takes more work and an unwavering commitment, real love is the combination of reality and dream. It is the answer to our hopes, yet is also the firm foundation from which our personal and spiritual renewal is born. We need to break the bubble and banish the ethereal fairy tale so that we can buckle down to our commitment to find real love.

This doesn't mean kissing every frog we find. But it does mean finding the best in each frog and using our dates to move us ahead in our own process. By bringing your Imago techniques to your dates, you can transform a boring movie and humdrum dinner into an enriching evening for you both. In this way, every date you have becomes more meaningful and enjoyable. By practicing your skills, you keep the end in sight during every date and offer yourself a chance for growth. Your frog may never turn into a prince—or princess—but what you may find is a really good friend!

🐸 *Look back over all the units in this book and choose two of the realtionship skills you've learned. Promise yourself that you will try out these skills on your next date.*

During this time of contemplation, I recognize that creating relationship requires more than sitting back and waiting for the other person to fill my empty spaces. I hold this truth: "Every relationship is a chance to take another step on my journey toward wholeness."

Romantic love is not at all what it appears to be. The notion that we love other people for themselves, just as they are, with their peculiar needs and quirks, is an illusion. We are in love with the projection of our lost self and with the expectation of what our beloved can give us through association.

The Imago bond creates a spurious wholeness. Having a partner who is confident, generous, or calm under pressure is not the same as having those qualities ourselves. Inevitably, our attempt to get through another person what is missing in ourselves never works.

Romantic love is a time bomb. It carries within it the mechanism for its own destruction. It is *supposed* to shatter, for it is only an attachment and *not* real love. When it does, we are left with reality— and a unique opportunity to work through power struggles with our partner to achieve a genuine, lasting love relationship, one which helps both us and our partner to become whole individuals together.

❞ *Today, refamiliarize yourself with the qualities you identified as your lost self qualities on Days 215–220. These are the qualities that you will seek in another during the romantic stage of love and that you can ultimately develop in yourself through a committed, real-love relationship.*

Breathing deeply, I relax and enter the sacred stillness today. I marvel at the truth that what attracts me most in the other is a mirror of what is most undeveloped in myself. I decided to become what I love.

*I love you no matter what you do, but do you have
to do so much of it?*
                                          —JEAN ILLSLEY CLARKE

When we're in love with someone, we enjoy letting our romantic
fantasies and tender feelings run wild. The sheer fact that we don't
have to be as emotionally controlled around our lover as we are
around other people is exhilarating. Unfortunately, we often wind up
having the same lack of inhibition in regard to our critical impulses.
Whenever we're upset or dissatisfied, we lash out. Sometimes, we
get into this blaming mode just because we're feeling generally
cranky. Since misery loves company, we stand ready to let all the
little criticisms that come to mind simply run out of our mouths.

Whenever we feel the urge to blame or criticize someone we care
about, we should take it as a signal to *stop!* Then, we should examine
our complaint more closely. Criticism is the adult version of crying
and whining. Unconsciously, we're inflicting pain in a childish effort
to get our needs met. We fault others for not being perfect, for not
intuiting what we want. To build a more conscious relationship, we
should first identify the need behind our criticism and then convey
that need through a behavior-change request.

❧ *Today, identify one particular criticism you harbor about
someone close to you. How could you translate that criticism into
a behavior-change request? Once you've made that translation,
consider actually approaching the other person with the behavior-
change request sometime during the coming week.*

**I am amazed how committed I sometimes seem to be to holding on to
my frustrations and complaining rather than asking directly for what
I want. In my moments of quiet reflection today, I choose to take joy
in the satisfaction of desire rather than to take satisfaction in the
expression of frustration.**

Convictions are more dangerous enemies of truth than lies.

—FRIEDRICH NIETZSCHE

As we grow up, we develop a set of beliefs about how the world and, more specifically, about how families and relationships work. These beliefs help us create order, explain discord, and assuage our fears.

These beliefs come in many forms: "The best thing to do when I'm scared or angry is to withdraw into myself." "If I flatter and flirt with people enough, I'll get what I want." "I can only get what I want if I take it." The more troubled the family, the tighter we cling to our beliefs to preserve our sense of safety and belonging in the face of conflicting messages and emotional turmoil. Embedded in stone within our minds, they serve as secure models for our day-to-day thoughts and behaviors, giving us the mental and emotional stability we long for.

But however useful these beliefs may be in a stressful environment, their rigidity has to be examined, challenged, and tempered. If we're ever going to find and build effective relationships as adults, we must weed through our "convictions" and update our beliefs to fit the changing world we find ourselves in.

Throughout the coming day, consider how your own convictions—fixed beliefs you developed as a child—are influencing your thoughts and behaviors. Can you catch yourself behaving just as you used to behave when you were a child? Can you hear yourself actually make a statement that reflects one of your "inert ideas"?

Today, in my twenty minutes of silence, I see the area of myself that has become stagnant, and visualize a cool breeze ruffling through the murky waters, allowing myself to transcend my beliefs.

When considering partners we must be cautious about making a commitment to someone who isn't aware of his or her own self-completion issues. But more important, we must look for someone who is willing to grow and change. We may not have much choice about whom we are attracted to, thanks to our Imago, but we *can* choose to remain only with someone who wants and values a conscious partnership. It's hard to make this determination when we're blinded by romantic illusions.

But at some point, we must assess our prospective mate's desire and ability to be conscious. The person we're assessing doesn't have to be *equally* motivated or fluent in the language of self-development. He or she just needs to be ready and able to change to a somewhat *similar* degree. In relationships that succeed, it often happens that one person will do significantly more work than the other person for a while, but the other person must catch up eventually. We need to remember this law of human nature: Just as our character defenses have to change for us to heal our partner's wounds, our partner's character defenses have to change before *we* can be healed.

❧ *Consider your past romantic relationships. For each relationship, ask yourself: How much was my partner willing and able to work toward change and growth, compared to me? Write your answers down.*

Today, as I enter into the deep place where God dwells, I recognize the beautiful symmetry created by partners who are willing to be consciously aware of healing their own and each other's wounds.

*If we make our goal to live a life of compassion and
unconditional love, then the world will indeed become
a garden where all kinds of flowers can bloom
and grow.*

— ELISABETH KÜBLER-ROSS

When we achieve a real love relationship, something glorious occurs
that is far greater than our personal healing or the healing of our
partner. Through these healings, nature as a whole comes closer to
completing itself. We are all a part of the tapestry of being. What
happens to one thread affects the whole. When we are in pain, our
woundedness is felt throughout nature. When we are healed, nature's
pain is assuaged.

Today, nature is in extreme travail due to human insensitivity,
thoughtlessness, and suffering. Wounded ourselves, we have become
nature's wounders. We are polluting the land, the sea, and the air.
We are decimating the plants and the animals. Fortunately, hope still
exists, for we are not only a thread in the tapestry of nature, we are
nature's apex. Because nature has equipped our brain with a frontal
lobe—and with it the capacity for self-awareness and self-knowledge—we have as well the potential for self-correction. We are that
part of nature through which it knows itself and, therefore, through
which it can repair itself. By learning to develop a conscious love that
restores ourselves and our partners to our original wholeness, we
become more capable of helping to heal the universe.

☙ *Today, identify at least three specific and doable ways in which
you could help to make the natural world around you a better,
healthier place.*

**I see all of life and nature as being inextricably woven together, so
that when one thread is pulled, all others grow taught. I offer this
prayer: "May the thread that I am add to the weave of healing."**

*Inside you there's an artist you don't know about.
. . . Say yes quickly, if you know, if you've known
it from before the beginning of the universe.*

—JALAI UD-DIN RUMI

There are many aspects of ourselves that we don't realize until we
see those same aspects in the people who are close to us. The
characteristics of our disowned self can fall into this category: the
positive attributes that we possess but do not consciously acknowledge until another person somehow brings them to our attention.

When we're attracted to another person's way with words, for
example, we must consider whether we ourselves also have a similar
verbal capability but just don't give ourselves credit for it. Perhaps
the other person will actually let us know that we *do* have this
capability. Alternatively, maybe we never bothered to develop our
latent verbal talents but, instead, chose to focus our efforts on some
other aspect of our identity that received more support from the
people who surrounded us during our childhood: our athletic skills,
our handiness with tools, or our capacity to be silent and take
direction. In this case, perhaps the other person's facility with the
language will inspire us to start cultivating, at last, our own, natural
way with words. In either situation, we will be reclaiming our
disowned self and, in the process, becoming more whole as individuals.

*Thinking about your intimate relationships in the past and
present, identify at least three traits that you tend to admire in
other people but disown in yourself. Then choose one of these
traits and make a special effort to express it during the coming
week.*

**I am becoming aware that I sometimes surrender aspects of myself
through admiration of others. In this moment of solitude, I reclaim
all of myself and allow others to have all of themselves. I honor this
thought: "Envy and admiration are forms of self-rejection."**

When we open our hearts to our own inner sadness, we enlarge our capacity to be compassionate· toward others. And when we extend compassion to others, we increase our ability to manage our own inner hurt. Dealing with sadness brings us closer in tune with the universal energy.

To process our own sadness, we must first take a full and final account of our losses. Then, we must develop ways to transform that sadness, so that we can be more alive toward others.

The process of helping *others* to deal with their sadness can be as simple as lending an ear or a shoulder, as needed. We must guard against trying to "fix" others' hurts. Only they are capable of doing that. But we can try to distract them from their sorrow by inviting them out for dinner and a movie, soliciting their help in a project we know they'll like, or steering them toward an activity that seems likely to restore their sense of aliveness. There are times when all someone needs is a warm hug. In the search for ways to overcome sorrow, we learn not only by working through our own pain, but also by sharing the pain of others.

🍃 *Today, identify three people you know who are sad and could use some comforting. Then, choose one of them and think of one thing you could do this week to help that person overcome his or her sadness and feel more alive.*

Moving into my inner sanctuary, I allow myself to access the past loss I feel in my heart, recognizing that we are fully alive when we are fully experiencing all of our emotional states.

What you will do matters. All you need is to do it.
— JUDY GRAHN

The secret to mastering relationship skills is to apply them in every possible situation. We are now well aware of our own childhood wounds and character defenses. Using this awareness, we can start working to overcome them right away because every interaction with the important people in our lives is an opportunity for practice. Furthermore, we have some idea of what our future, Imago-match partner's wounds and defenses will be, so we can begin now to deal with these wounds and defenses more effectively when we see them exhibited by anyone we care about.

For example, if we know that we tend to cling to people because we fear they'll abandon us, we can consciously try to avoid being overly possessive of our friends or to cease worrying so much when a member of our family doesn't contact us for a while. Also, knowing that we're likely to be attracted to someone who isolates him- or herself out of a fear of rejection, we can practice engaging in intentional dialogue with "isolator" people. This will train us in validating and empathizing with their points of view. Whatever areas we choose to work on, it is important that we consistently engage in our own journey to wholeness. In this way we fertilize the field where love can eventually flourish.

❧ *Today, identify at least two people in your regular, day-to-day life with whom you have difficulty getting along. Consider each person's character defense. Then, choose one of them and make a vow to practice a particular relationship skill that you feel may help to improve matters.*

In the deepest part of me where God dwells, I hold this important truth: "I can begin the healing work on myself in preparation for the partner that will come into my life."

*If you haven't forgiven yourself something, how can
you forgive others?*

—DOLORES HUERTA

As children, we were careful to hide from our peers any of our
"weird" traits and behaviors. Since conformity is the number one
rule, this type of concealment becomes an automatic reflex, a basic
tenet of survival. The macho sixth-grade boy won't let anyone find
out that he still sleeps with a teddy bear. The way-cool ninth-grade
girl would die of embarrassment if anyone peeked into her diary and
discovered her crush on a ninth-grade loner.

As adults, it is difficult to shake this deeply ingrained habit of
protecting our private lives. We never reveal our love of sleeping into
the afternoon, the great deal of comfort we get from talking "cutsie"
to our German shepherd, or our need to run out to the local fast-food
outlet in the middle of the night for a mandarin orange milkshake.
Somehow, we can't help but be ashamed of these personal quirks
just because they *are* so personal—no one else seems to do them.
But there's nothing intrinsically wrong about many of the traits and
behaviors that make up our hidden self, and if we don't share them,
we won't be able to get closer to others. Nor will we learn that
others have similar quirks and that these traits don't make us wrong,
silly, or bad—they just make us human.

❧ *Today, begin the process of forgiving yourself for being yourself. Let someone else know about one trait or behavior that is
part of your hidden self. Work a humorous "confession" into the
course of a conversation or make a mock-serious announcement
of a secret trait or behavior as a way of letting someone know
that you feel close to them.*

**I move into the courage that is alive and present in my core, and
draw on the strength to accept the quirks that I've worked so hard to
hide from others.**

As single people we can be especially susceptible to brooding over hurts from past relationships. Again and again, we return to the soul-lacerating moment when a colleague stole our idea to impress our boss, when a favorite date cruelly ditched us for someone else, or when a trusted partner laughed at our ambition to write a best-seller. We're still attached to these incidents in our lives not necessarily because they were so unfair, but because they were so *dramatic*. Regardless of the fact that they were negative, they were comparatively *intense* experiences in our emotional life. In the absence of similarly intense emotional experiences now, we keep recalling those past hurts to feel once more the old, addictive charge of adrenaline. In order to release ourselves to feel more positively and passionately about the future, we need to break away from these past attachments.

❧ *Today, think of someone in your recent or distant past toward whom you still feel angry or vengeful. If this person is no longer a part of your present life, use the saying-good-bye process (Days 104–108) to achieve a final release. If this person remains a part of your life, forgive the old hurt—if possible, face to face.*

I am aware that I tend to carry painful memories from the past that give me a sense of aliveness and importance. In quiet today I choose to surrender those memories and to feel alive and important through forgiveness.

And someday there shall be such closeness that when one cries the other shall taste salt.
— ANONYMOUS

Real love offers far more satisfaction than superficial romance ever can. A romantic's compulsive search for meaning—sometimes seen as a yearning for a genuine sense of aliveness—is replaced in real love by a transcendent *experiencing*. Dream stuff gives way to an actuality that is much more vibrant and substantial. While romance is filled with hopes, vows, and declarations of faith, real love is the hope made true, the vow honored, the declaration in action.

Such is the certainty and transformative power of real love, compared to romance. Vivid life replaces imagined ideals. Lasting knowledge succeeds temporary delirium. Real love is built upon the rock of permanent character change. It doesn't blow away when storms come, nor does it sink into doubts or fears, as "sand-castle" romance so easily can. Instead, it is an enduring source of surety, comfort, and joy.

❧ *Today, think of a long-term positive relationship that you've enjoyed with a family member or friend. What makes this relationship so special to you? What rock-solid sureties do you find in this relationship that you don't find in others?*

I see the journey of real love as a mountain I must climb. Though the path may be steep, I recognize that each step will bring me closer to the sacred in myself and others.

The story of love is not important. What is
important is that one is capable of love. It is perhaps
the only glimpse we are permitted of eternity.

—HELEN HAYES

On the surface, we are each distinctly different individuals. Directly beneath that surface, we remain uniquely ourselves, with a psyche that's been shaped, nurtured, and wounded by our own unique experience in life. But all human beings share a common core deep within, an essence of life that some people call the human spirit or soul, and others refer to as the God within us. It is from this essence that real love emanates, once we have broken through the layers of self that keep it encased.

As individual human beings, we filter this real love through our own, distinct personalities and behaviors, so that it takes on our own particular color. When we bond with another person in a committed partnership, we are surrounded by a sphere of love that blends each partner's color and illuminates each partner's life in a prism of miraculous possibility. As we learn to tap the deepest power of love within us, and then to share that love with another human being, we come to feel the power that energizes all life in the universe.

❧ *Today, recall at least three moments in life when you've felt a very deep stirring in your soul about someone—a feeling of warmth, joy, and benevolence that had nothing to do with your own, immediate self-interests. Perhaps you once felt this way looking at a newborn baby or at a beloved grandparent's sleeping face. Maybe it happened when you heard about a friend's act of kindness or when you first realized how brave, or how vulnerable, a lover was.*

I breathe deeply into this time of prayer, and visualize the various parts of me as the vivid colors in an abstract painting. I recognize that the one painting will come into focus as I move through the steps toward consciousness.

To achieve any sort of real and lasting change for the better, we need to be conscious and intentional about who we are and how we behave. As we practice new behaviors we become aware of the evolution in ourselves. It's an energetic and energizing process. New attitudes and behaviors will create new experiences, which will create new internal images. The cycle is endless!

Difficult and daunting as it may be for us to break out of our old familiar territory and start the wheels of change rolling, it is essential if we're going to make any progress. And it is much harder to get the wheel out of our familiar rut than it is to keep it rolling. We have to choose to be a pioneer. Sometimes this means going against the forces of society that are holding us back—especially in regard to gender roles and stereotypes. But, as they say, if we're not part of the solution, we're part of the problem. The solution lies in moving ahead, so that we can reach the destination our inner self most longs to reach.

Today, identify at least two ways in which you are afraid to change, even though you believe these changes would be good for you. Then, with a brave, pioneer spirit, choose one of these ways and think of a specific thing you can do during the coming week to get started on this way.

Drawing upon an inner strength, I hold this truth: "My commitment to my process will spin the wheel and keep the momentum going so that I can truly accomplish the change that I seek."

*No man can produce great things who is not
thoroughly sincere in dealing with himself.*

—JAMES RUSSELL LOWELL

Now that you are nearing the end of this book, it's time to start thinking of starting a new one—a book that you write yourself. Maintaining a daily or weekly journal is perhaps the single best way to ensure that we lead a conscious life and increase our awareness of the longstanding or subtle patterns that might go undetected. And when we've set the vital goal of finding and keeping a conscious, committed love relationship, it's especially important to note our day-to-day or week-to-week progress.

Too often, journals are used only to process disappointment, discharge frustration, and ventilate anger. An Imago journal can—and should—be much more motivating and creative. In this journal, we can record what seemed to work and why. We can give ourselves credit for our gains, and we can inspire ourselves to set our sights even higher—expanding our vision of love and imagining all sorts of new ways we can empower ourselves and our future partners to achieve that vision.

The more we are aware of the positive changes that are happening in our life, the more fuel we will have to go further. A journal can be our passport to this awareness. It can capture the meaning behind the moment, the idea behind the action, the spirit behind the flesh.

❧ *Today, decide how you could go about maintaining a journal in a consistent fashion. Consider how often you want to write, the best time for you during the day, and how lengthy you want the entries to be.*

Today, in sacred stillness, I recognize that the work must continue even after this book is finished. This truth is mine: "My commitment to this work is ultimately my commitment to my own process of finding wholeness."

We all seek meaning in our lives: knowledge about ourselves and others, answers to the questions raised by our hopes and fears, explanations of the behaviors that puzzle us, and reasons for the seemingly random and inscrutable events that we live through. But the search for meaning can become compulsive, shutting us off from a freer, more spontaneous experience of life. If we are constantly focused on the goal, then we forget to take in the beauty of the journey. And, in reality, most of the important work and meaning that we seek is cultivated by engaging daily in the journey! In order to prevent a compulsive attitude from taking over, we must tap the spirit of divine peace within, from which we can simply enjoy the world around us. Rather than thinking about life's mysteries, we have to turn off our minds for a while and let our full range of feelings roam free—reveling in the marvelous moment of life at hand without worrying about analyzing it. We must cease to *do* and, instead, simply, *be*.

ᴥ *Declare that today will be a day of being, not doing. Take advantage of every opportunity you have simply to enjoy watching, listening, tasting, touching, smelling, and feeling, instead of having to think.*

Today, I enter a restful place and release myself from compulsive activity. I vow to carry this inner peace with me into this day and savor the moment, deepening my awareness of how I use thinking and analyzing to separate myself from experiencing.

We need an Imago partner in order to grow and heal. Like it or not, our issues of self-completion paradoxically require relationship for resolution. Learning to live more consciously and effectively with our partners is the dynamic process by which we attain wholeness.

Aware of what our Imago is like, we know the kind of person with whom we must finish our business. We understand the issues we will have to confront and deal with. We recognize what is going on in our search for a mate, and we appreciate that we cannnot avoid facing our childhood wounds by trying to choose a "perfect" mate who promises to spare us the pains. When we meet our Imago match, we are prepared for what's in store.

An Imago-match partner has the potential to hurt us deeply as well as to heal us. If we hope to be healed in our partnership rather than suffer further injury, we must be willing to look at our Imago issues, however difficult; otherwise we will be unconsciously driven by those issues. Until we familiarize ourselves with our Imago, acknowledge the journey we face, and then work consciously and conscientiously with our partners to heal those issues, we are sleepwalking through life, fated to repeat the same mistakes over and over again.

&❧ *Today, refamiliarize yourself with the Imago portrait you created on Day 50.*

Turning to the God within, I open myself to full consciousness. Becoming fully awake is my goal.

*Fear nothing, for every renewed effort raises all
former failures into lessons, all sins into experiences.*
                                    —KATHERINE TINGLEY

Throughout nature, safety is the necessary precondition for optimal
well-being. Creating safety within a human relationship requires two
different types of activity. First, we must surrender our own fears:
our fear of being ourselves; our fear of being wrong, foolish, or
unattractive; our fear of changing; our fear of losing the other person;
and, perhaps the hardest fear of all to relinquish, our fear that the
other person will hurt us. We must learn to relax in our partner's
company, which means cultivating love, trust, and faith.

Second, we need to cease being an object of fear for our partner.
Instead, we must create a welcoming and restorative environment of
safety for our partner, as well as for our trusted friends. To achieve
that goal, we have to redirect our self-preservation instincts toward
the other person, by putting an end to criticism and other forms of
abuse and working toward guaranteeing his or her emotional and
spiritual welfare. Thus, our own life force is translated into unconditional love—a concern for the other person's welfare that lifts us out
of our narrow, fearful, shaky world of self and into a much grander,
sounder world of harmony and connectedness.

🍂 *Focus on at least two of your past romantic relationships and
ask yourself these questions: In what ways was I afraid of my
partner? In what ways was my partner afraid of me?*

**Drawing upon an inner wisdom, I acknowledge this truth: "I have
the choice of living my life from a place of love or fear." I choose love.**

*He that will not apply new remedies must expect
new evils; for time is the greatest innovator.*

—FRANCIS BACON

Each new day gives us an opportunity for a fresh start, a chance to try out a more promising attitude or a more useful behavior. This is especially true in terms of relationships. Each new encounter with someone, even if it's someone we've known for years, can be turned into an experience that revitalizes both parties.

We don't have to let our past mistakes continually haunt us. Nor do we have to keep boring ourselves and others with our old routines. Just as our bodies continuously generate new cells and discard worn-out ones, so that we aren't the same physical person from day to day, our minds can continuously generate fresh ideas and actions and let go of the stale ones, so that we don't become mentally and emotionally stagnant. Self-renewal can only happen when we stay focused on the future and what it *can* be like. If we're too caught up in past wounds and never move through them, we will never move forward. We will never discover the excitement of each new day.

❧ *Promise yourself that tomorrow you'll do something creative in one of your relationships: try out a new attitude, a new behavior, or a new plan.*

In a reverential time of stillness, I let go of any judgment I may still carry about my past mistakes. This wisdom is my guide: "I can focus on a future that holds the promise of new growth."

All along our path toward self-development, we need to keep our eyes open for opportunities to bring others into the process: to share our thoughts; to elicit our powers of mirroring, validation, and empathy; to hear us confess our fears and shortcomings; to help us realize at-one-ment. The idea is to continue practicing our new attitudes, skills, and behaviors in increasingly larger doses and in increasingly "risky" situations. At first, we might try them out with a supportive friend or in a therapy group. As we gain confidence, we can move on to situations where we perceive the stakes to be greater: with coworkers, then with dates who aren't "the one"— perhaps ongoing, utilitarian dates whom we actually introduce to the ideas in this book.

The more we can invite others' participation on all sorts of levels, the richer our experience will be and the faster we will grow. The more we can become comfortable with new behaviors in low- or medium-risk arenas, the more we can be our better, more authentic self when true love finally comes into view!

Today, promise yourself that you will take advantage of at least two opportunities every day for the next three days to practice a new attitude, skill, or behavior.

As I relax and breathe deeply, I recognize that the work I've done has already created a greater feeling of safety. From this place of greater safety, I acknowledge the need to bring my new skills to those I trust in my life.

*When we were children, we used to think that when
we were grown-up we would no longer be vulnerable.
But to grow up is to accept vulnerability. . . . To be
alive is to be vulnerable.*

— MADELEINE L'ENGLE

A conscious relationship is an ever-evolving journey, not a destination. Each partner is continually working on reclaiming his or her own lost strengths and abilities. Both are busy developing their contrasexual selves, so that they can live fuller lives. As they grow both individually and as a couple, they begin to shift their awareness to the world around them. In this way, all the work that has brought them into wholeness as an individual can help to create wholeness and healing in our world as well.

Unfortunately, many couples have trouble really believing in the concept of "till death do us part." They hope their marriage will last forever, but they know that if they run into trouble, they can always get divorced. Prospective marriage partners need to take that vow far more seriously: not for the sake of morality, but for their own emotional, mental, and spiritual well-being. We can't find ourselves by leaving a marriage. We can only find ourselves *through* becoming conscious in a committed relationship. The journey of a conscious relationship is the most effective means of uncovering and recovering our original wholeness.

❧ *Today, imagine you were composing your own marriage vow, a vow that ends with the words "till death do us part." What promises would you make to the other person? What goals would you set for the two of you as a couple?*

Opening to a broader perspective, I hold in mind the wonder that I am a creature with goals built into me, a wisdom that is not an outcome of my life experience, but an outcome built into my genes. All I have to do is cooperate with what is trying to happen.

Congratulations! You have completed a year of working on the Imago process and have now graduated into a higher state of living. You've identified your childhood wounds and your Imago portrait, thus achieving a much better understanding of the type of person to whom you're attracted and the type of relationship issues you're most likely to encounter with this person. You've learned a great deal about the value of a committed relationship—one in which both partners work toward healing each other and assisting each other to realize self-fulfillment. And you've developed many of the skills that will help you build that kind of relationship. Look back over the past year and celebrate how far you've come! Then, look forward to the brighter future you will have as you continue to apply the Imago process to your day-to-day life. That adventure begins tomorrow.

🍃 *Today, recommit yourself to your "Vision of Love" (Day 342) by reading it out loud.*

In a place of prayer today, I accept the challenge of learning that keeping the love I find and getting the love I want depends upon my giving the love my future partner needs.